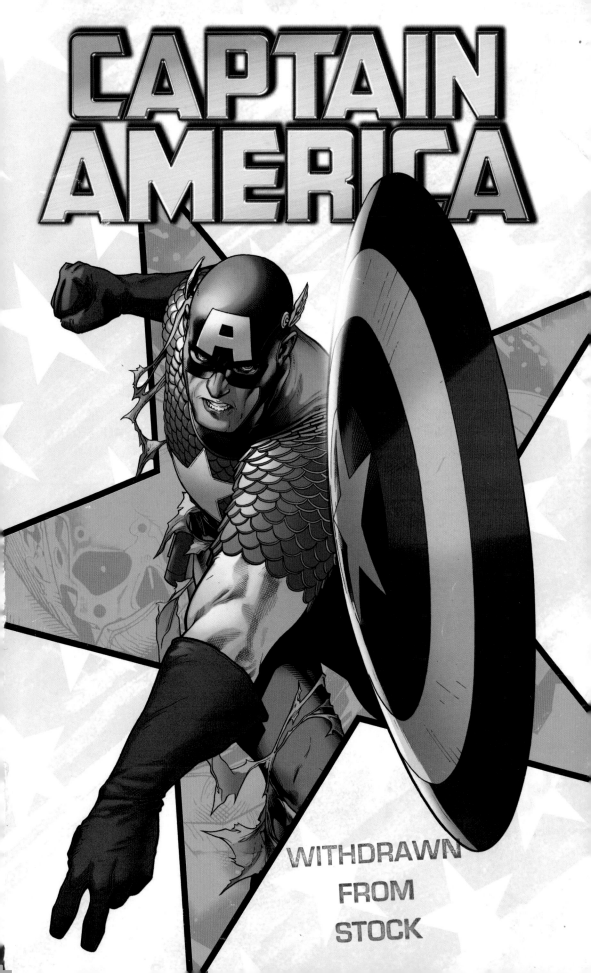

CAPTAIN AMERICA

DURING THE DARK DAYS OF THE EARLY 1940S, A COVERT MILITARY EXPERIMENT TURNED STEVE ROGERS INTO AMERICA'S FIRST SUPER-SOLDIER, CAPTAIN AMERICA. THROUGHOUT THE WAR, CAP AND HIS PARTNER BUCKY FOUGHT ALONGSIDE OUR INFANTRY AND WITH A GROUP OF HEROES KNOWN AS THE INVADERS. IN THE CLOSING MONTHS OF WWII, CAPTAIN AMERICA AND BUCKY WERE BOTH PRESUMED DEAD IN AN EXPLOSION OVER THE ENGLISH CHANNEL.

DECADES LATER, A FIGURE WAS FOUND TRAPPED IN ICE, AND CAPTAIN AMERICA WAS REVIVED. HAVING SLEPT THROUGH THE MAJORITY OF THE 20TH CENTURY, STEVE ROGERS AWAKENED TO A WORLD HE NEVER IMAGINED, A WORLD WHERE WAR HAD MOVED FROM THE BATTLEFIELD TO THE CITY STREETS...A WORLD IN DIRE NEED OF...

CAPTAIN AMERICA

CAPTAIN AMERICA BY ED BRUBAKER VOL. 1. Contains material originally published in magazine form as CAPTAIN AMERICA #1-5. First printing 2012, Hardcover ISBN# 978-0-7851-5708-3. Softcover ISBN# 978-0-7851-5709-0. Published by MARVEL WORLDWIDE, INC., a subsidiary of MARVEL ENTERTAINMENT, LLC. OFFICE OF PUBLICATION: 135 West 50th Street, New York, NY 10020. Copyright © 2011 and 2012 Marvel Characters, Inc. All rights reserved. Hardcover: $19.99 per copy in the U.S. and $21.99 in Canada (GST #R127032852). Softcover: $16.99 per copy in the U.S. and $18.99 in Canada (GST #R127032852). Canadian Agreement #40668537. All characters featured in this issue and the distinctive names and likenesses thereof, and all related indicia are trademarks of Marvel Characters, Inc. No similarity between any of the names, characters, persons, and/or institutions in this magazine with those of any living or dead person or institution is intended, and any such similarity which may exist is purely coincidental. **Printed in the U.S.A.** ALAN FINE, EVP - Office of the President, Marvel Worldwide, Inc. and EVP & CMO Marvel Characters B.V.; DAN BUCKLEY, Publisher & President - Print, Animation & Digital Divisions; JOE QUESADA, Chief Creative Officer; DAVID BOGART, SVP of Business Affairs & Talent Management; TOM BREVOORT, SVP of Publishing; C.B. CEBULSKI, SVP of Creator & Content Development; DAVID GABRIEL, SVP of Publishing Sales & Circulation; MICHAEL PASCIULLO, SVP of Brand Planning & Communications; JIM O'KEEFE, VP of Operations & Logistics; DAN CARR, Executive Director of Publishing Technology; SUSAN CRESPI, Editorial Operations Manager; ALEX MORALES, Publishing Operations Manager; STAN LEE, Chairman Emeritus. For information regarding advertising in Marvel Comics or on Marvel.com, please contact John Dokes, SVP Integrated Sales and Marketing, at jdokes@marvel.com. For Marvel subscription inquiries, please call 800-217-9158. **Manufactured between 12/12/2011 and 1/9/2012 (hardcover), and 12/12/2011 and 7/30/2012 (softcover), by R.R. DONNELLEY, INC., SALEM, VA, USA.**

10 9 8 7 6 5 4 3 2 1

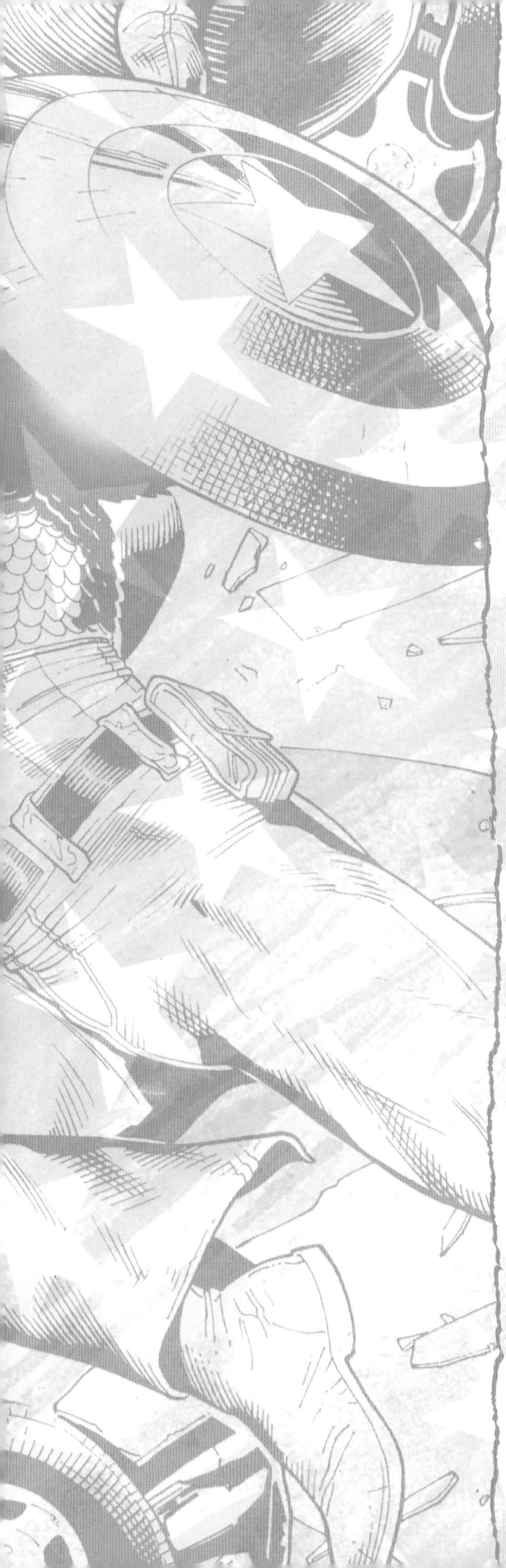

WRITER
ED BRUBAKER

PENCILERS
STEVE McNIVEN
WITH
GIUSEPPE CAMUNCOLI (#5)

INKERS
MARK MORALES (#1)
& JAY LIESTEN (#2-5)
WITH
DEXTER VINES (#2)
& MATTEO BUFFAGNI (#5)

COLORIST
JUSTIN PONSOR

LETTERERS
VC'S JOE CARAMAGNA
WITH **CLAYTON COWLES** (#2)

COVER ART
STEVE McNIVEN,
MARK MORALES &
JUSTIN PONSOR

ASSISTANT EDITOR
JOHN DENNING

ASSOCIATE EDITOR
LAUREN SANKOVITCH

EDITOR
TOM BREVOORT

CAPTAIN AMERICA CREATED BY
JOE SIMON & JACK KIRBY

COLLECTION EDITOR
JENNIFER GRÜNWALD
ASSISTANT EDITORS
ALEX STARBUCK & NELSON RIBEIRO
EDITOR, SPECIAL PROJECTS
MARK D. BEAZLEY
SENIOR EDITOR, SPECIAL PROJECTS
JEFF YOUNGQUIST
SENIOR VICE PRESIDENT OF SALES
DAVID GABRIEL
SVP OF BRAND PLANNING & COMMUNICATIONS
MICHAEL PASCIULLO
BOOK DESIGN
JEFF POWELL

EDITOR IN CHIEF
AXEL ALONSO
CHIEF CREATIVE OFFICER
JOE QUESADA
PUBLISHER
DAN BUCKLEY
EXECUTIVE PRODUCER
ALAN FINE

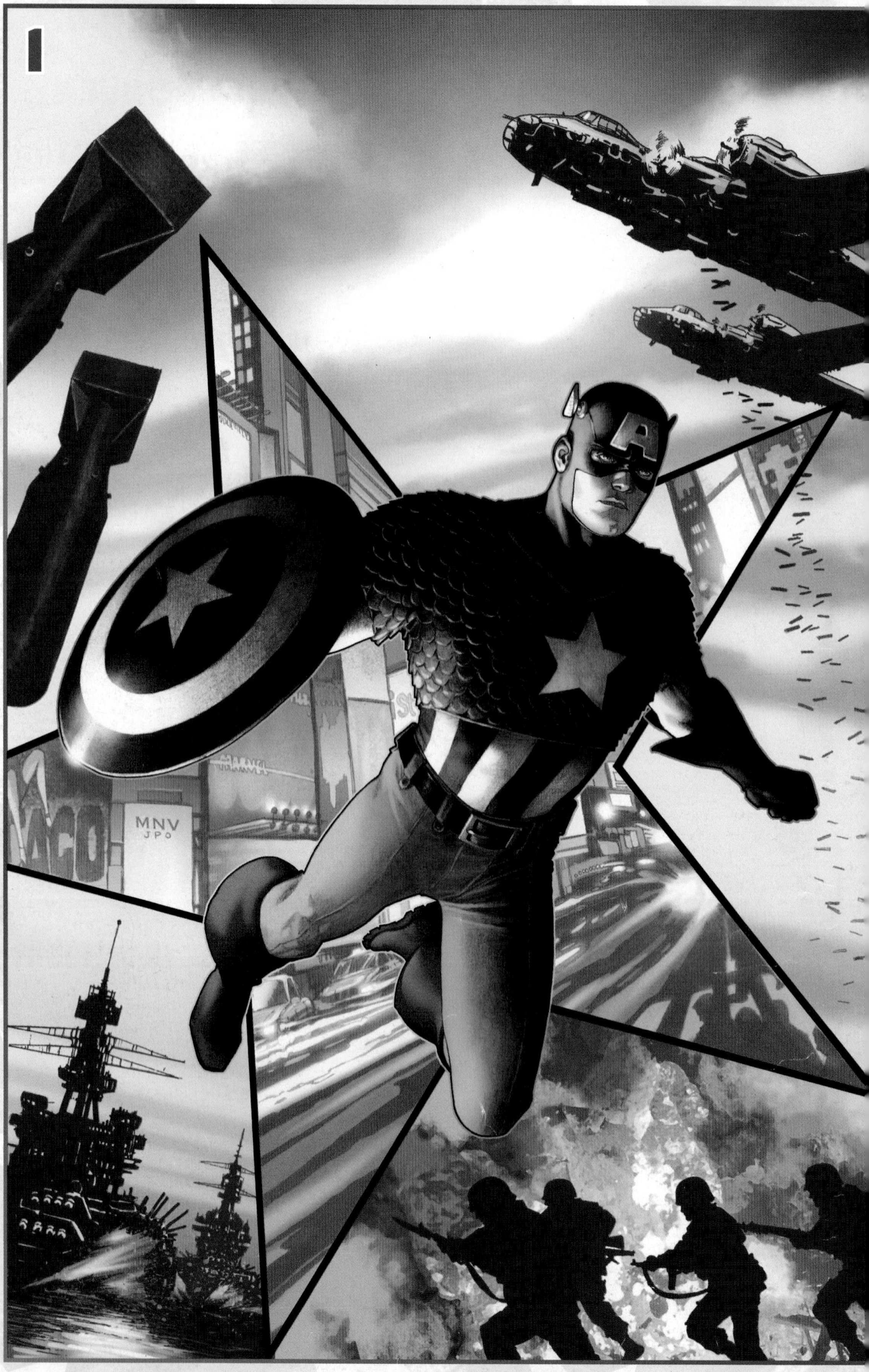
1
MNV
JPO

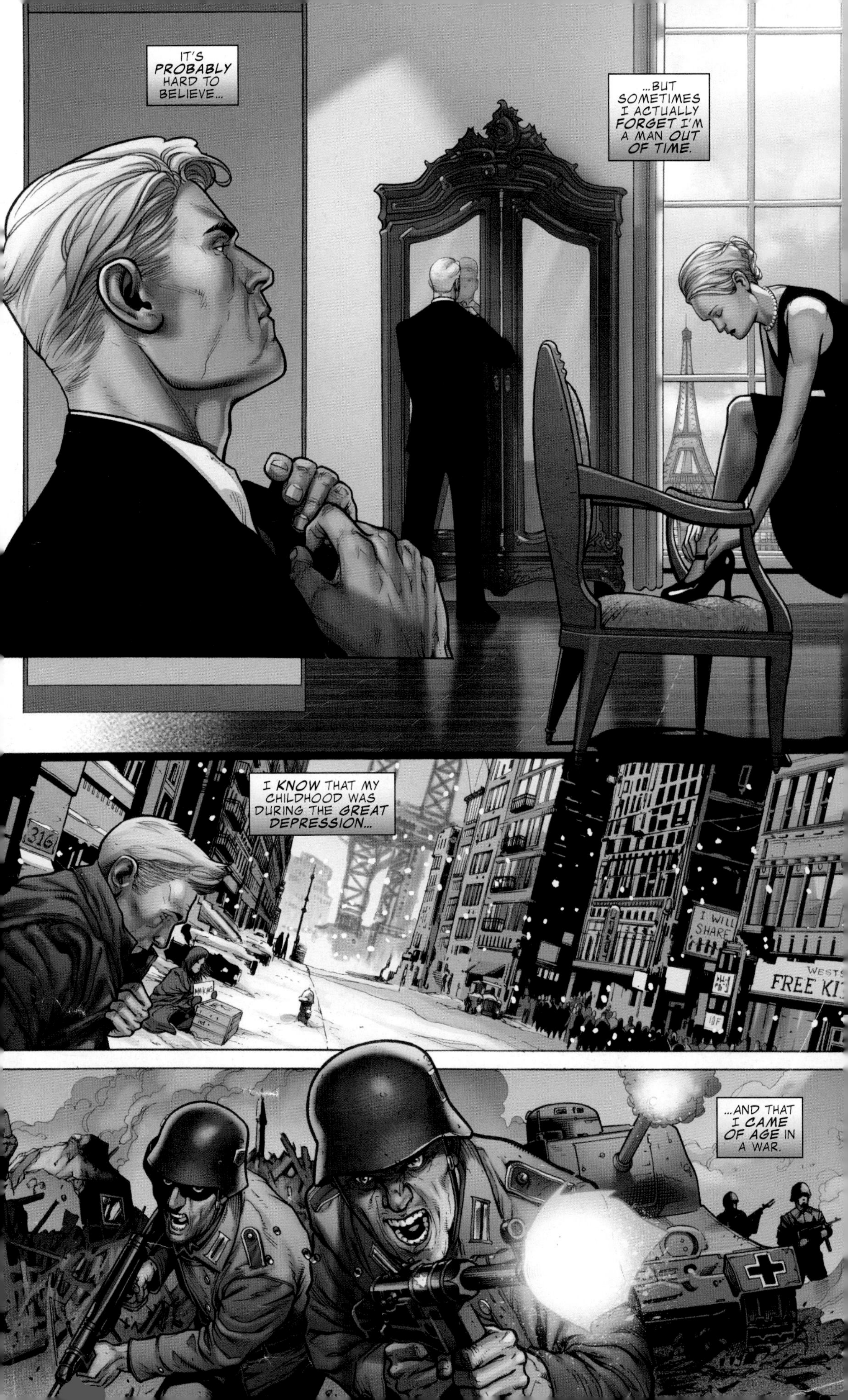
IT'S PROBABLY HARD TO BELIEVE...
...BUT SOMETIMES I ACTUALLY FORGET I'M A MAN OUT OF TIME.
I KNOW THAT MY CHILDHOOD WAS DURING THE GREAT DEPRESSION...
316
I WILL SHARE
...AND THAT I CAME OF AGE IN A WAR.

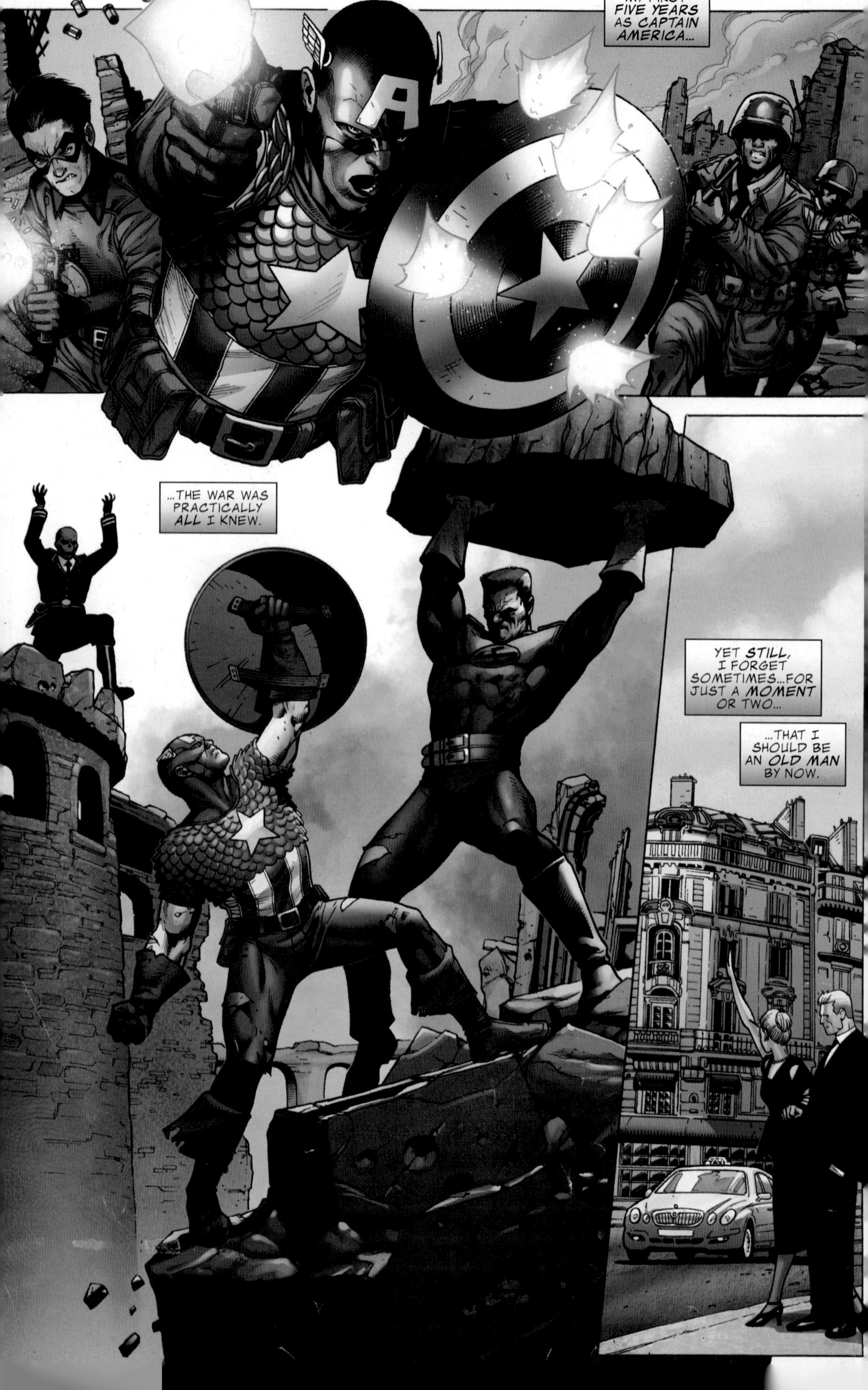
MY FIRST FIVE YEARS AS CAPTAIN AMERICA...
...THE WAR WAS PRACTICALLY ALL I KNEW.
YET STILL, I FORGET SOMETIMES...FOR JUST A MOMENT OR TWO...
...THAT I SHOULD BE AN OLD MAN BY NOW.

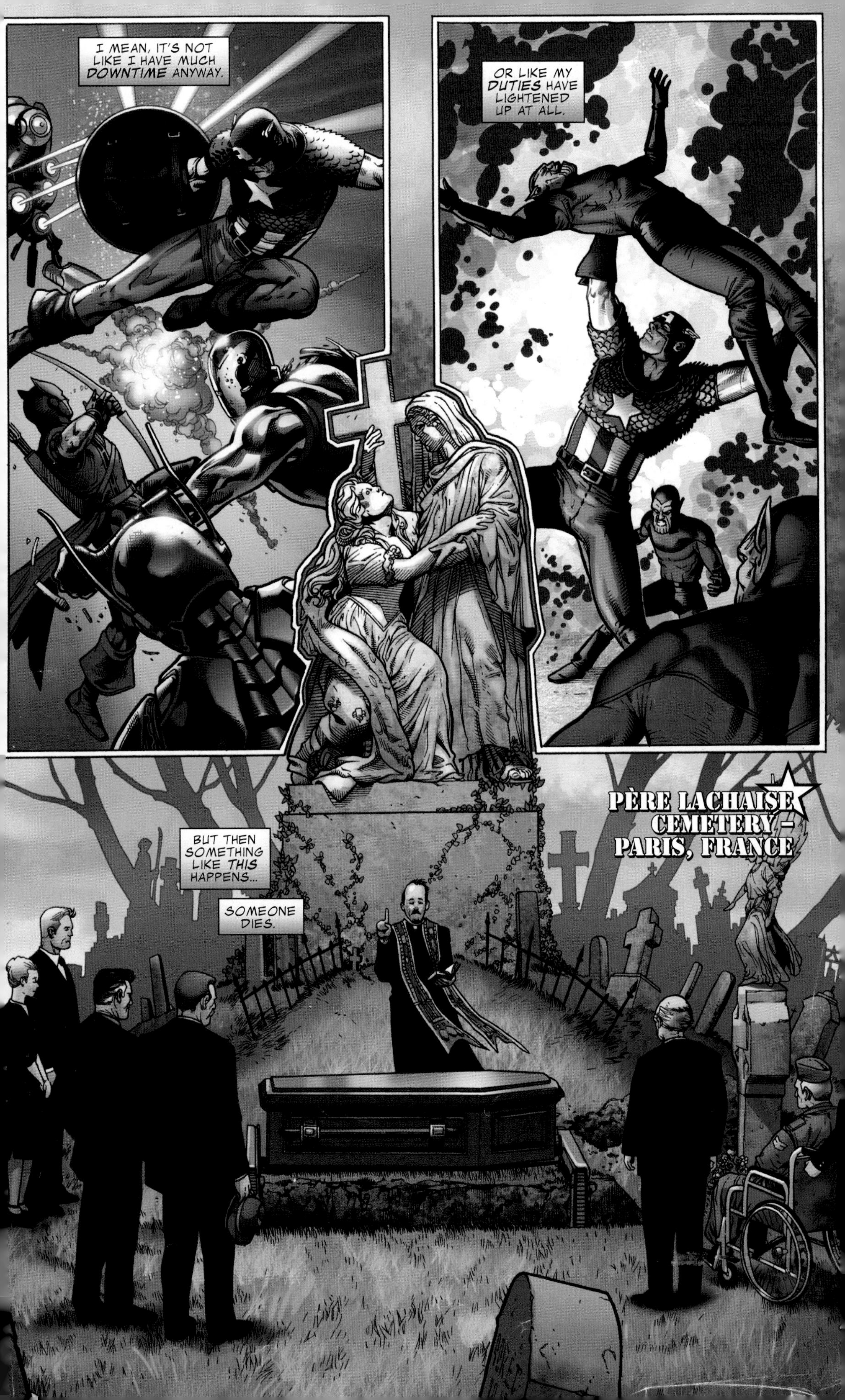

I MEAN, IT'S NOT LIKE I HAVE MUCH DOWNTIME ANYWAY.
OR LIKE MY DUTIES HAVE LIGHTENED UP AT ALL.
PÈRE LACHAISE CEMETERY – PARIS, FRANCE
BUT THEN SOMETHING LIKE THIS HAPPENS...
SOMEONE DIES.

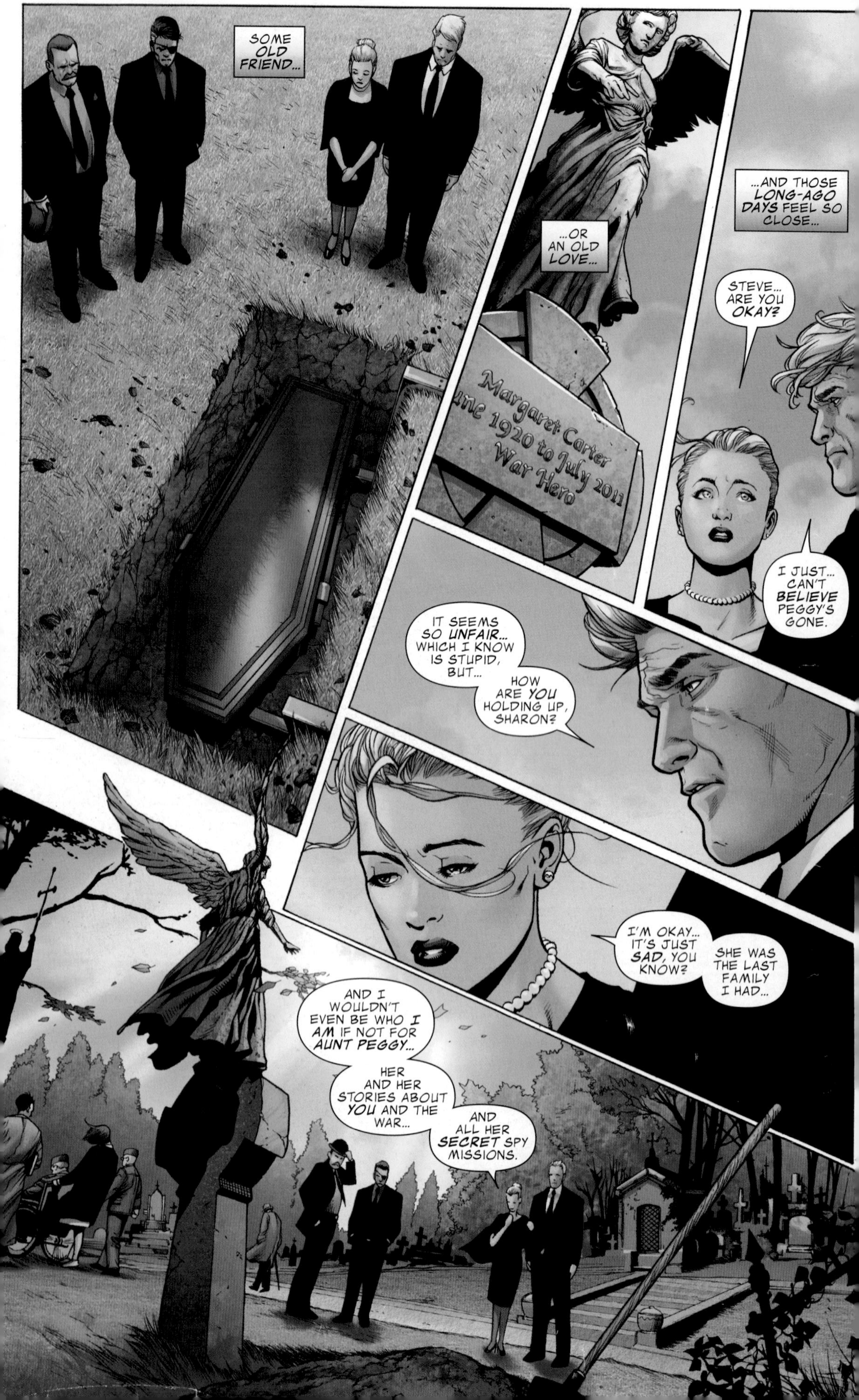
SOME OLD FRIEND...
...OR AN OLD LOVE...
Margaret Carter
June 1920 to July 2011
War Hero
...AND THOSE LONG-AGO DAYS FEEL SO CLOSE...
STEVE... ARE YOU OKAY?
I JUST... CAN'T BELIEVE PEGGY'S GONE.
IT SEEMS SO UNFAIR... WHICH I KNOW IS STUPID, BUT...
HOW ARE YOU HOLDING UP, SHARON?
I'M OKAY... IT'S JUST SAD, YOU KNOW?
SHE WAS THE LAST FAMILY I HAD...
AND I WOULDN'T EVEN BE WHO I AM IF NOT FOR AUNT PEGGY...
HER AND HER STORIES ABOUT YOU AND THE WAR...
AND ALL HER SECRET SPY MISSIONS.

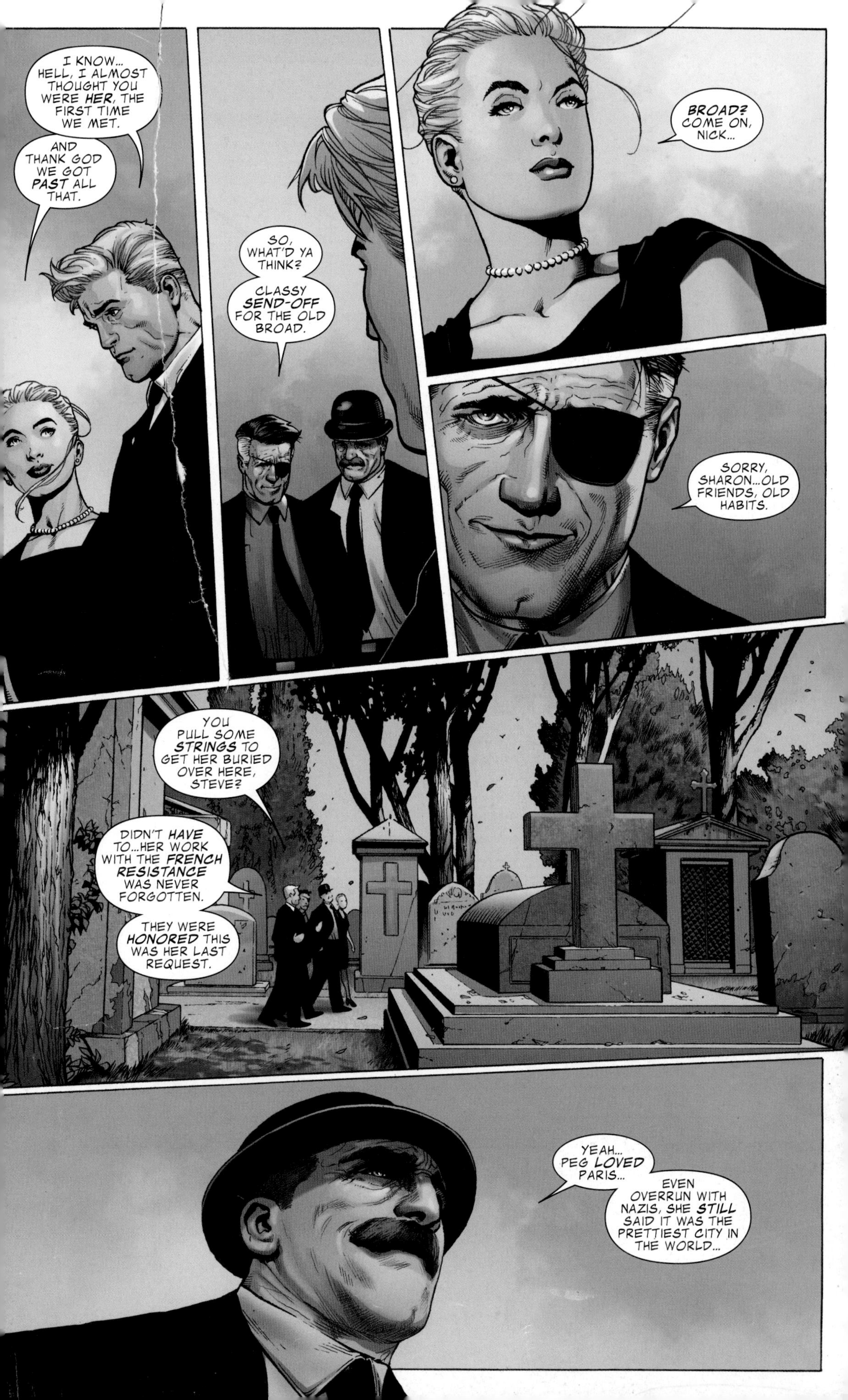
I KNOW... HELL, I ALMOST THOUGHT YOU WERE HER, THE FIRST TIME WE MET.
AND THANK GOD WE GOT PAST ALL THAT.
SO, WHAT'D YA THINK?
CLASSY SEND-OFF FOR THE OLD BROAD.
BROAD? COME ON, NICK...
SORRY, SHARON...OLD FRIENDS, OLD HABITS.
YOU PULL SOME STRINGS TO GET HER BURIED OVER HERE, STEVE?
DIDN'T HAVE TO...HER WORK WITH THE FRENCH RESISTANCE WAS NEVER FORGOTTEN.
THEY WERE HONORED THIS WAS HER LAST REQUEST.
YEAH... PEG LOVED PARIS...
EVEN OVERRUN WITH NAZIS, SHE STILL SAID IT WAS THE PRETTIEST CITY IN THE WORLD...

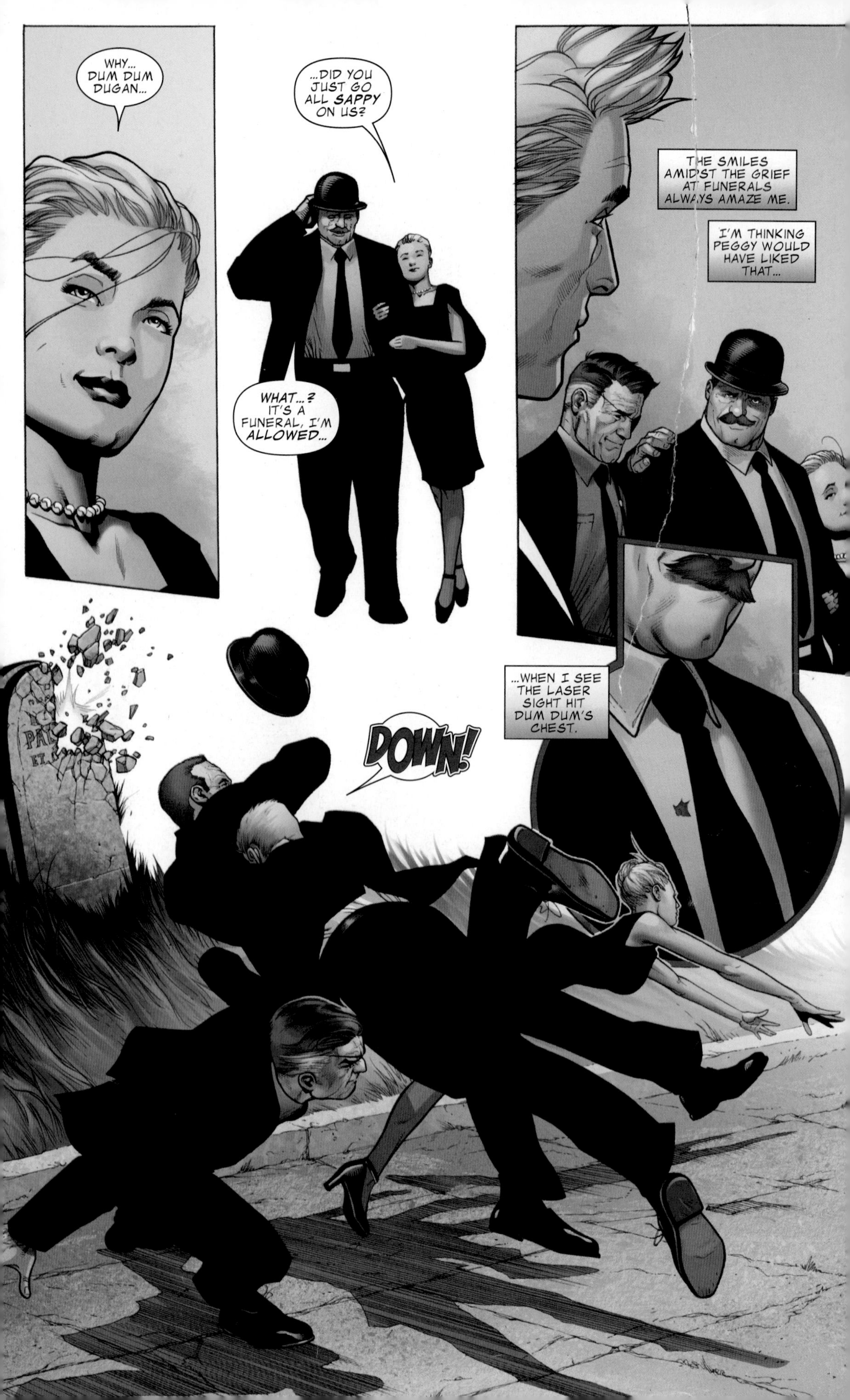
WHY... DUM DUM DUGAN...
...DID YOU JUST GO ALL SAPPY ON US?
WHAT...? IT'S A FUNERAL, I'M ALLOWED...
THE SMILES AMIDST THE GRIEF AT FUNERALS ALWAYS AMAZE ME.
I'M THINKING PEGGY WOULD HAVE LIKED THAT...
...WHEN I SEE THE LASER SIGHT HIT DUM DUM'S CHEST.
DOWN!

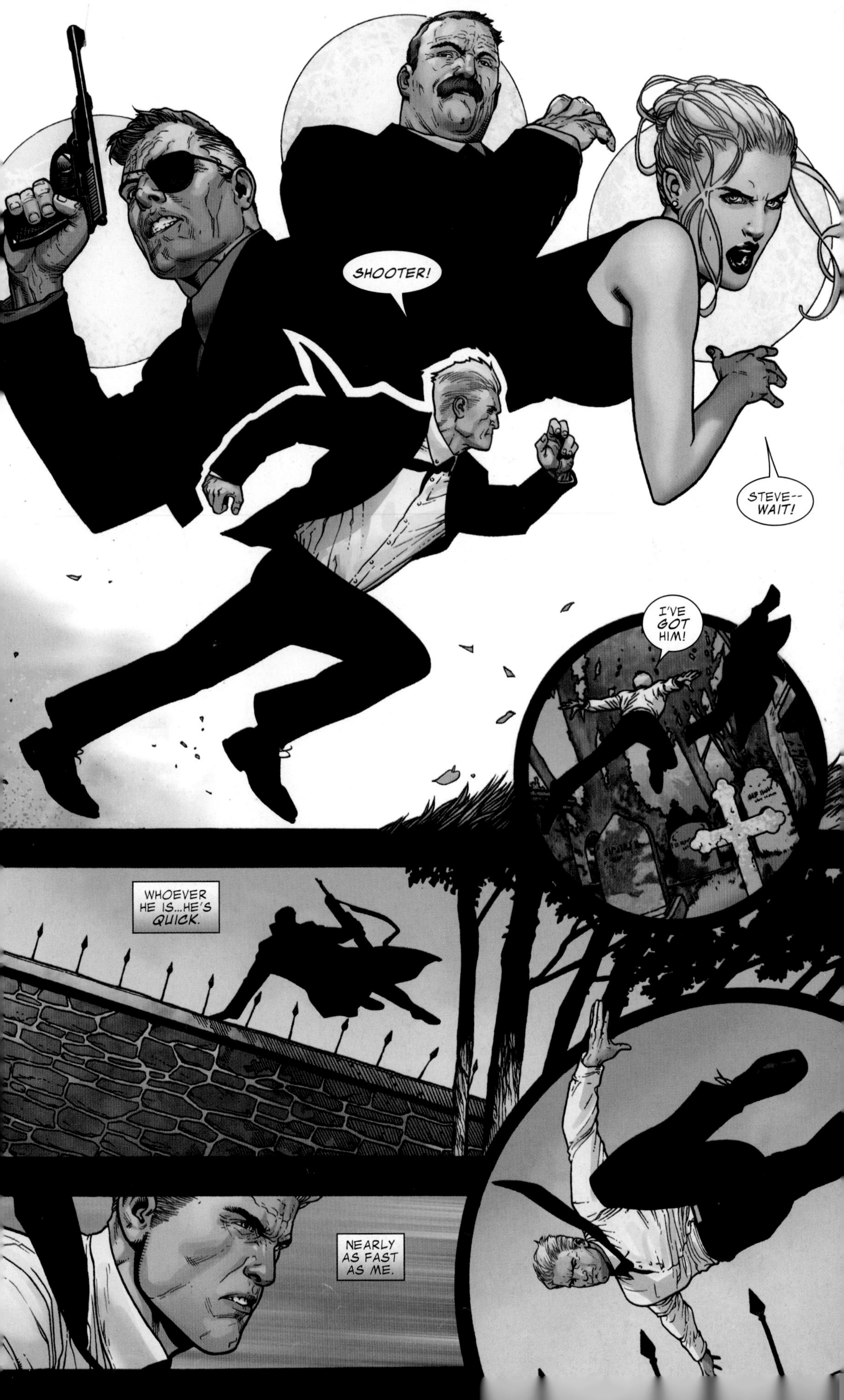
SHOOTER!
STEVE-- WAIT!
I'VE GOT HIM!
WHOEVER HE IS...HE'S QUICK.
NEARLY AS FAST AS ME.

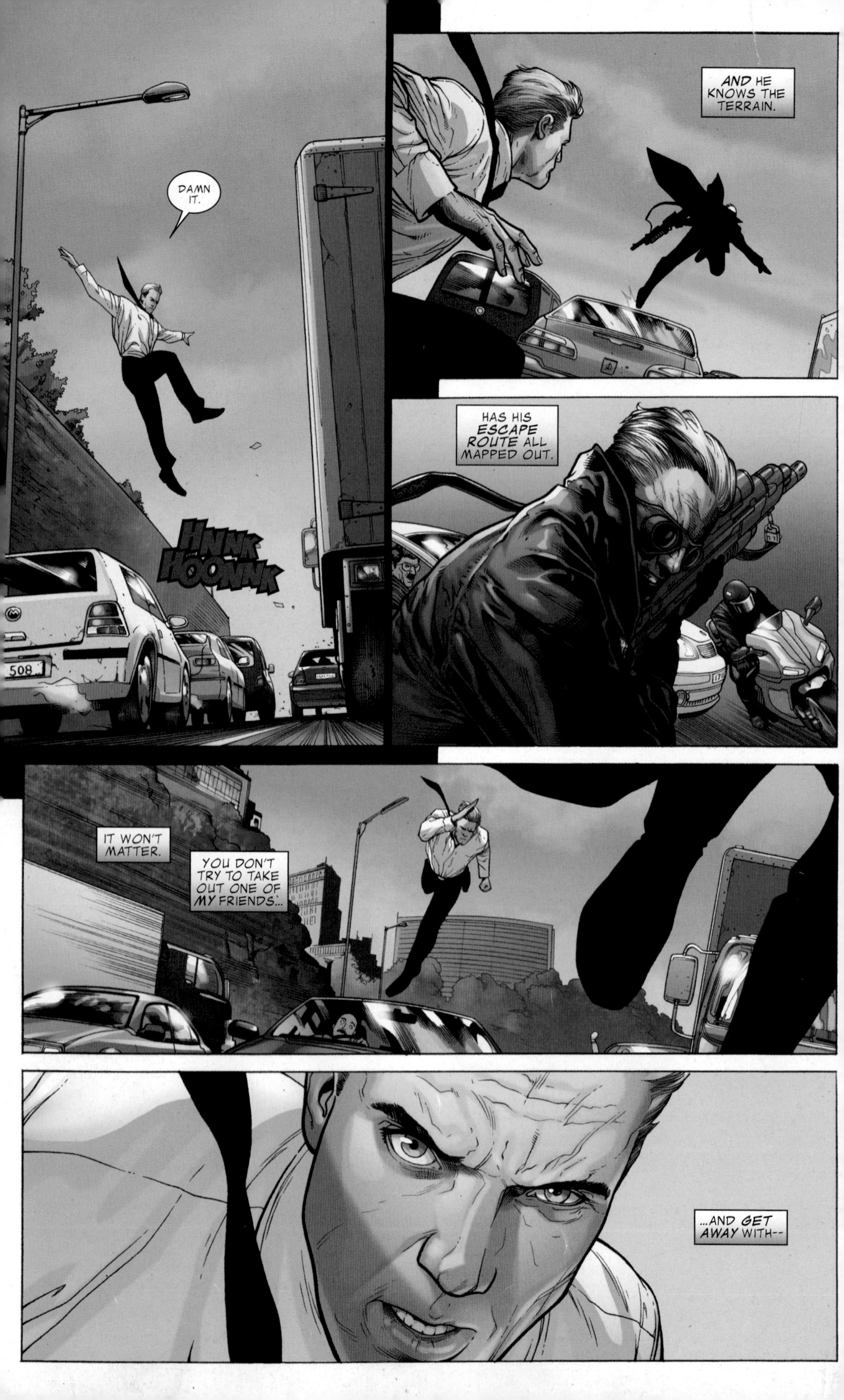
DAMN IT.
HNNK HOONNK
AND HE KNOWS THE TERRAIN.
HAS HIS ESCAPE ROUTE ALL MAPPED OUT.
IT WON'T MATTER.
YOU DON'T TRY TO TAKE OUT ONE OF MY FRIENDS...
...AND GET AWAY WITH--

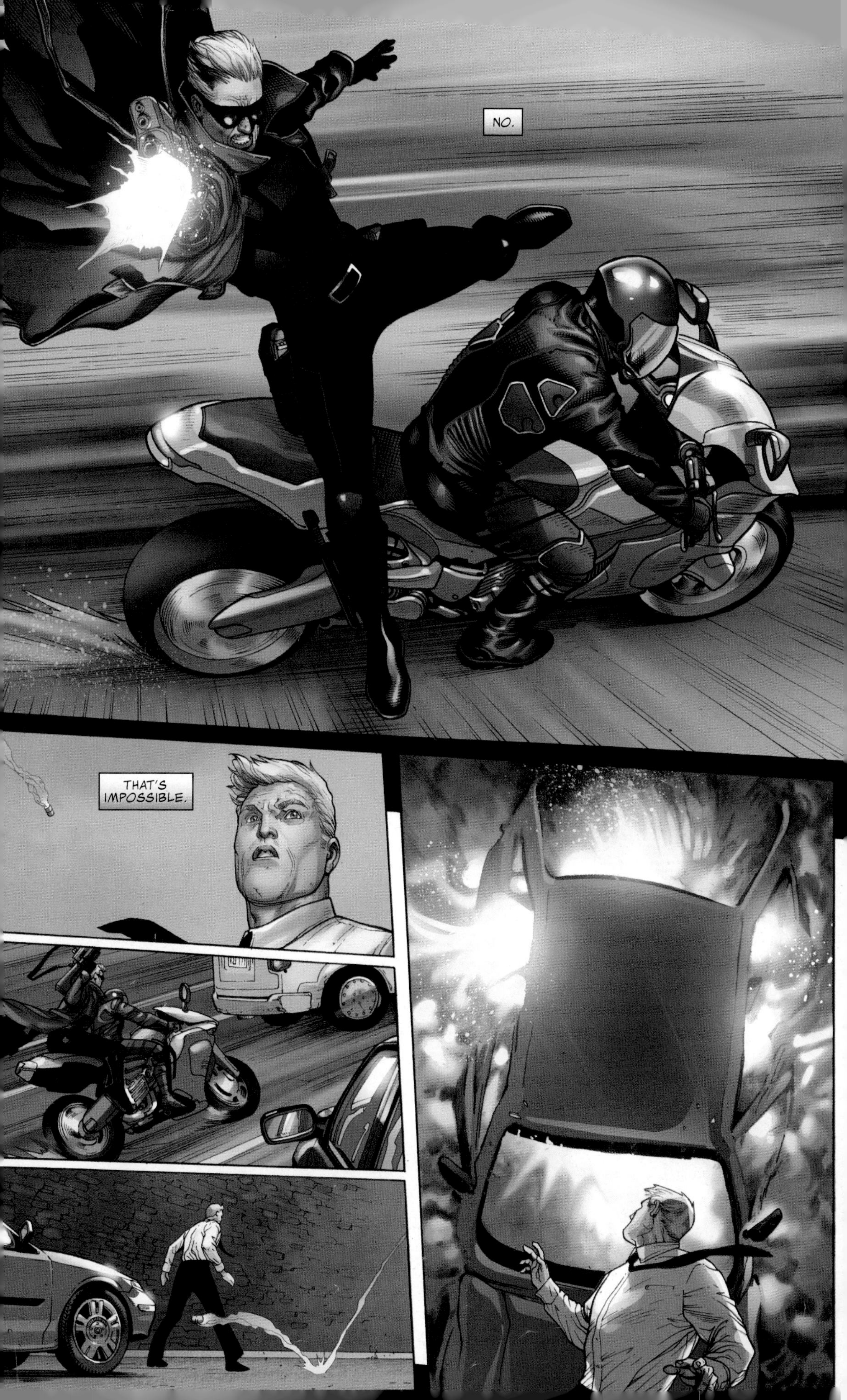
NO.
THAT'S IMPOSSIBLE.

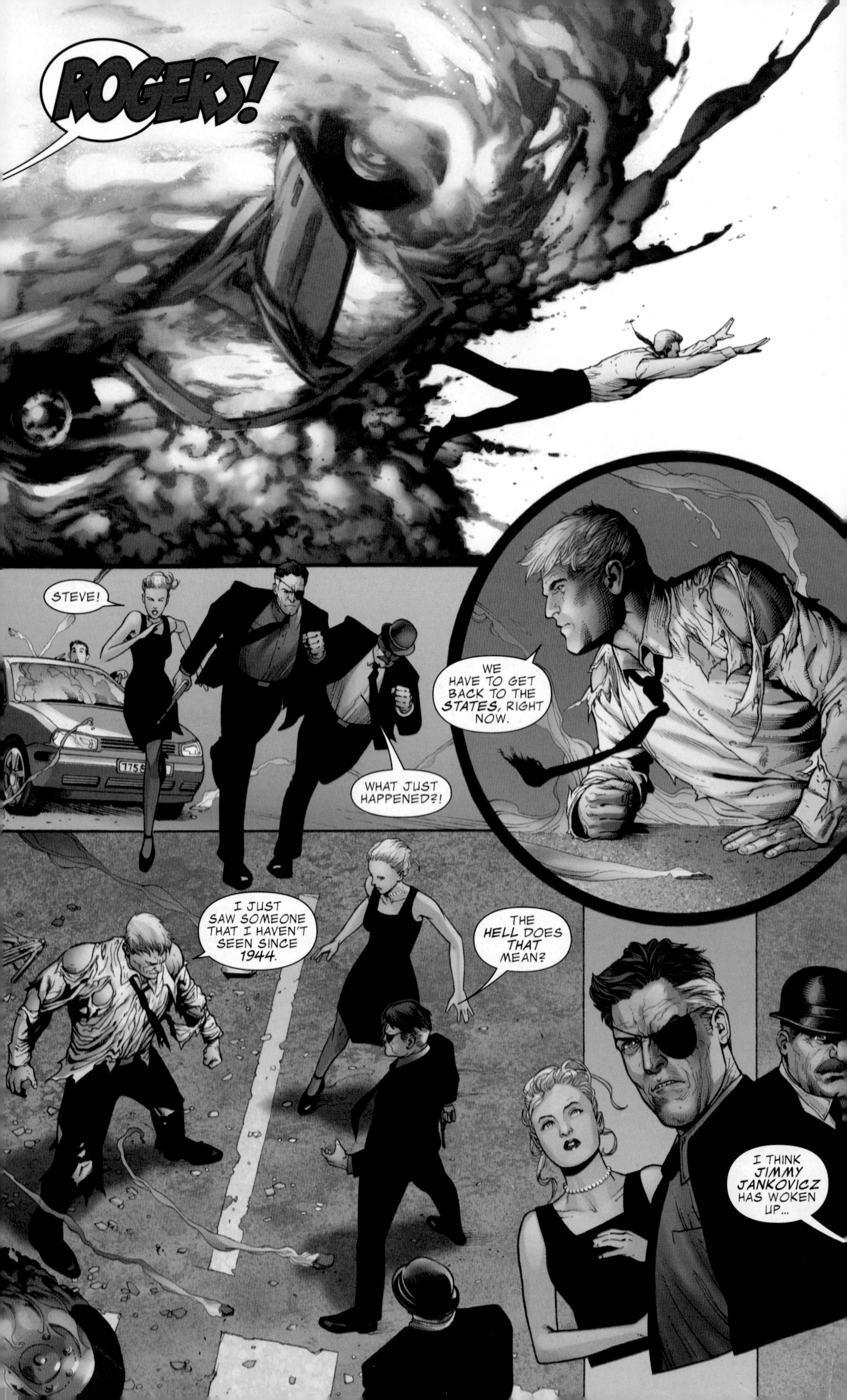
ROGERS!
STEVE!
WE HAVE TO GET BACK TO THE STATES, RIGHT NOW.
WHAT JUST HAPPENED?!
I JUST SAW SOMEONE THAT I HAVEN'T SEEN SINCE 1944.
THE HELL DOES THAT MEAN?
I THINK JIMMY JANKOVICZ HAS WOKEN UP...

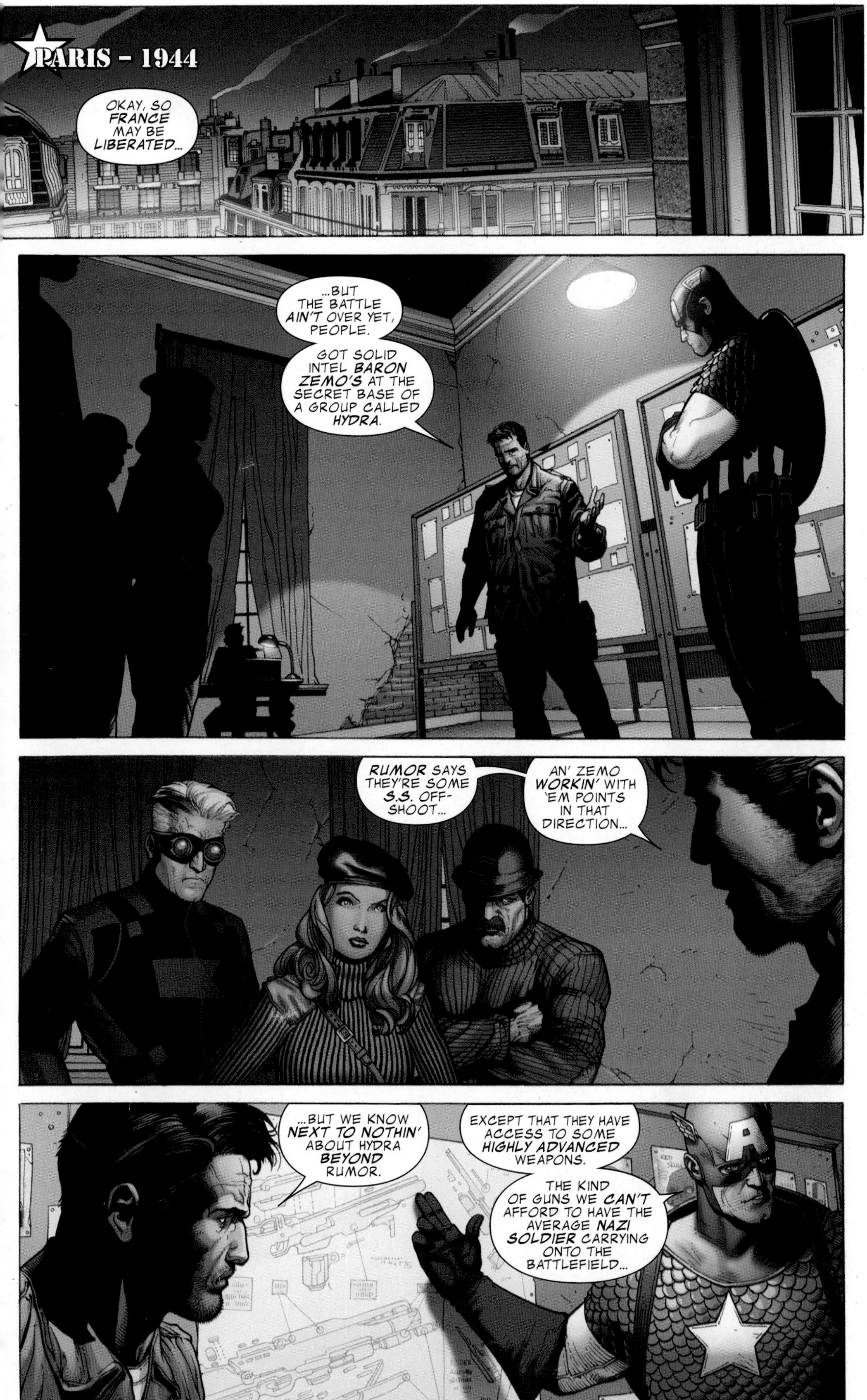
PARIS - 1944
OKAY, SO FRANCE MAY BE LIBERATED...
...BUT THE BATTLE AIN'T OVER YET, PEOPLE.
GOT SOLID INTEL BARON ZEMO'S AT THE SECRET BASE OF A GROUP CALLED HYDRA.
RUMOR SAYS THEY'RE SOME S.S. OFF-SHOOT...
AN' ZEMO WORKIN' WITH 'EM POINTS IN THAT DIRECTION...
...BUT WE KNOW NEXT TO NOTHIN' ABOUT HYDRA BEYOND RUMOR.
EXCEPT THAT THEY HAVE ACCESS TO SOME HIGHLY ADVANCED WEAPONS.
THE KIND OF GUNS WE CAN'T AFFORD TO HAVE THE AVERAGE NAZI SOLDIER CARRYING ONTO THE BATTLEFIELD...

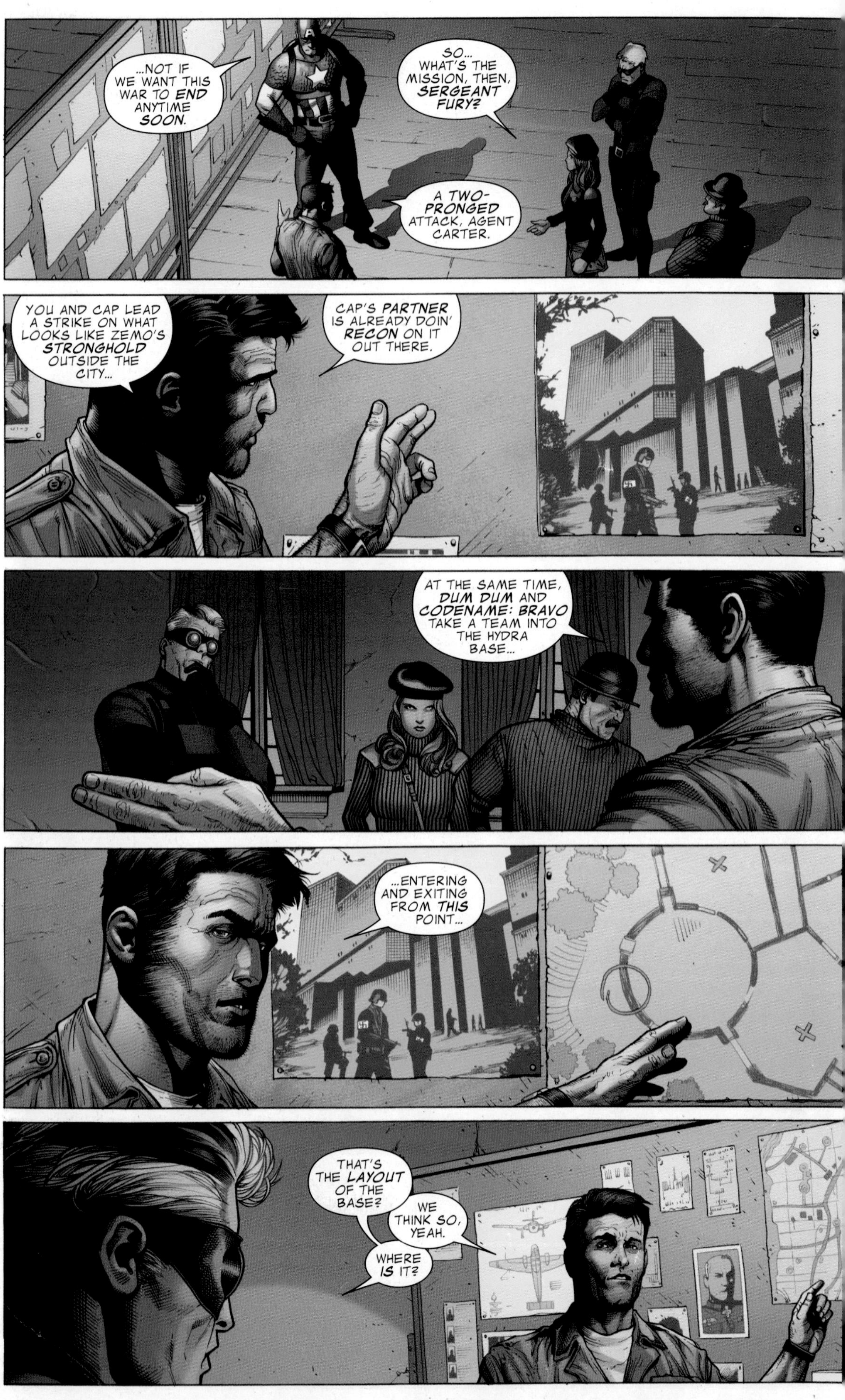
...NOT IF WE WANT THIS WAR TO END ANYTIME SOON.
SO... WHAT'S THE MISSION, THEN, SERGEANT FURY?
A TWO-PRONGED ATTACK, AGENT CARTER.
YOU AND CAP LEAD A STRIKE ON WHAT LOOKS LIKE ZEMO'S STRONGHOLD OUTSIDE THE CITY...
CAP'S PARTNER IS ALREADY DOIN' RECON ON IT OUT THERE.
AT THE SAME TIME, DUM DUM AND CODENAME: BRAVO TAKE A TEAM INTO THE HYDRA BASE...
...ENTERING AND EXITING FROM THIS POINT...
THAT'S THE LAYOUT OF THE BASE?
WE THINK SO, YEAH.
WHERE IS IT?

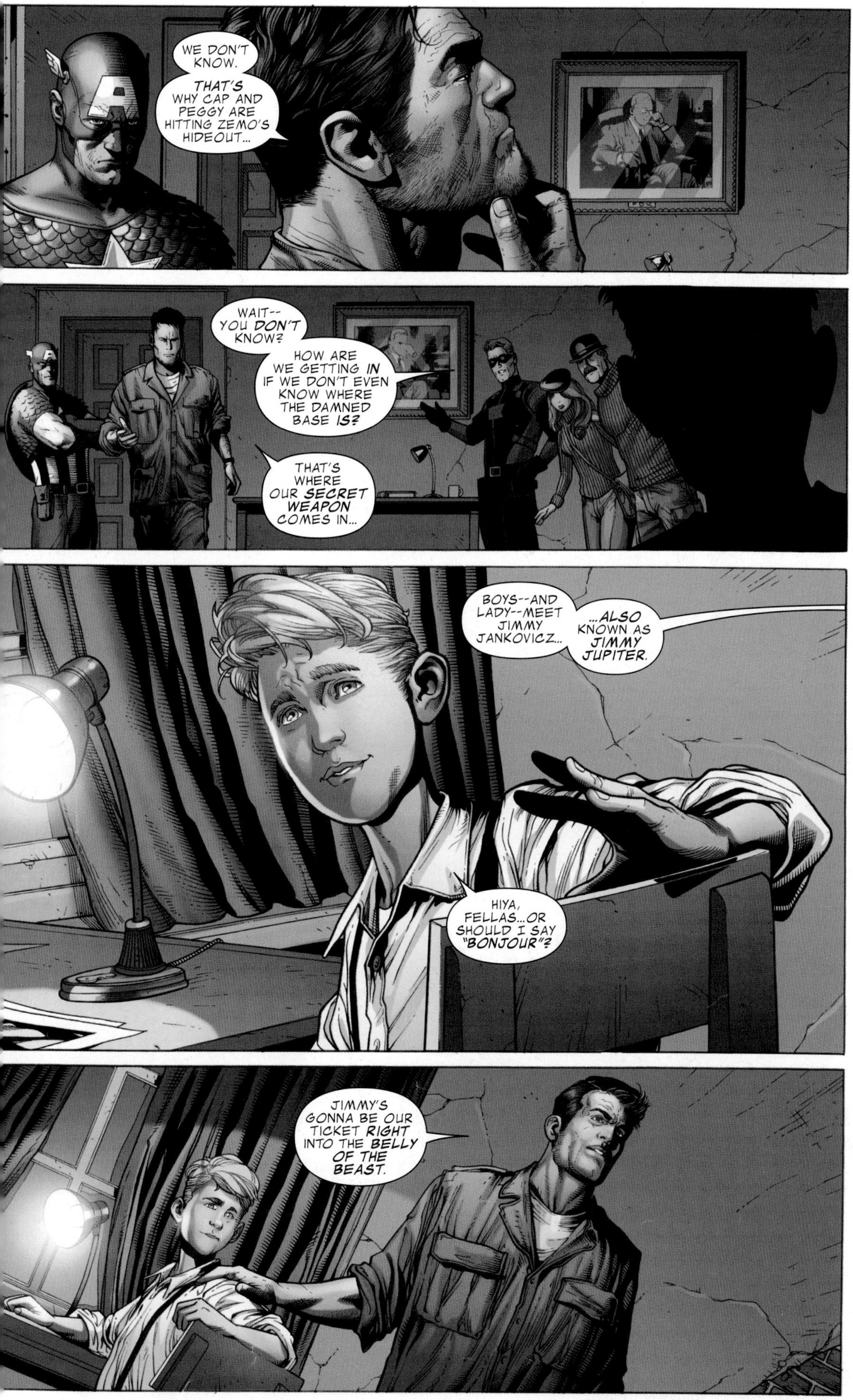
WE DON'T KNOW. THAT'S WHY CAP AND PEGGY ARE HITTING ZEMO'S HIDEOUT...
WAIT-- YOU DON'T KNOW?
HOW ARE WE GETTING IN IF WE DON'T EVEN KNOW WHERE THE DAMNED BASE IS?
THAT'S WHERE OUR SECRET WEAPON COMES IN...
BOYS--AND LADY--MEET JIMMY JANKOVICZ...
...ALSO KNOWN AS JIMMY JUPITER.
HIYA, FELLAS...OR SHOULD I SAY "BONJOUR"?
JIMMY'S GONNA BE OUR TICKET RIGHT INTO THE BELLY OF THE BEAST.

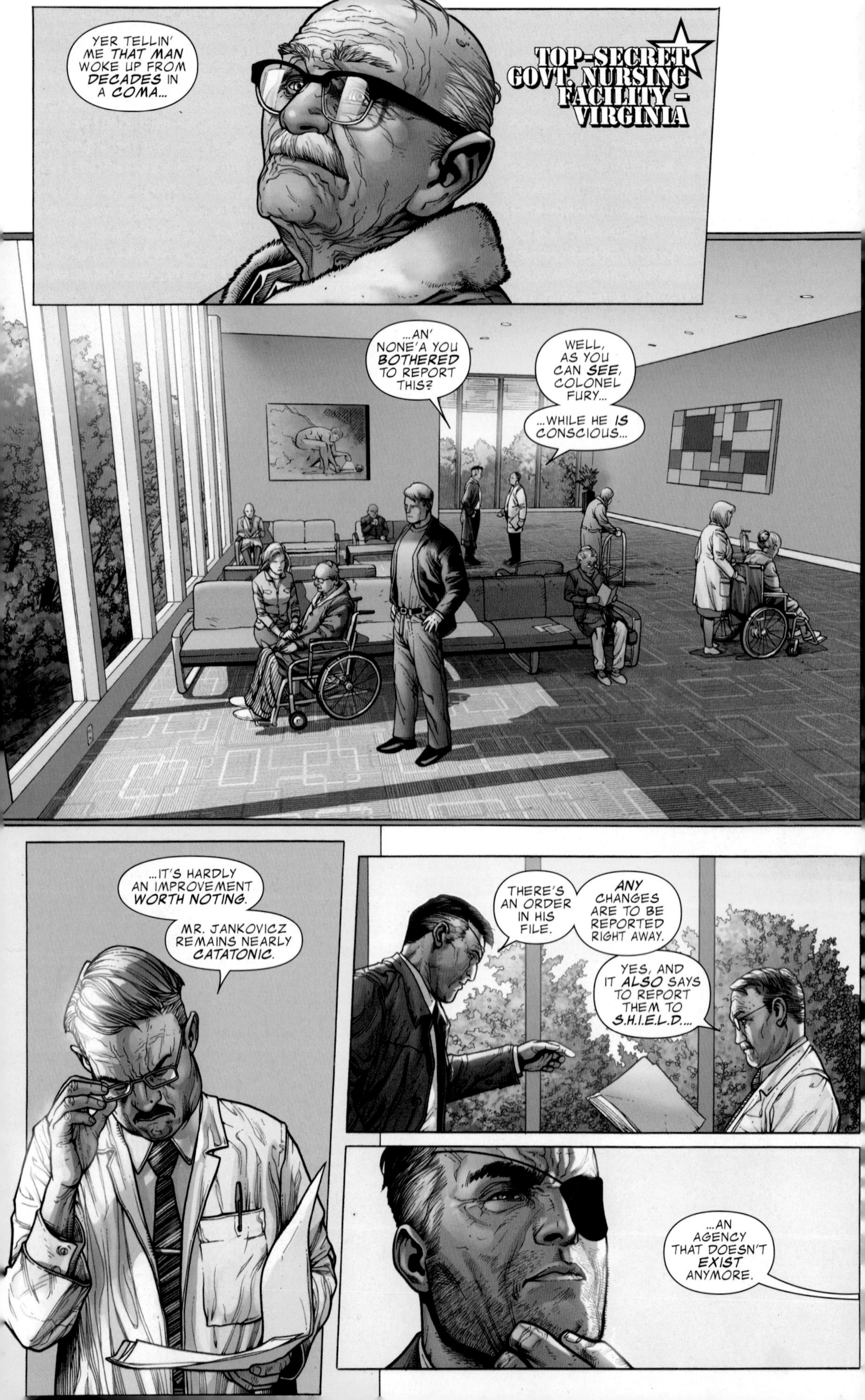

YER TELLIN' ME THAT MAN WOKE UP FROM DECADES IN A COMA...
TOP-SECRET GOVT. NURSING FACILITY - VIRGINIA
...AN' NONE'A YOU BOTHERED TO REPORT THIS?
WELL, AS YOU CAN SEE, COLONEL FURY...
...WHILE HE IS CONSCIOUS...
...IT'S HARDLY AN IMPROVEMENT WORTH NOTING.
MR. JANKOVICZ REMAINS NEARLY CATATONIC.
THERE'S AN ORDER IN HIS FILE.
ANY CHANGES ARE TO BE REPORTED RIGHT AWAY.
YES, AND IT ALSO SAYS TO REPORT THEM TO S.H.I.E.L.D....
...AN AGENCY THAT DOESN'T EXIST ANYMORE.

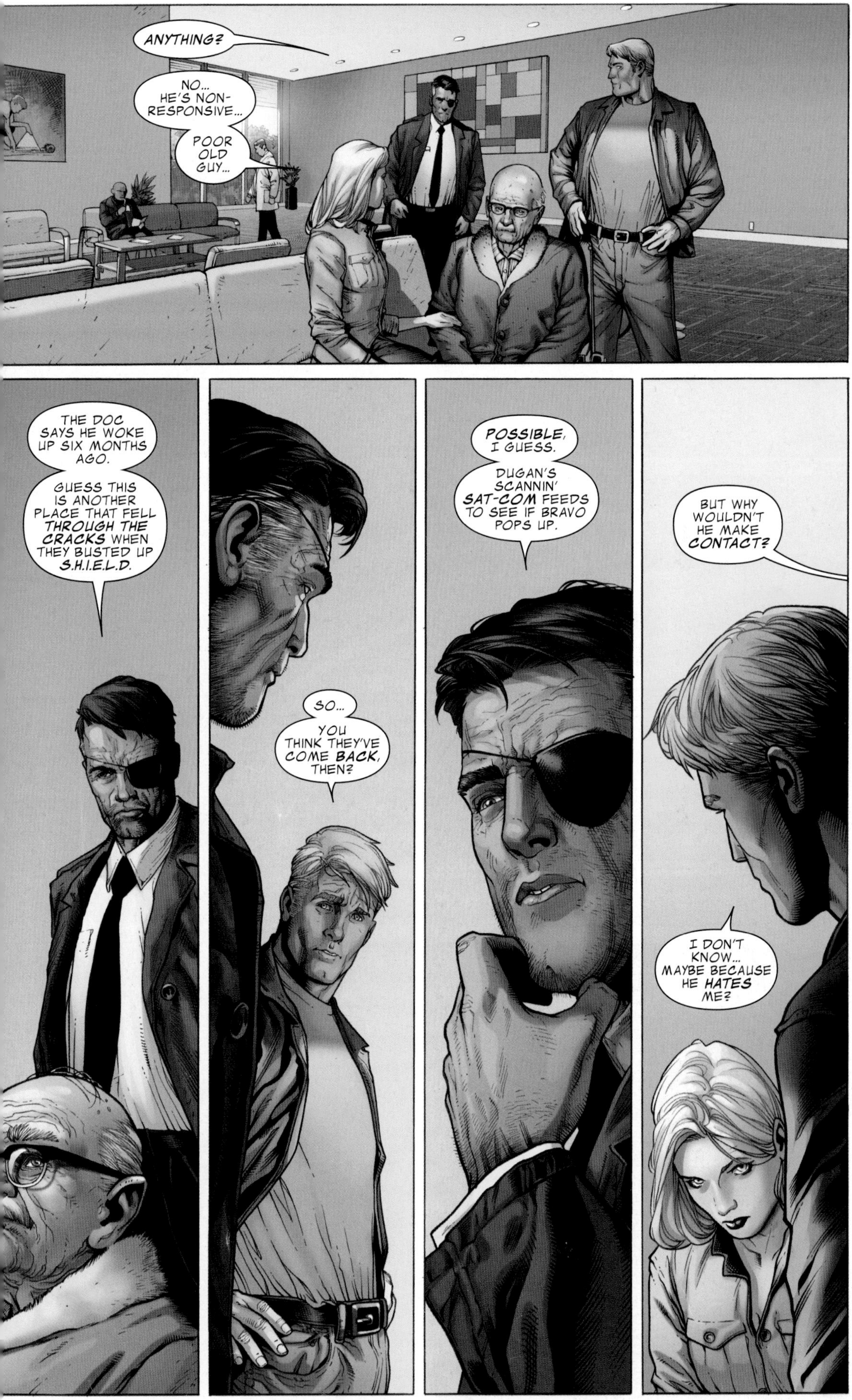
ANYTHING?
NO... HE'S NON-RESPONSIVE...
POOR OLD GUY...
THE DOC SAYS HE WOKE UP SIX MONTHS AGO.
GUESS THIS IS ANOTHER PLACE THAT FELL THROUGH THE CRACKS WHEN THEY BUSTED UP S.H.I.E.L.D.
SO... YOU THINK THEY'VE COME BACK, THEN?
POSSIBLE, I GUESS.
DUGAN'S SCANNIN' SAT-COM FEEDS TO SEE IF BRAVO POPS UP.
BUT WHY WOULDN'T HE MAKE CONTACT?
I DON'T KNOW... MAYBE BECAUSE HE HATES ME?

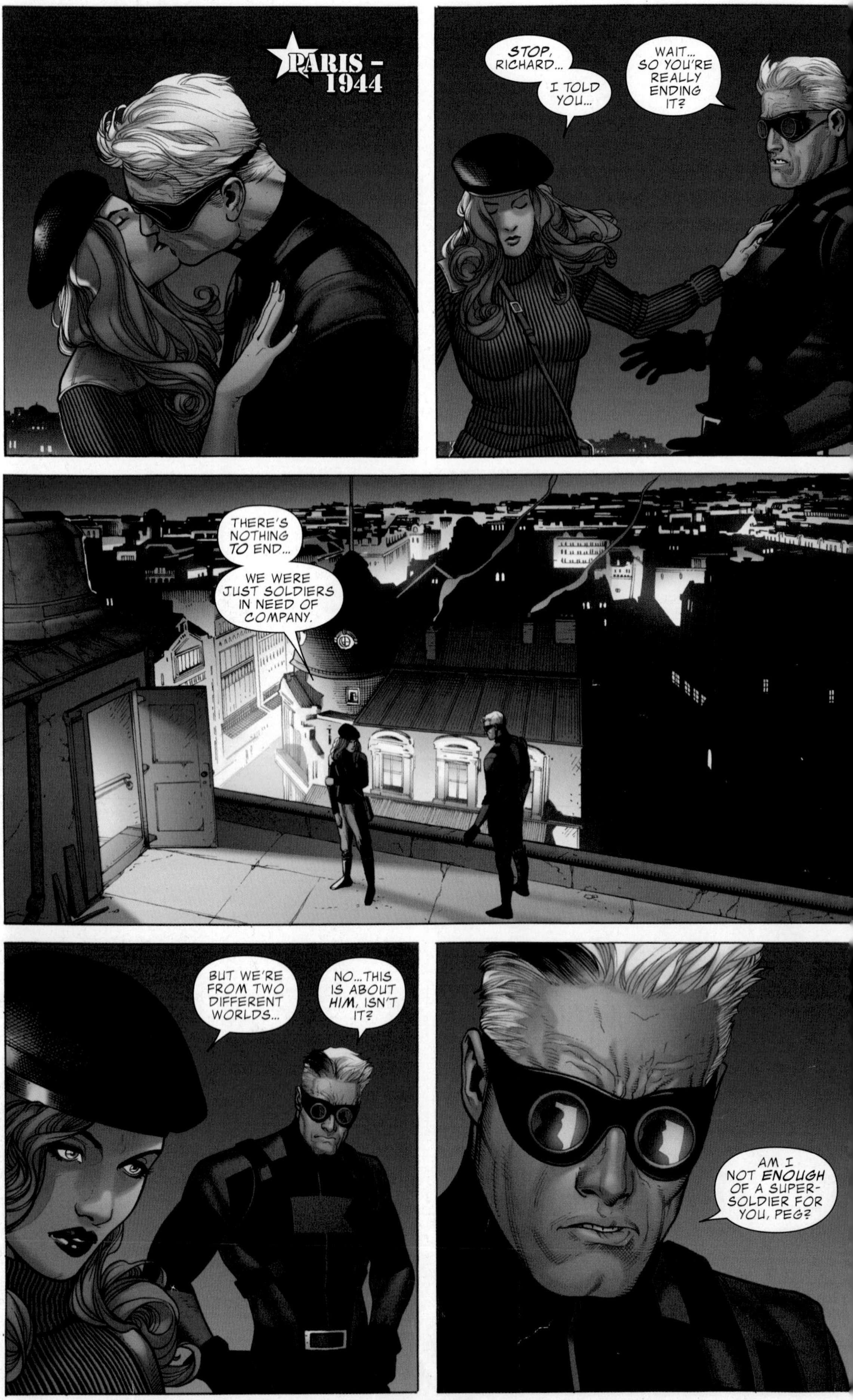
PARIS - 1944
STOP, RICHARD...
I TOLD YOU...
WAIT... SO YOU'RE REALLY ENDING IT?
THERE'S NOTHING TO END...
WE WERE JUST SOLDIERS IN NEED OF COMPANY.
BUT WE'RE FROM TWO DIFFERENT WORLDS...
NO...THIS IS ABOUT HIM, ISN'T IT?
AM I NOT ENOUGH OF A SUPER-SOLDIER FOR YOU, PEG?

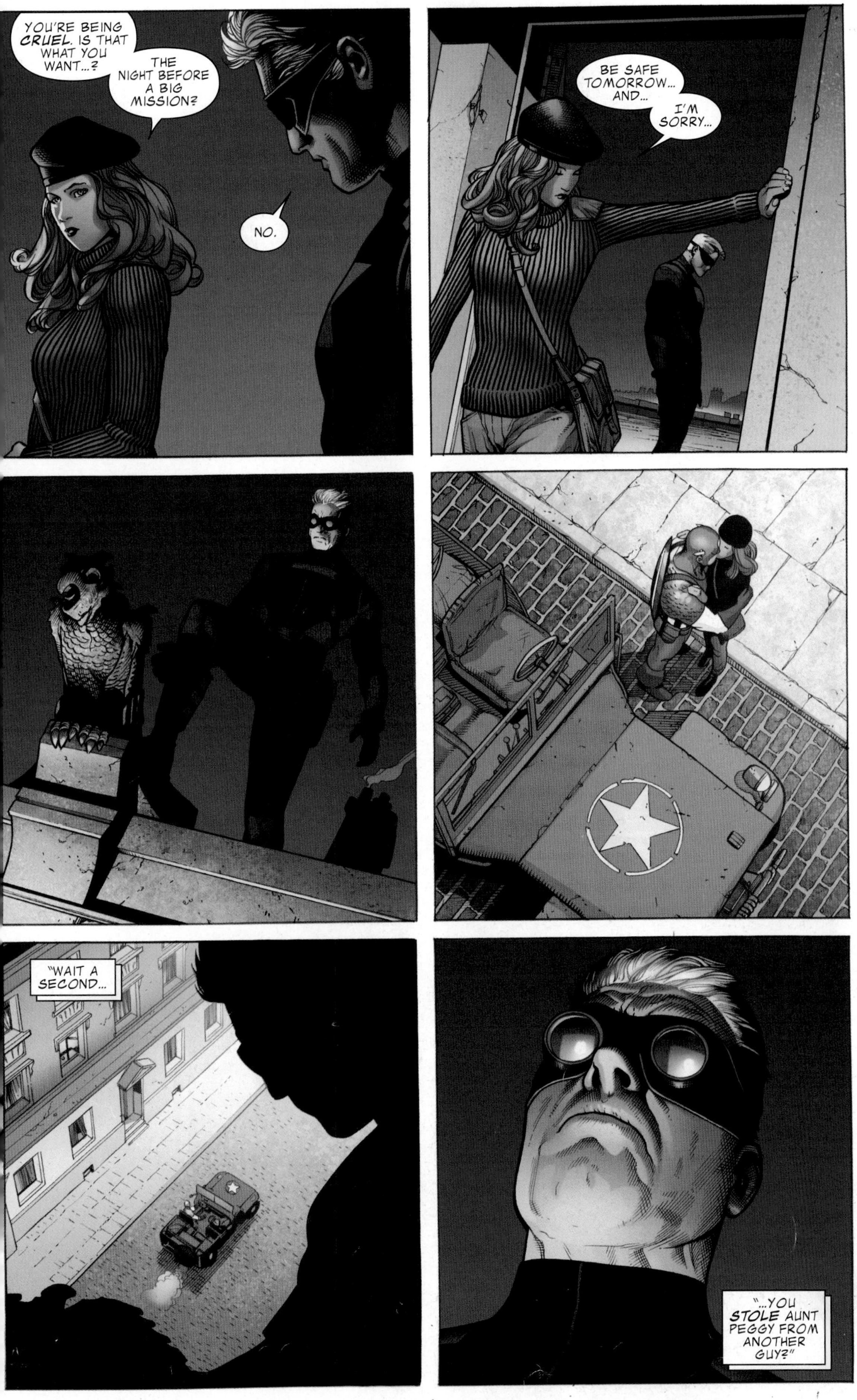
YOU'RE BEING CRUEL. IS THAT WHAT YOU WANT...?
THE NIGHT BEFORE A BIG MISSION?
NO.
BE SAFE TOMORROW... AND...
I'M SORRY...
"WAIT A SECOND...
"...YOU STOLE AUNT PEGGY FROM ANOTHER GUY?"

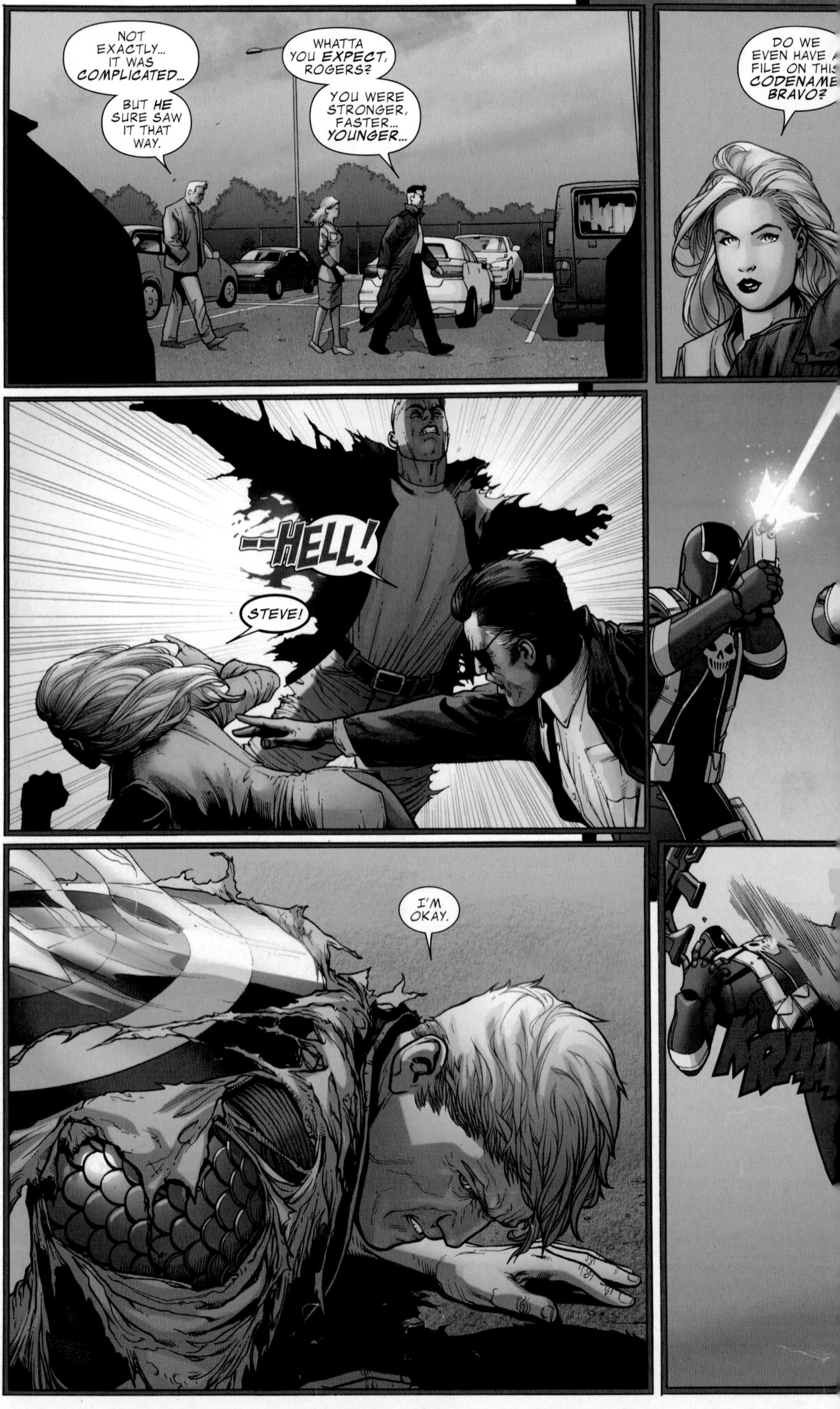
NOT EXACTLY... IT WAS COMPLICATED...
BUT HE SURE SAW IT THAT WAY.
WHATTA YOU EXPECT, ROGERS?
YOU WERE STRONGER, FASTER... YOUNGER...
DO WE EVEN HAVE A FILE ON THIS CODENAME BRAVO?
--HELL!
STEVE!
I'M OKAY.

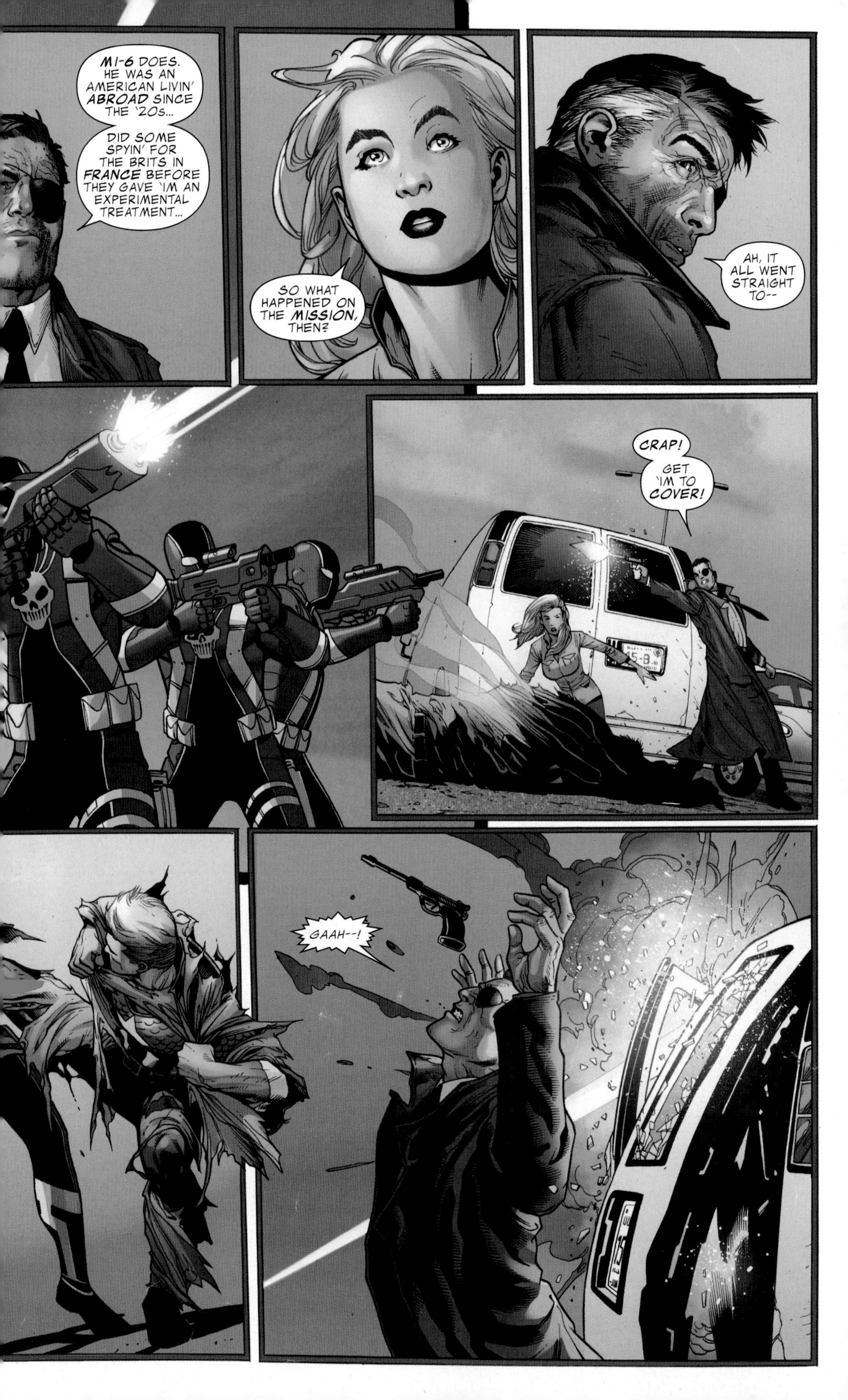
M I-6 DOES. HE WAS AN AMERICAN LIVIN' ABROAD SINCE THE '20s...
DID SOME SPYIN' FOR THE BRITS IN FRANCE BEFORE THEY GAVE 'IM AN EXPERIMENTAL TREATMENT...
SO WHAT HAPPENED ON THE MISSION, THEN?
AH, IT ALL WENT STRAIGHT TO--
CRAP! GET 'IM TO COVER!
GAAH--!

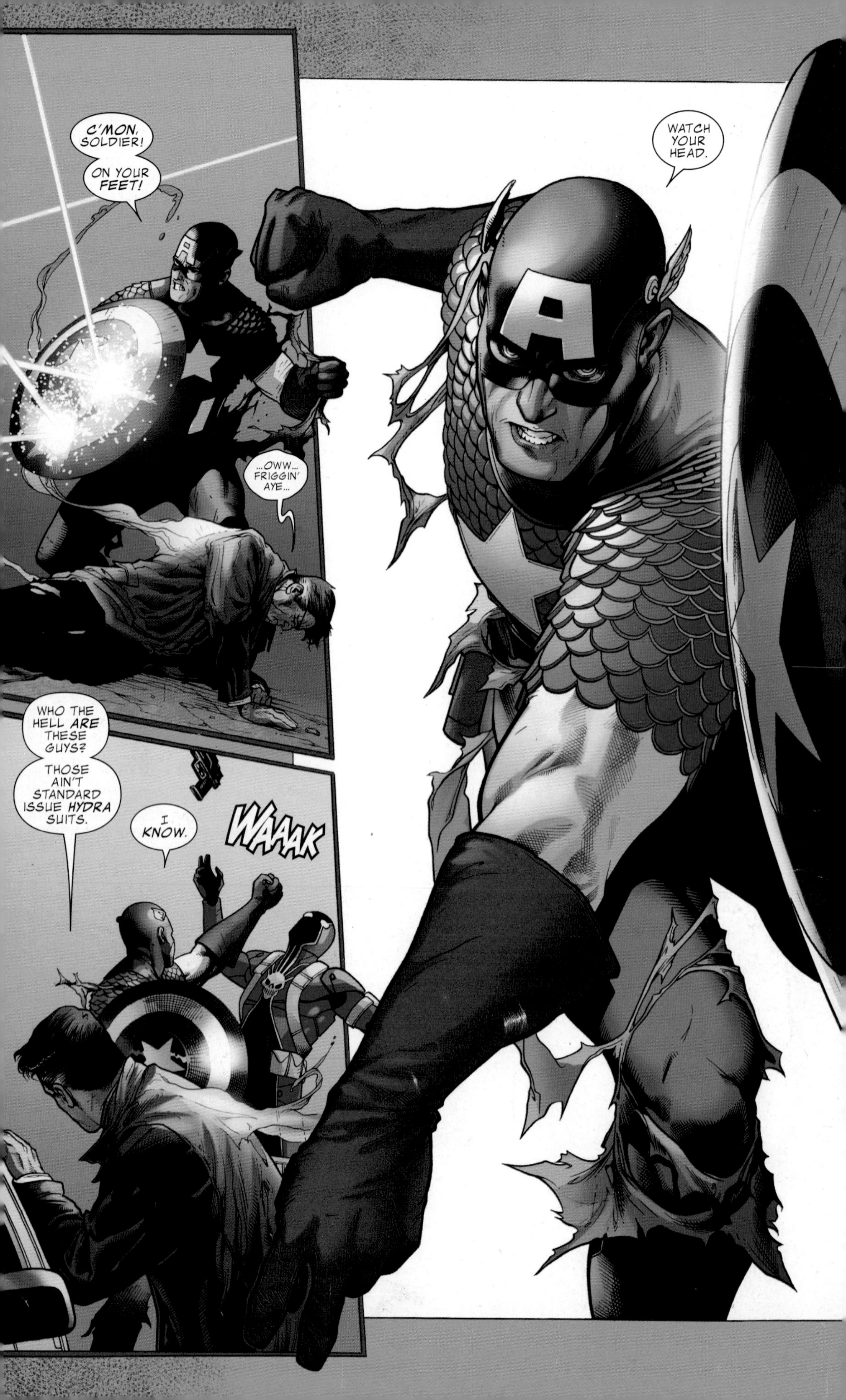

C'MON, SOLDIER!
ON YOUR FEET!
...OWW... FRIGGIN' AYE...
WATCH YOUR HEAD.
WHO THE HELL ARE THESE GUYS?
THOSE AIN'T STANDARD ISSUE HYDRA SUITS.
I KNOW.
WAAAK

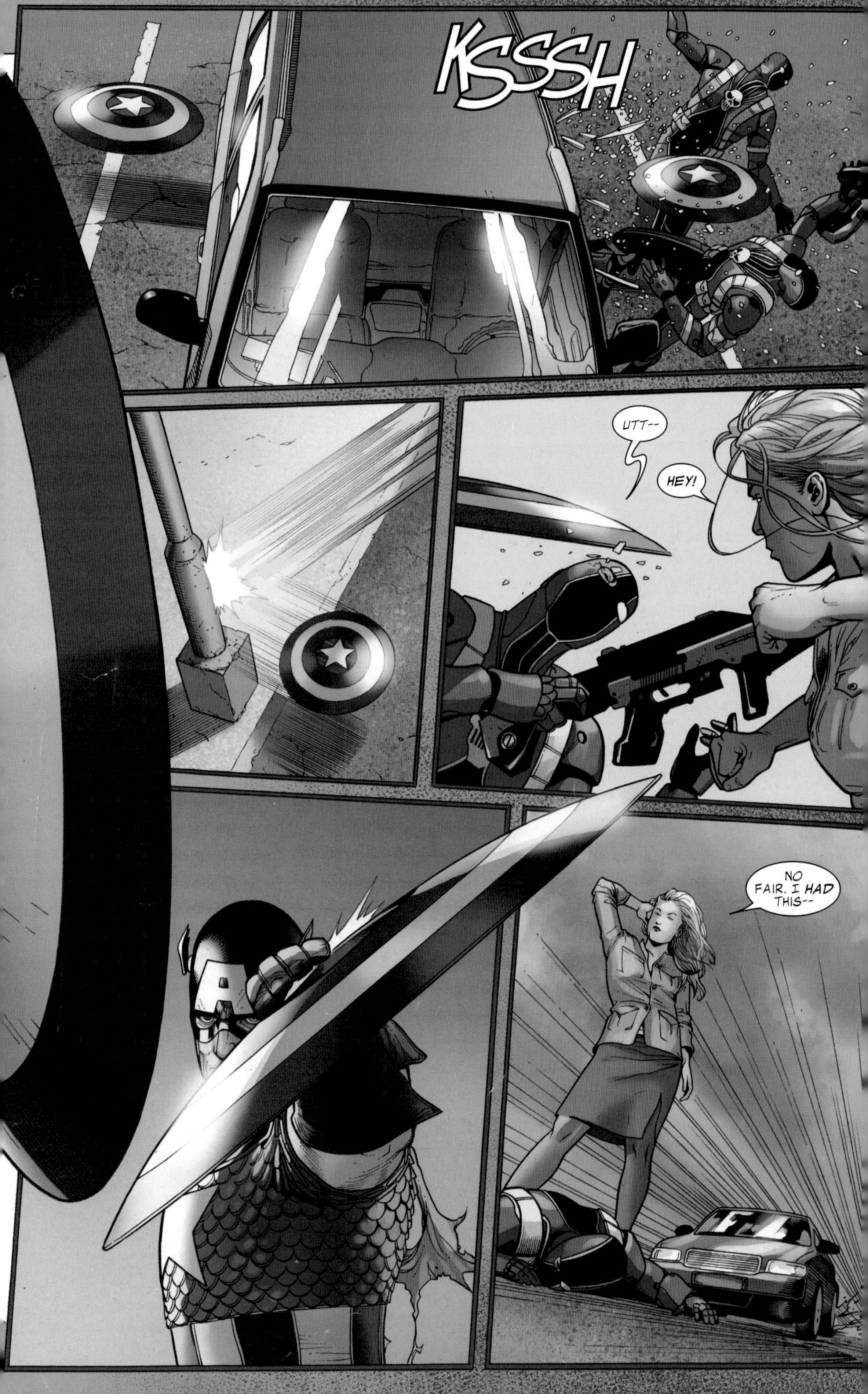
KSSSH
UTT--
HEY!
NO FAIR. I HAD THIS--

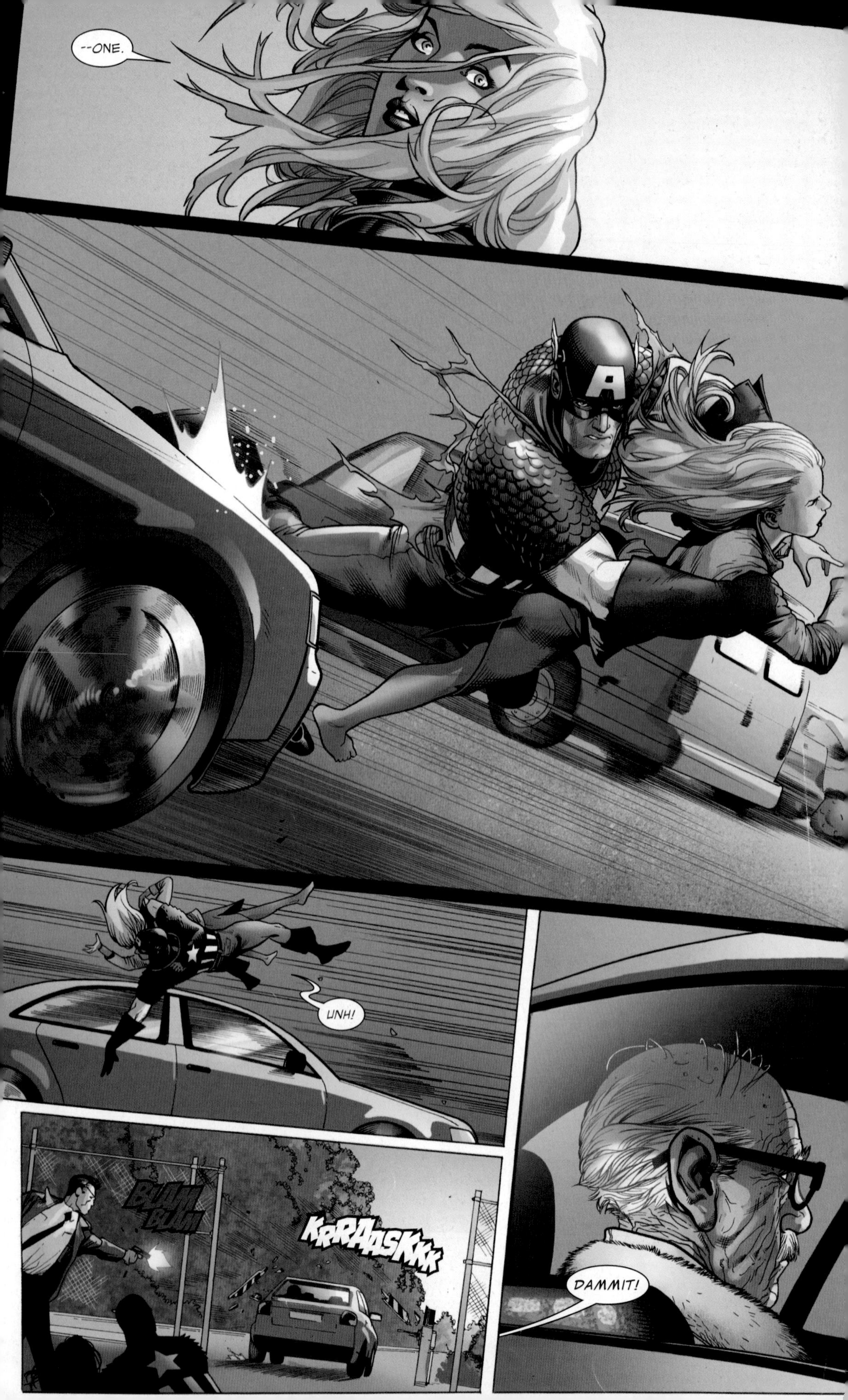
--ONE.
UNH!
BLAM BLAM
KRRAASKKK
DAMMIT!

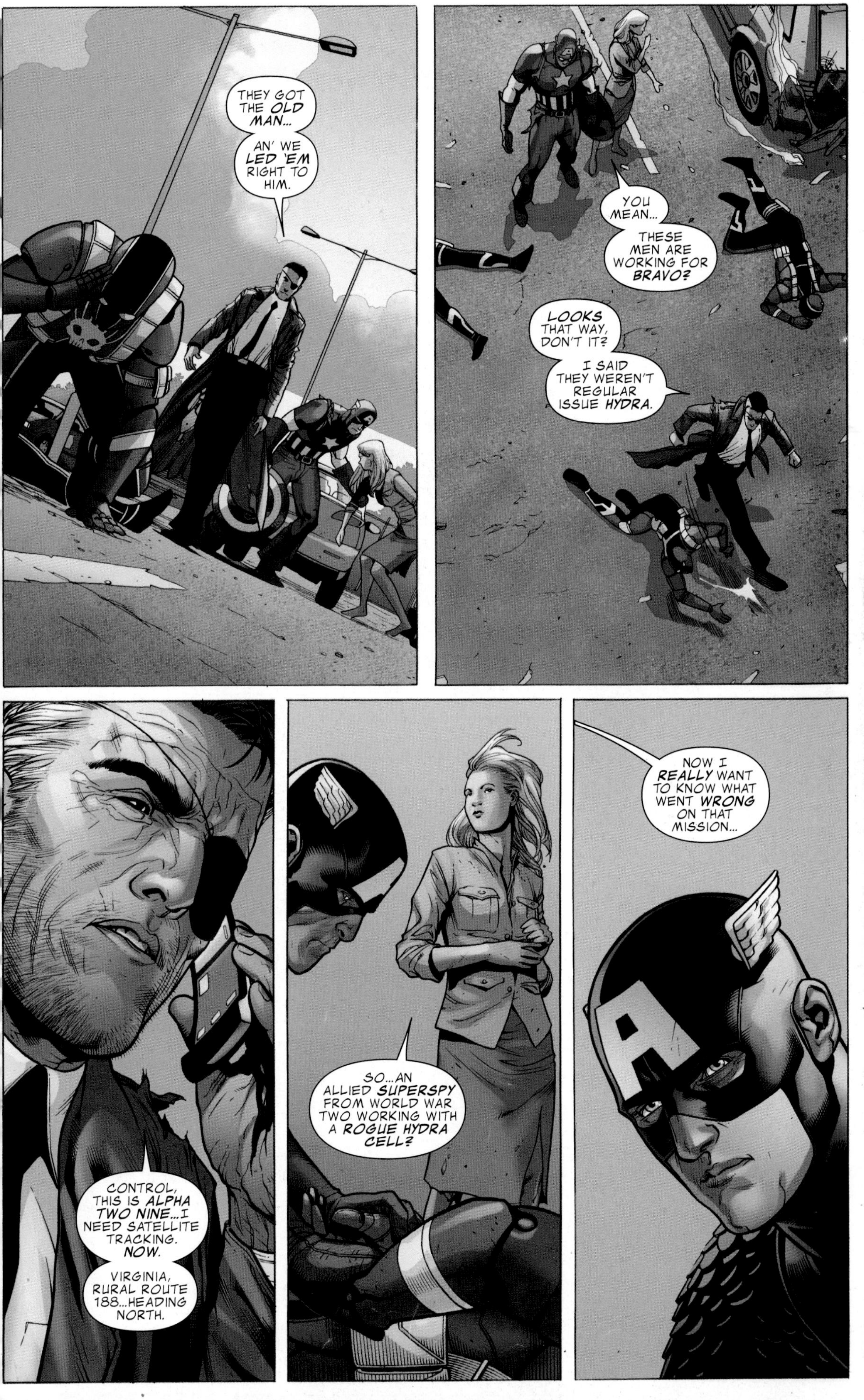
THEY GOT THE OLD MAN...
AN' WE LED 'EM RIGHT TO HIM.
YOU MEAN...
THESE MEN ARE WORKING FOR BRAVO?
LOOKS THAT WAY, DON'T IT?
I SAID THEY WEREN'T REGULAR ISSUE HYDRA.
CONTROL, THIS IS ALPHA TWO NINE...I NEED SATELLITE TRACKING. NOW.
VIRGINIA, RURAL ROUTE 188...HEADING NORTH.
SO...AN ALLIED SUPERSPY FROM WORLD WAR TWO WORKING WITH A ROGUE HYDRA CELL?
NOW I REALLY WANT TO KNOW WHAT WENT WRONG ON THAT MISSION...

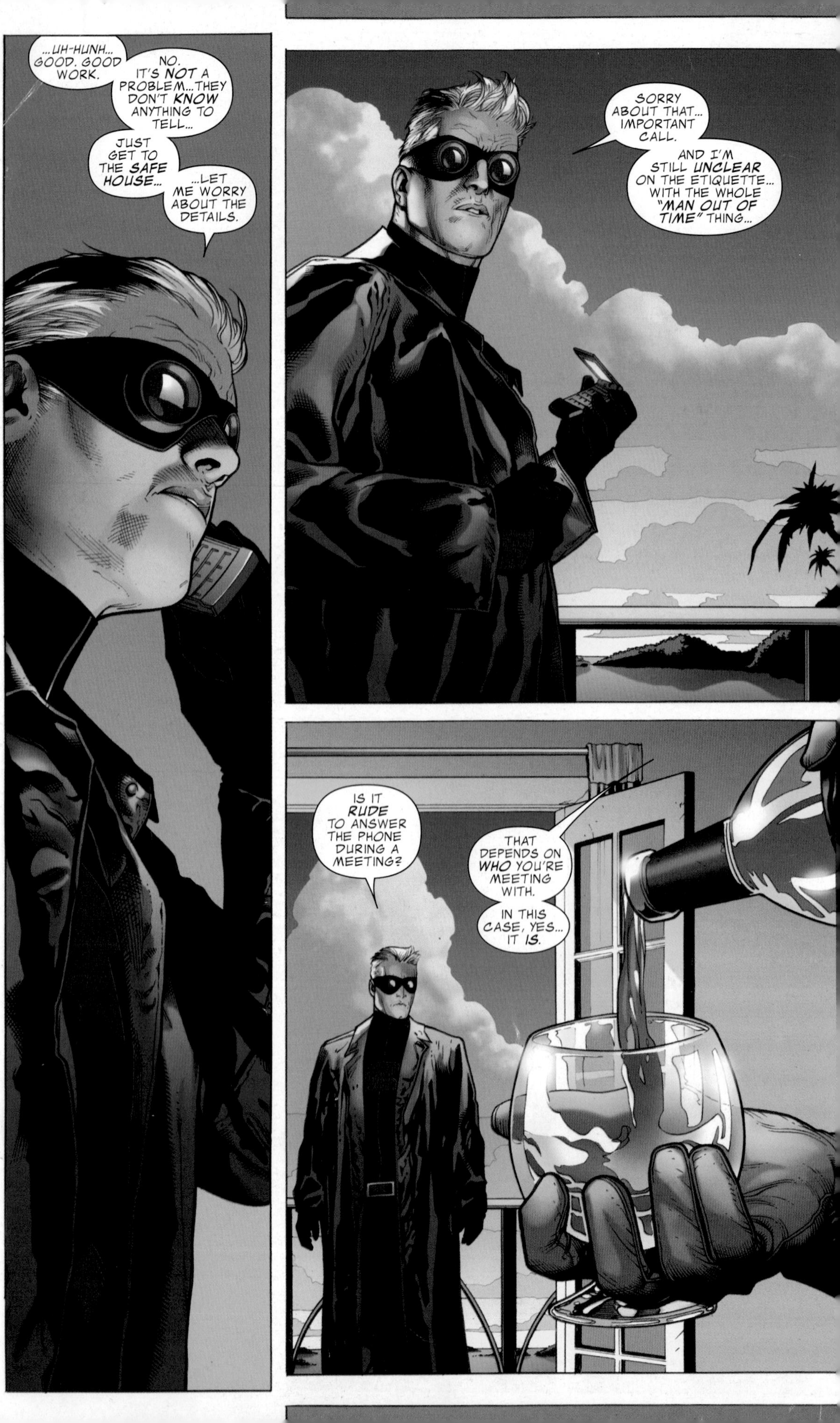

...UH-HUNH... GOOD. GOOD WORK.
NO. IT'S NOT A PROBLEM...THEY DON'T KNOW ANYTHING TO TELL...
JUST GET TO THE SAFE HOUSE...
...LET ME WORRY ABOUT THE DETAILS.
SORRY ABOUT THAT... IMPORTANT CALL.
AND I'M STILL UNCLEAR ON THE ETIQUETTE... WITH THE WHOLE "MAN OUT OF TIME" THING...
IS IT RUDE TO ANSWER THE PHONE DURING A MEETING?
THAT DEPENDS ON WHO YOU'RE MEETING WITH.
IN THIS CASE, YES... IT IS.

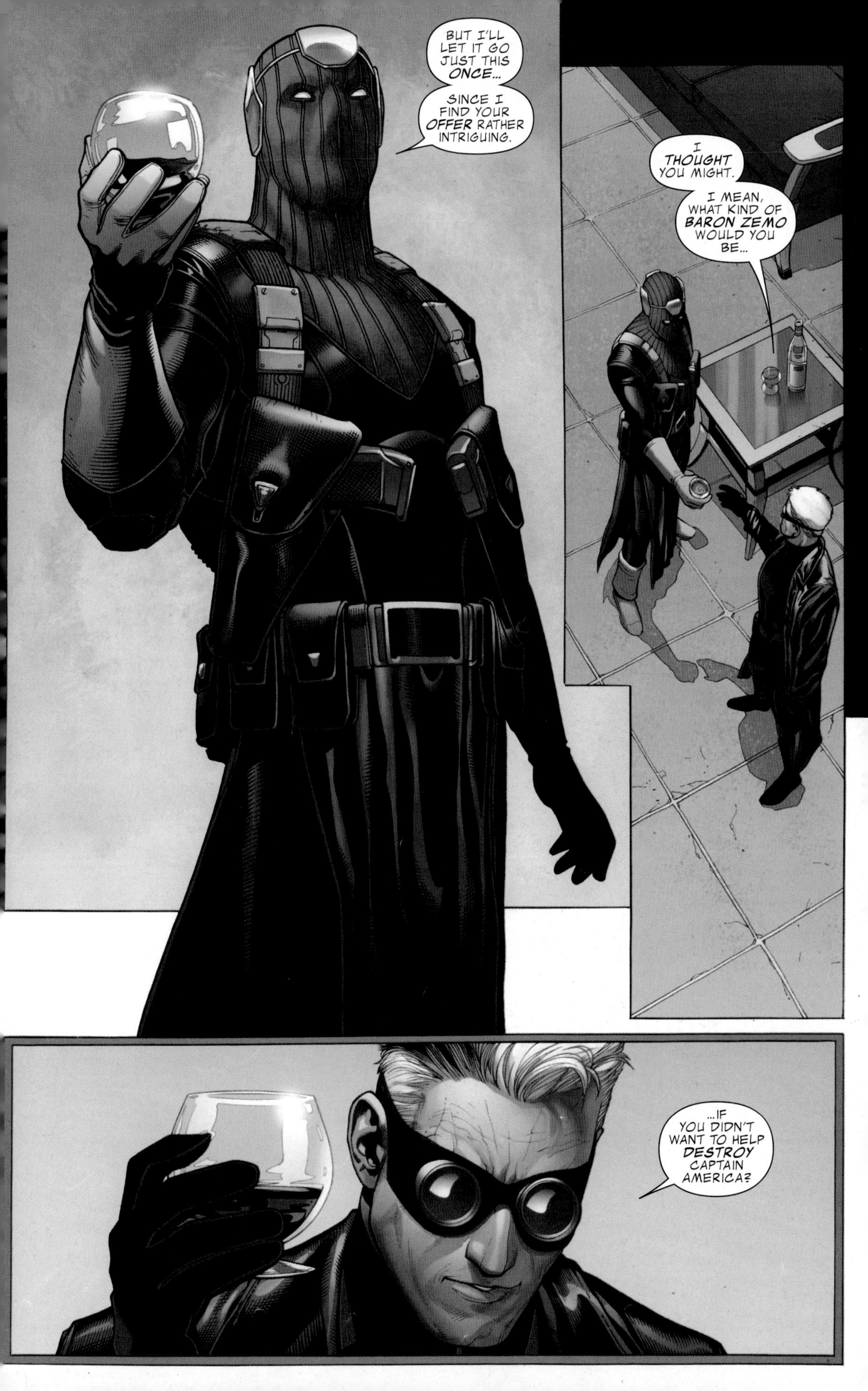
BUT I'LL LET IT GO JUST THIS ONCE...
SINCE I FIND YOUR OFFER RATHER INTRIGUING.
I THOUGHT YOU MIGHT.
I MEAN, WHAT KIND OF BARON ZEMO WOULD YOU BE...
...IF YOU DIDN'T WANT TO HELP DESTROY CAPTAIN AMERICA?

#1 VARIANT BY JOHN ROMITA SR., JOE SINNOTT & VAL STAPLES

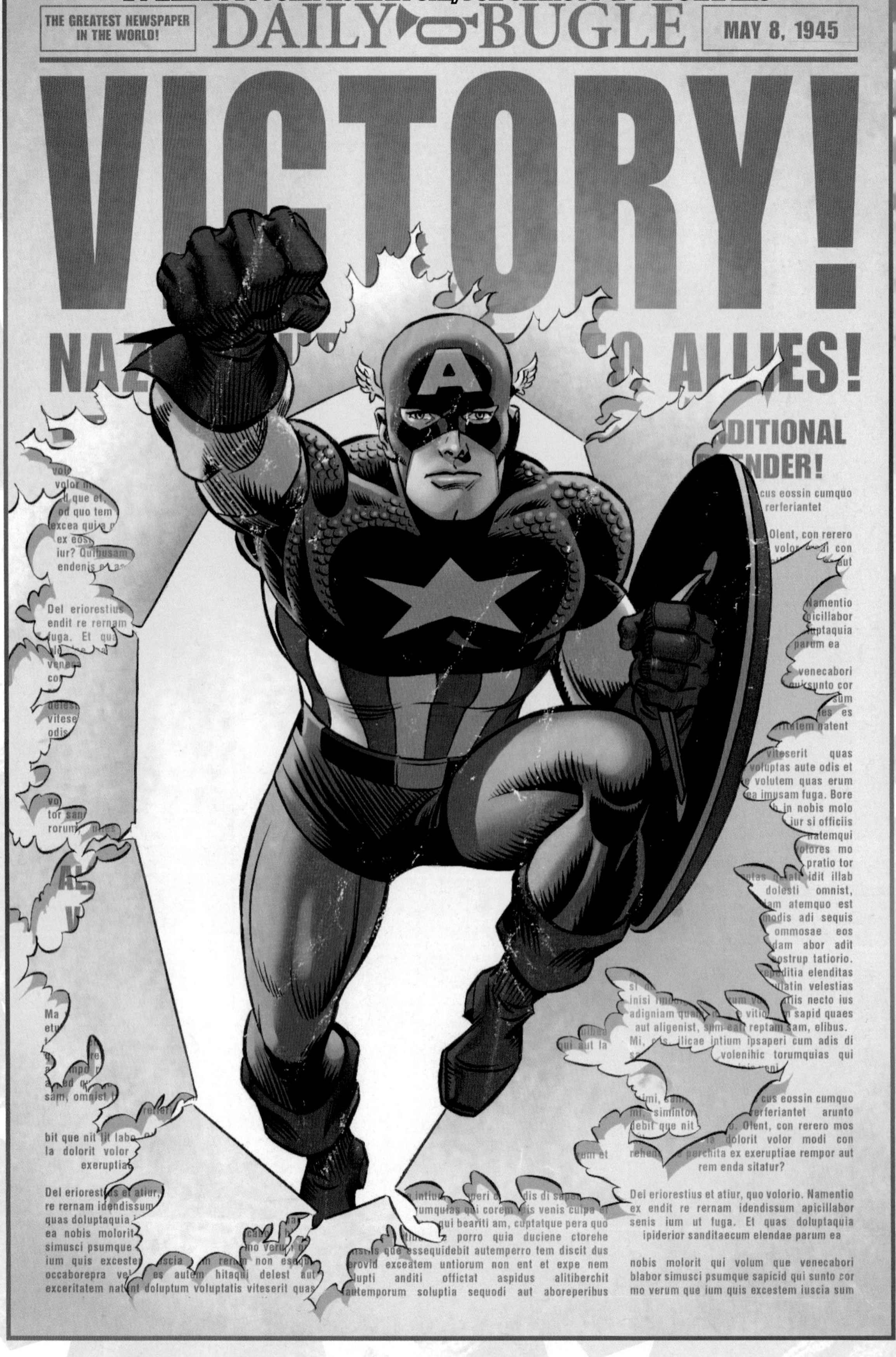

THE GREATEST NEWSPAPER IN THE WORLD!
DAILY BUGLE
MAY 8, 1945
VICTORY!
Del eriorestius et atiur, quo volorio. Namentio ex endit re rernam idendissum apicillabor senis ium ut fuga. Et quas doluptaquia ipiderior sanditaecum elendae parum ea
nobis molorit qui volum que venecabori blabor simusci psumque sapicid qui sunto cor mo verum que ium quis excestem iuscia sum

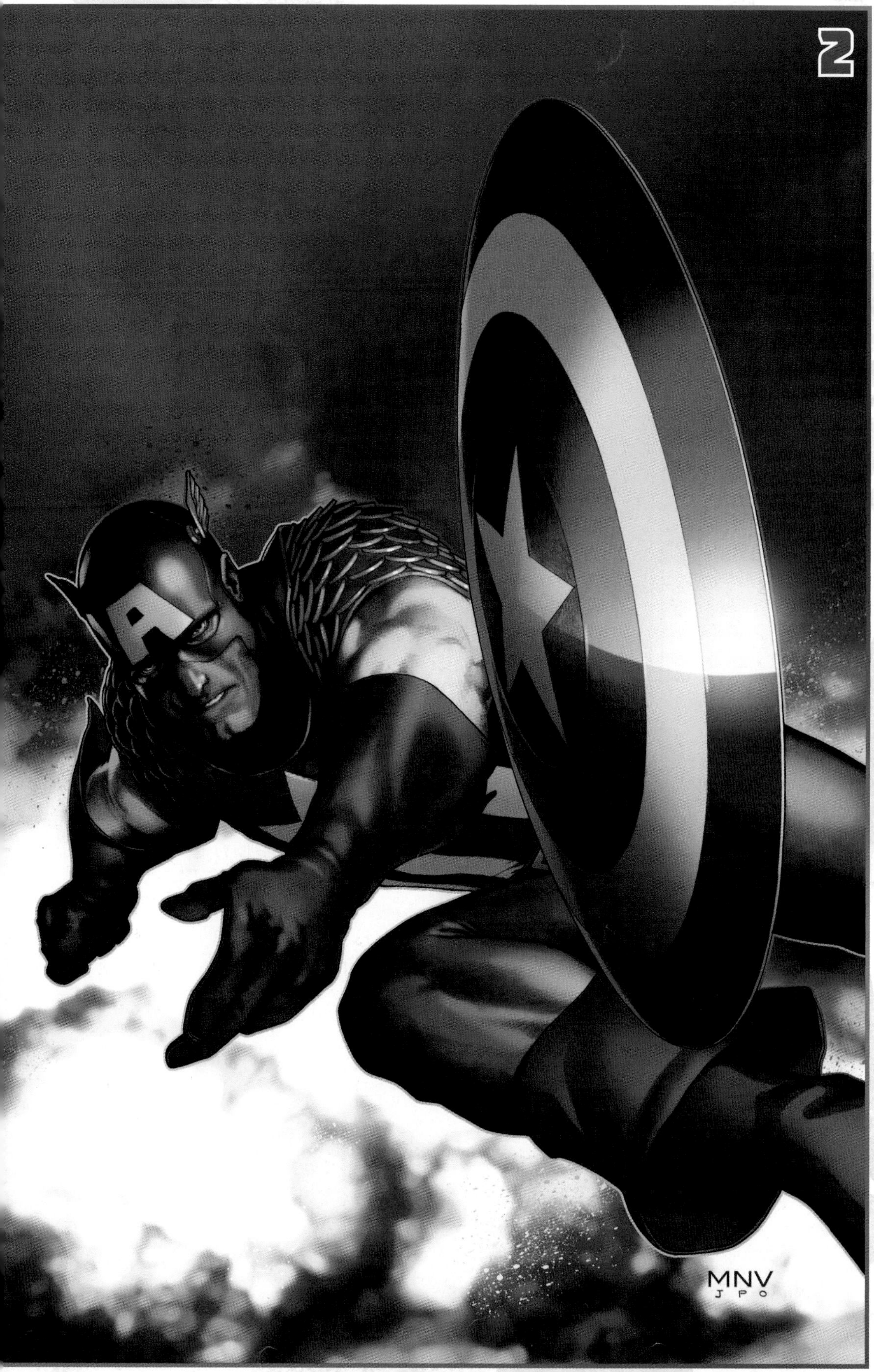
2
MNV
JPO

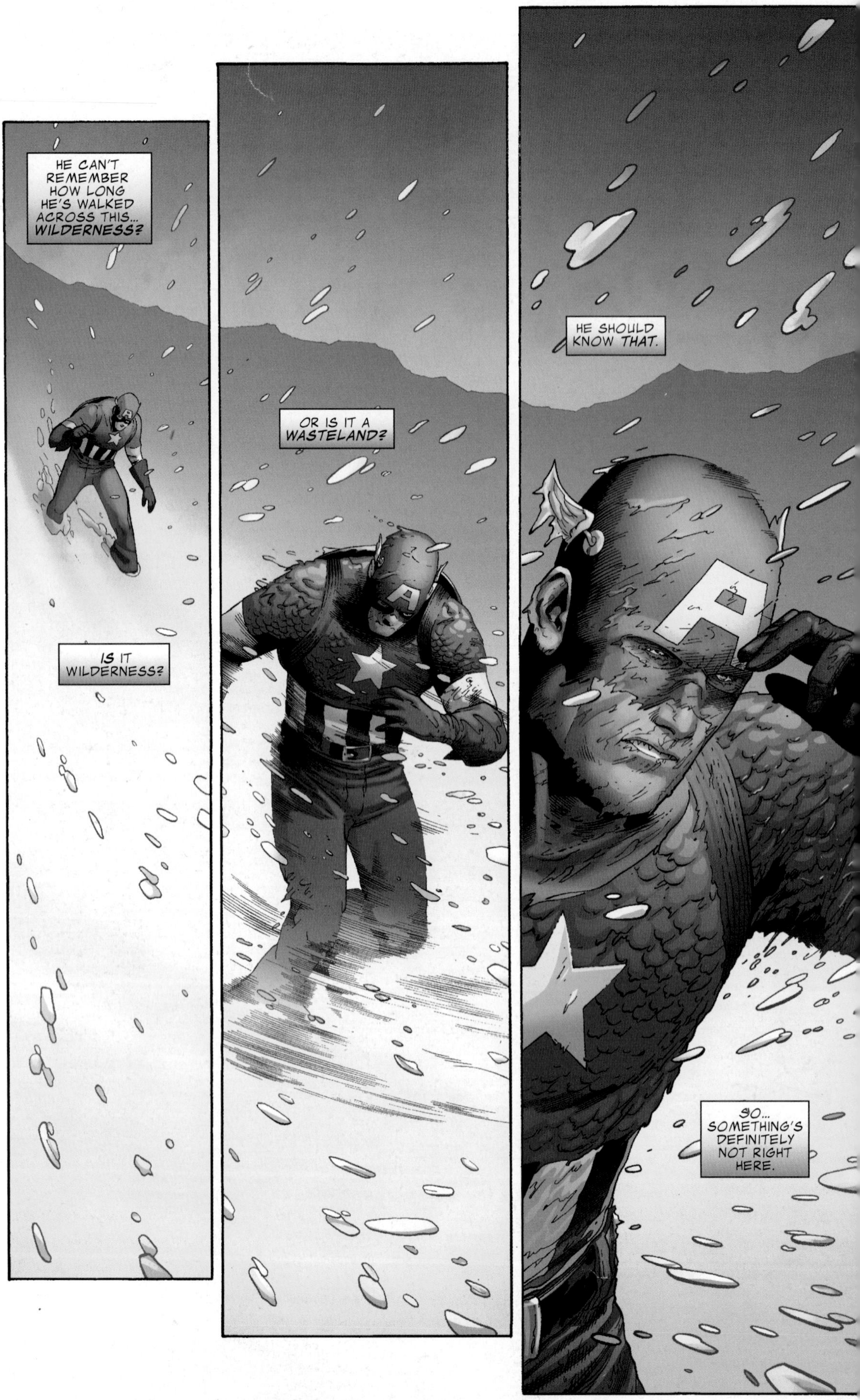
HE CAN'T REMEMBER HOW LONG HE'S WALKED ACROSS THIS... WILDERNESS?
IS IT WILDERNESS?
OR IS IT A WASTELAND?
HE SHOULD KNOW THAT.
SO... SOMETHING'S DEFINITELY NOT RIGHT HERE.

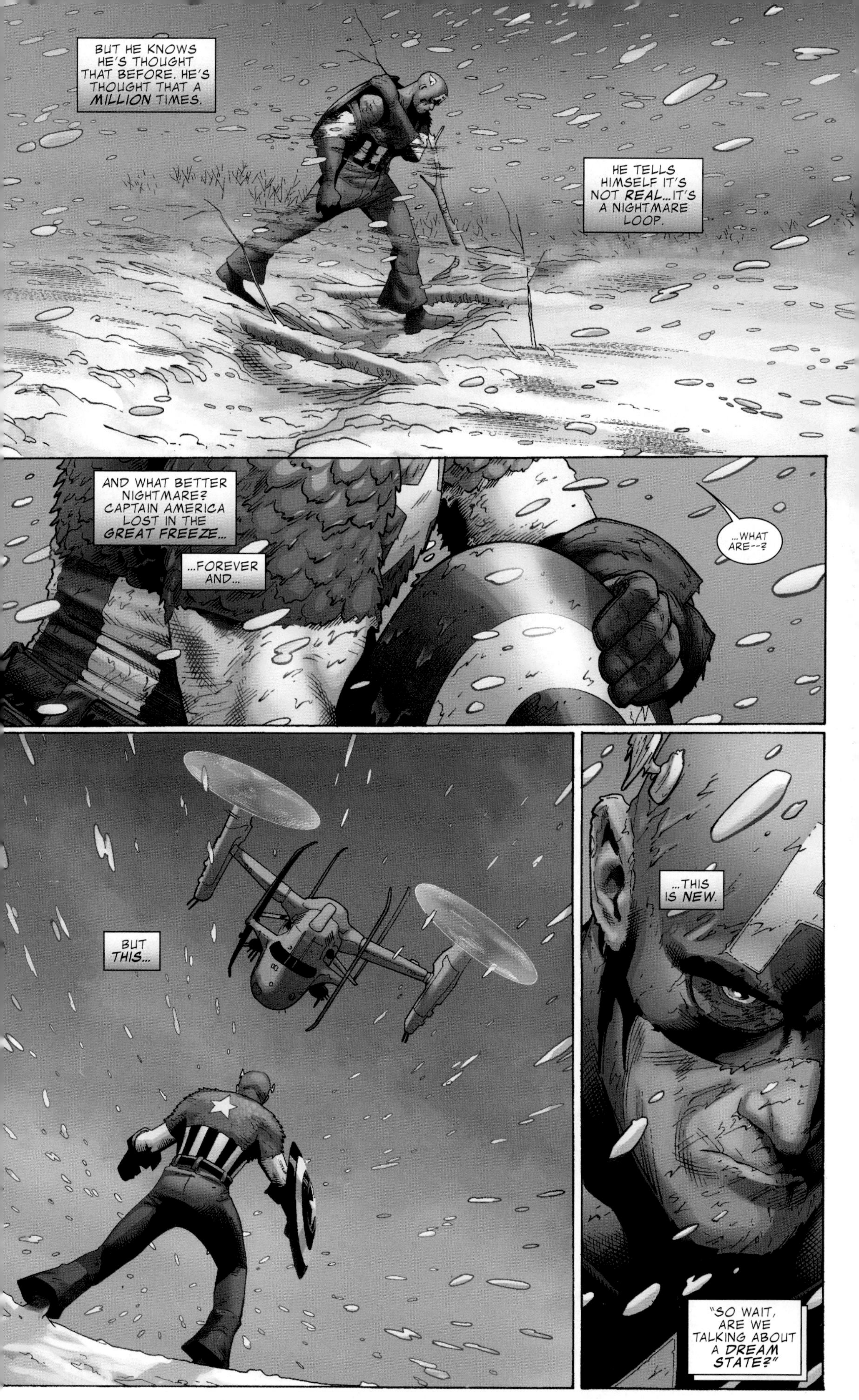
BUT HE KNOWS HE'S THOUGHT THAT BEFORE. HE'S THOUGHT THAT A MILLION TIMES.
HE TELLS HIMSELF IT'S NOT REAL...IT'S A NIGHTMARE LOOP.
AND WHAT BETTER NIGHTMARE? CAPTAIN AMERICA LOST IN THE GREAT FREEZE...
...FOREVER AND...
...WHAT ARE--?
BUT THIS...
...THIS IS NEW.
"SO WAIT, ARE WE TALKING ABOUT A DREAM STATE?"

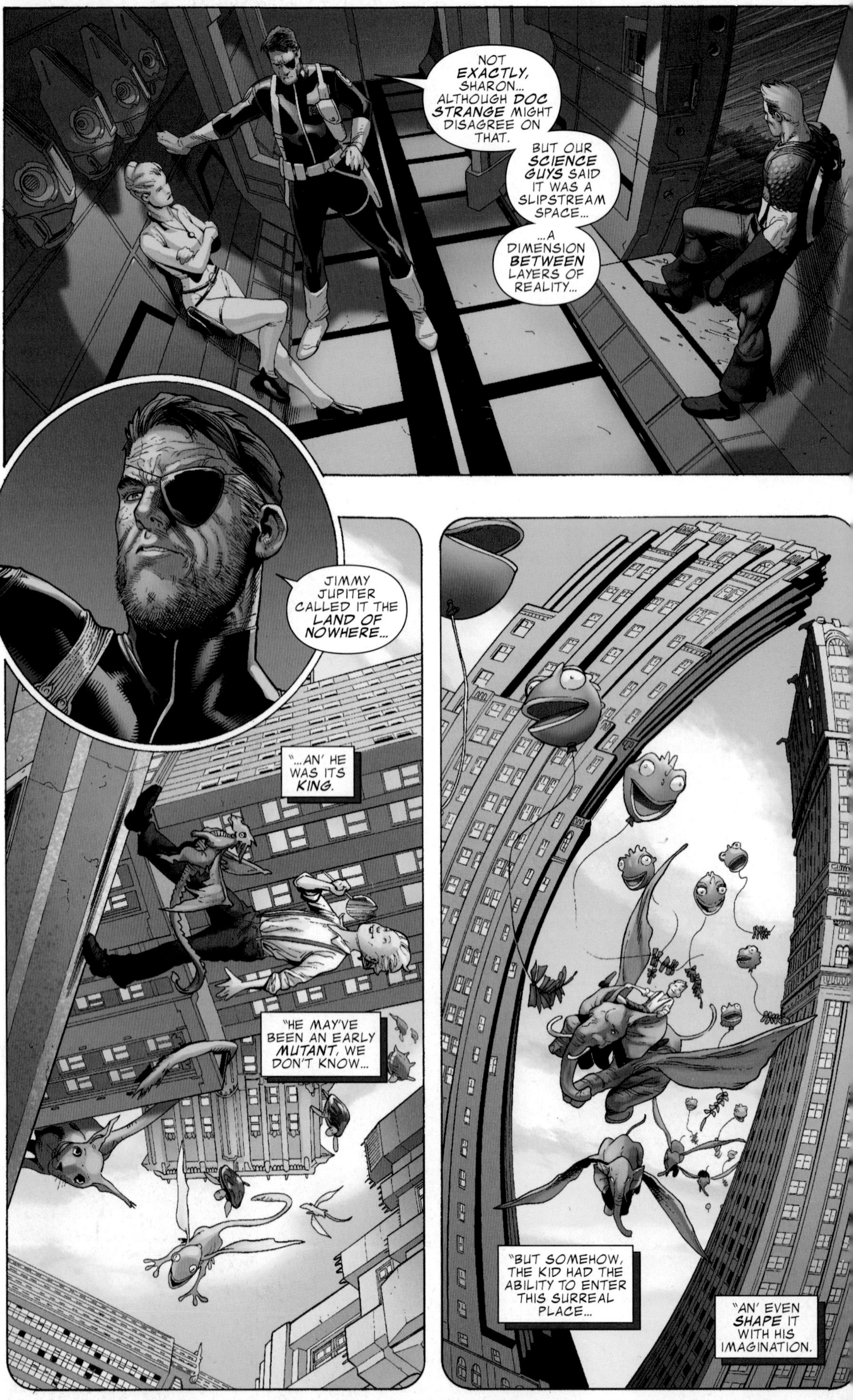
NOT EXACTLY, SHARON... ALTHOUGH DOC STRANGE MIGHT DISAGREE ON THAT.
BUT OUR SCIENCE GUYS SAID IT WAS A SLIPSTREAM SPACE...
...A DIMENSION BETWEEN LAYERS OF REALITY...
JIMMY JUPITER CALLED IT THE LAND OF NOWHERE...
"...AN' HE WAS ITS KING.
"HE MAY'VE BEEN AN EARLY MUTANT, WE DON'T KNOW...
"BUT SOMEHOW, THE KID HAD THE ABILITY TO ENTER THIS SURREAL PLACE...
"AN' EVEN SHAPE IT WITH HIS IMAGINATION.

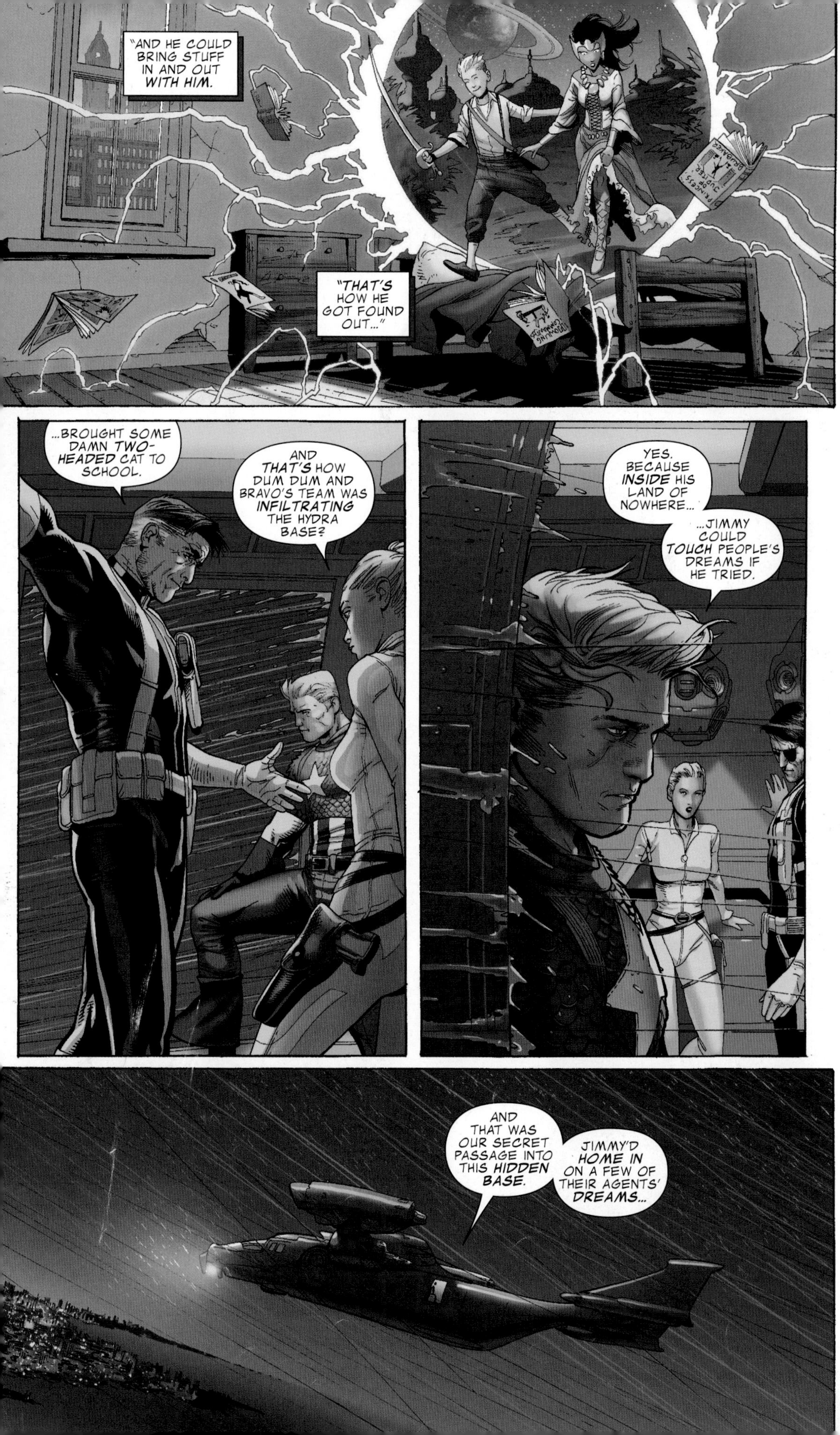
"AND HE COULD BRING STUFF IN AND OUT WITH HIM.
"THAT'S HOW HE GOT FOUND OUT..."
...BROUGHT SOME DAMN TWO-HEADED CAT TO SCHOOL.
AND THAT'S HOW DUM DUM AND BRAVO'S TEAM WAS INFILTRATING THE HYDRA BASE?
YES. BECAUSE INSIDE HIS LAND OF NOWHERE...
...JIMMY COULD TOUCH PEOPLE'S DREAMS IF HE TRIED.
AND THAT WAS OUR SECRET PASSAGE INTO THIS HIDDEN BASE.
JIMMY'D HOME IN ON A FEW OF THEIR AGENTS' DREAMS...

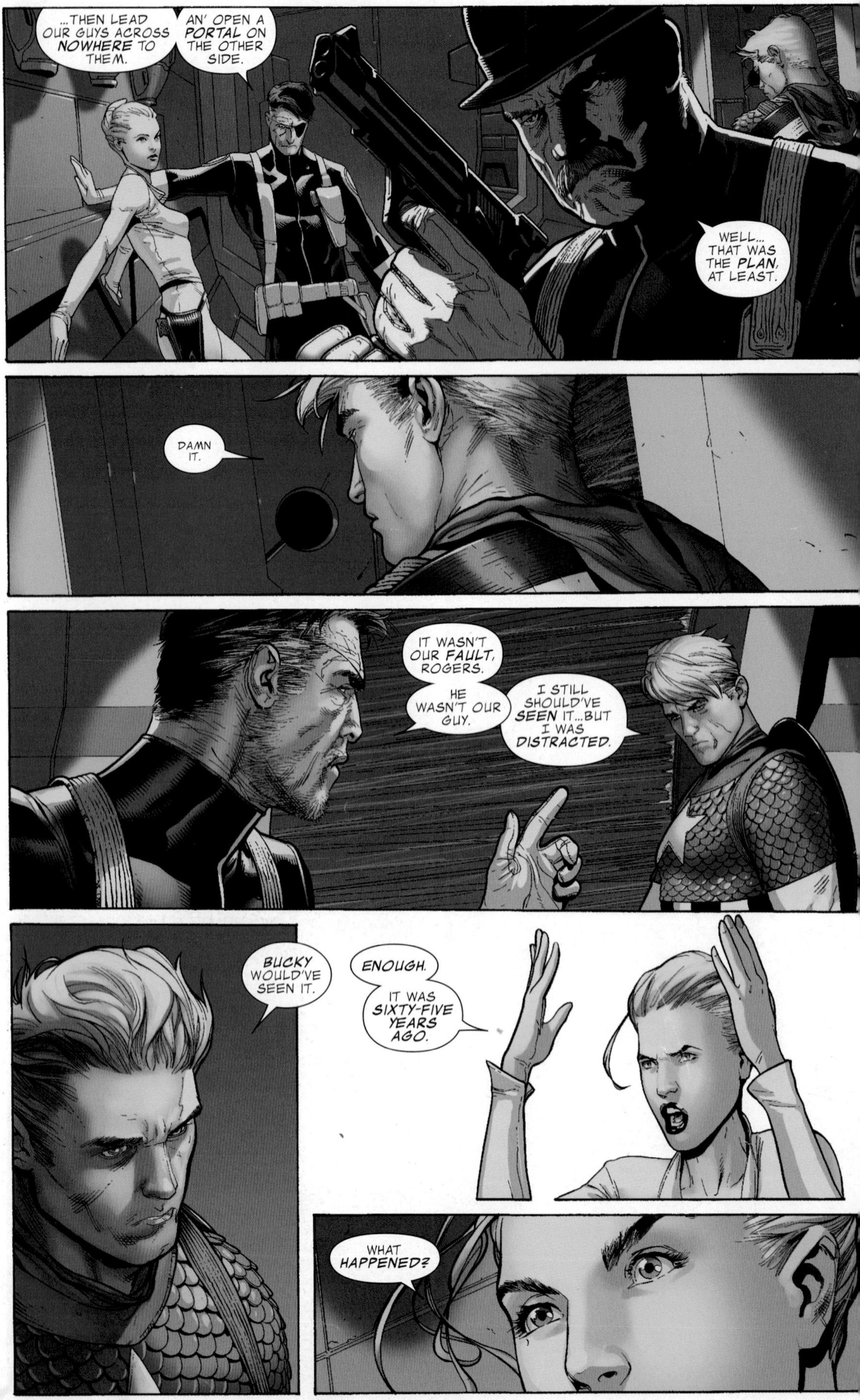
...THEN LEAD OUR GUYS ACROSS NOWHERE TO THEM.
AN' OPEN A PORTAL ON THE OTHER SIDE.
WELL... THAT WAS THE PLAN, AT LEAST.
DAMN IT.
IT WASN'T OUR FAULT, ROGERS.
HE WASN'T OUR GUY.
I STILL SHOULD'VE SEEN IT...BUT I WAS DISTRACTED.
BUCKY WOULD'VE SEEN IT.
ENOUGH.
IT WAS SIXTY-FIVE YEARS AGO.
WHAT HAPPENED?

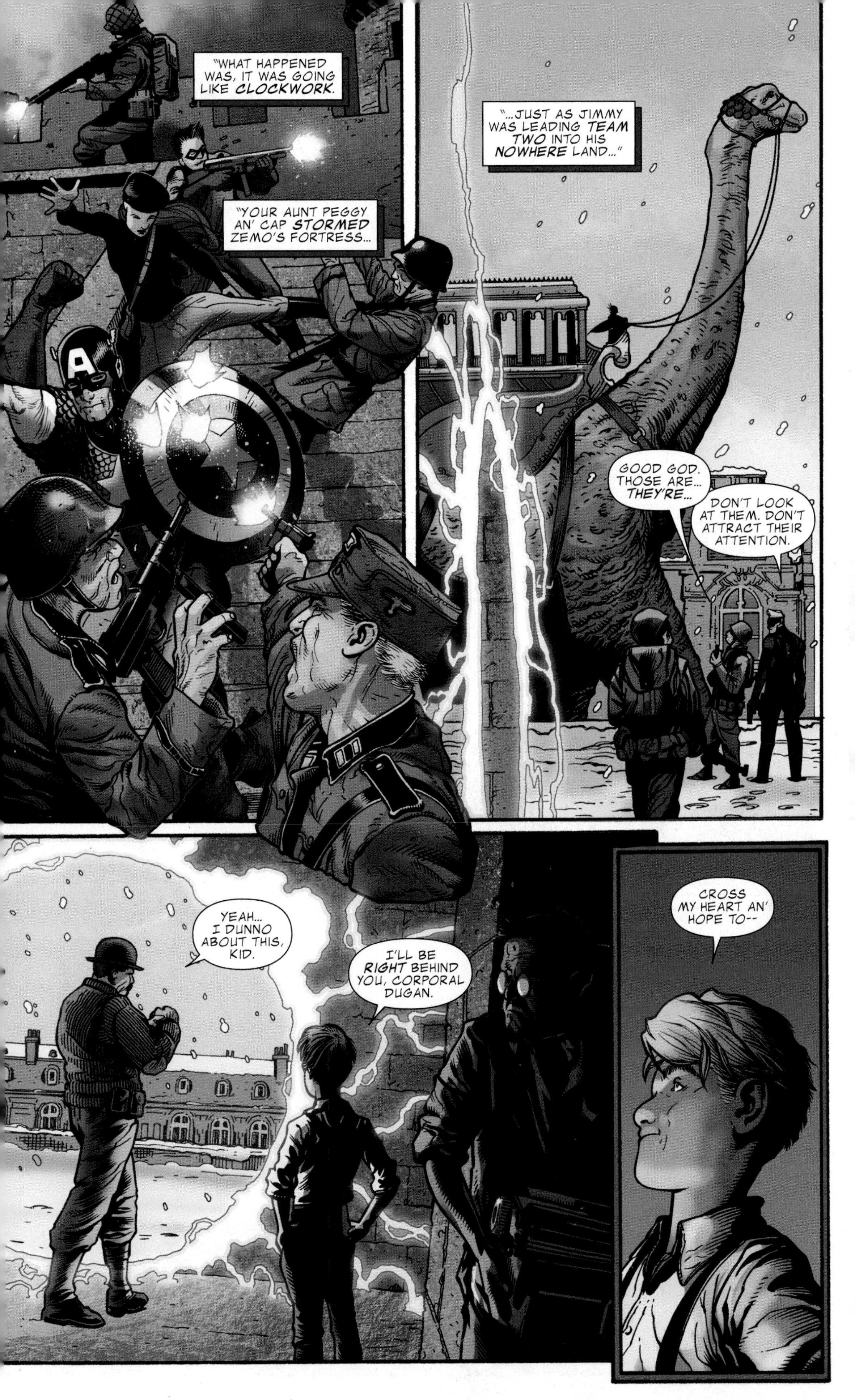
"WHAT HAPPENED WAS, IT WAS GOING LIKE CLOCKWORK.
"YOUR AUNT PEGGY AN' CAP STORMED ZEMO'S FORTRESS...
"...JUST AS JIMMY WAS LEADING TEAM TWO INTO HIS NOWHERE LAND..."
GOOD GOD. THOSE ARE... THEY'RE...
DON'T LOOK AT THEM. DON'T ATTRACT THEIR ATTENTION.
YEAH... I DUNNO ABOUT THIS, KID.
I'LL BE RIGHT BEHIND YOU, CORPORAL DUGAN.
CROSS MY HEART AN' HOPE TO--

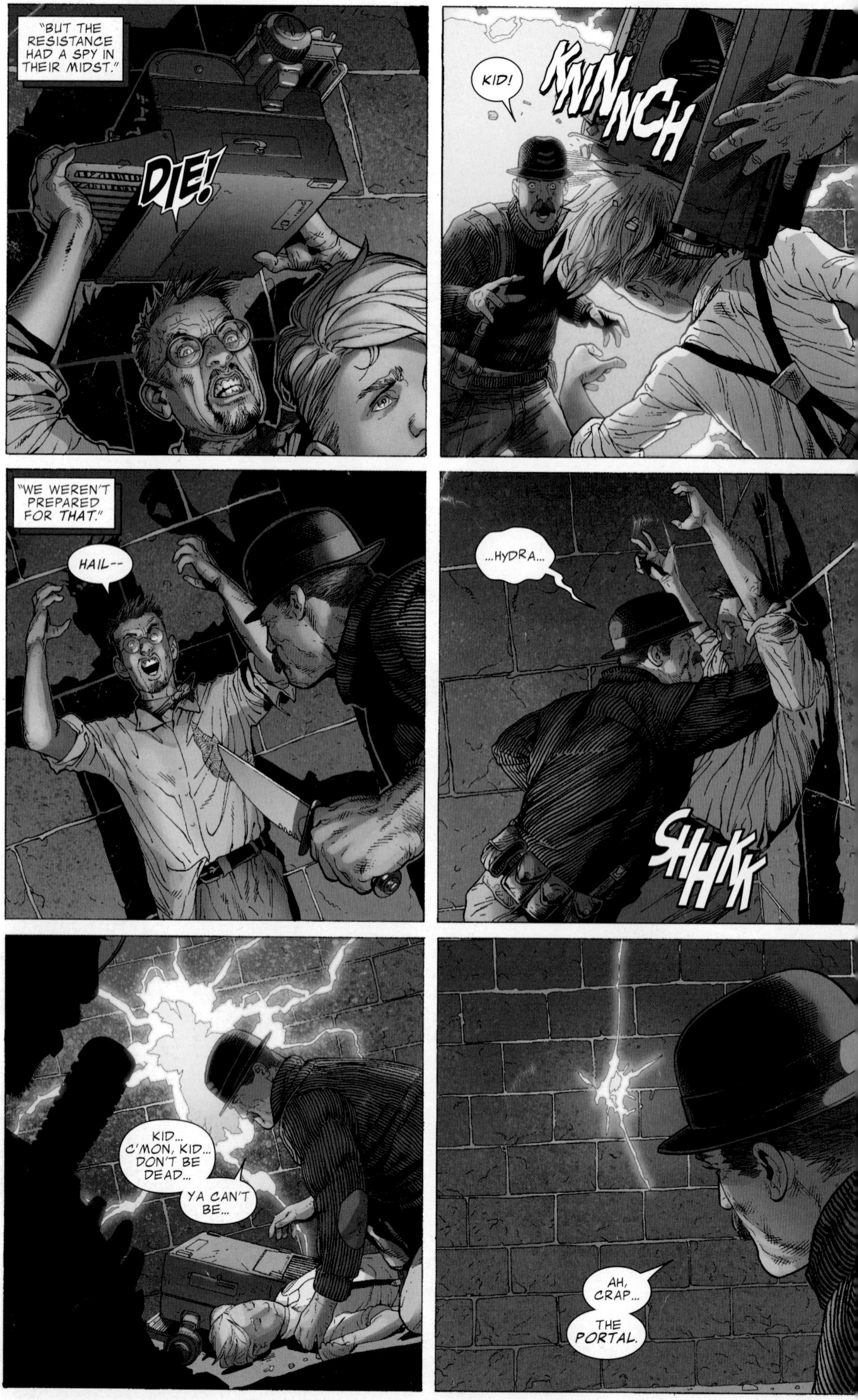
"BUT THE RESISTANCE HAD A SPY IN THEIR MIDST."
DIE!
KID!
KNNNCH
"WE WEREN'T PREPARED FOR THAT."
HAIL--
...HYDRA...
SHHKK
KID... C'MON, KID... DON'T BE DEAD...
YA CAN'T BE...
AH, CRAP...
THE PORTAL.

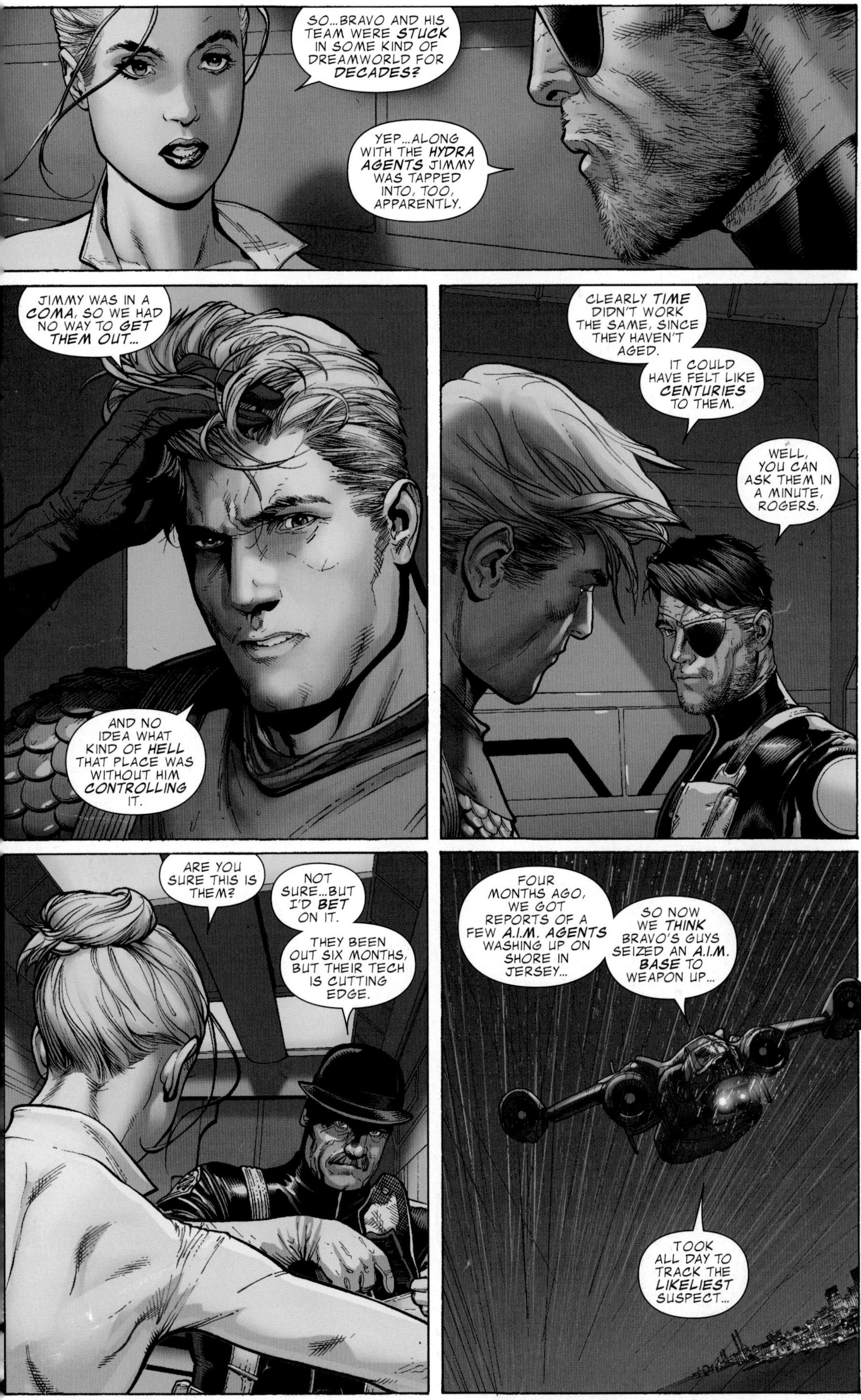
SO...BRAVO AND HIS TEAM WERE STUCK IN SOME KIND OF DREAMWORLD FOR DECADES?
YEP...ALONG WITH THE HYDRA AGENTS JIMMY WAS TAPPED INTO, TOO, APPARENTLY.
JIMMY WAS IN A COMA, SO WE HAD NO WAY TO GET THEM OUT...
AND NO IDEA WHAT KIND OF HELL THAT PLACE WAS WITHOUT HIM CONTROLLING IT.
CLEARLY TIME DIDN'T WORK THE SAME, SINCE THEY HAVEN'T AGED.
IT COULD HAVE FELT LIKE CENTURIES TO THEM.
WELL, YOU CAN ASK THEM IN A MINUTE, ROGERS.
ARE YOU SURE THIS IS THEM?
NOT SURE...BUT I'D BET ON IT.
THEY BEEN OUT SIX MONTHS, BUT THEIR TECH IS CUTTING EDGE.
FOUR MONTHS AGO, WE GOT REPORTS OF A FEW A.I.M. AGENTS WASHING UP ON SHORE IN JERSEY...
SO NOW WE THINK BRAVO'S GUYS SEIZED AN A.I.M. BASE TO WEAPON UP...
TOOK ALL DAY TO TRACK THE LIKELIEST SUSPECT...

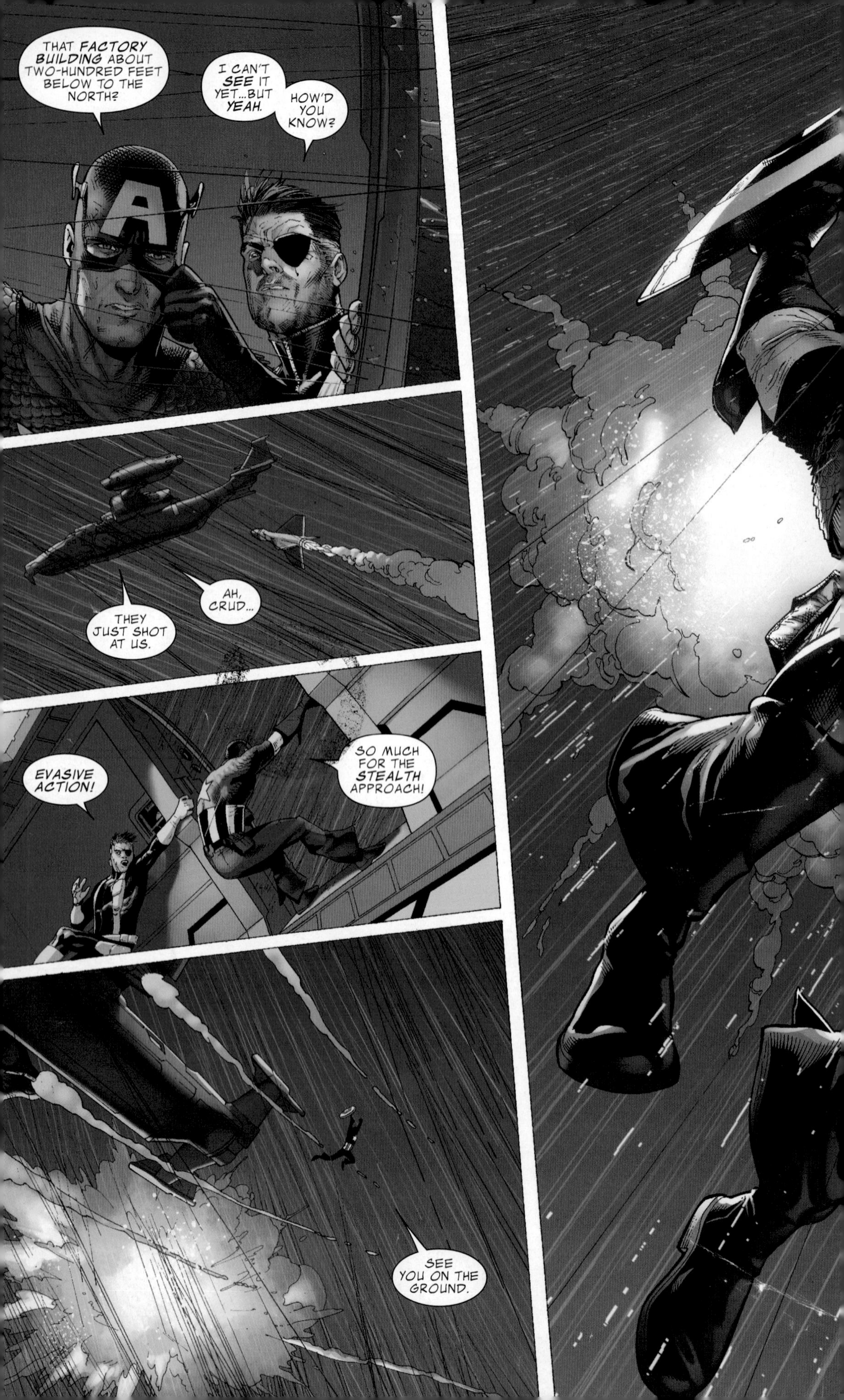

THAT FACTORY BUILDING ABOUT TWO-HUNDRED FEET BELOW TO THE NORTH?
I CAN'T SEE IT YET...BUT YEAH.
HOW'D YOU KNOW?
AH, CRUD...
THEY JUST SHOT AT US.
EVASIVE ACTION!
SO MUCH FOR THE STEALTH APPROACH!
SEE YOU ON THE GROUND.

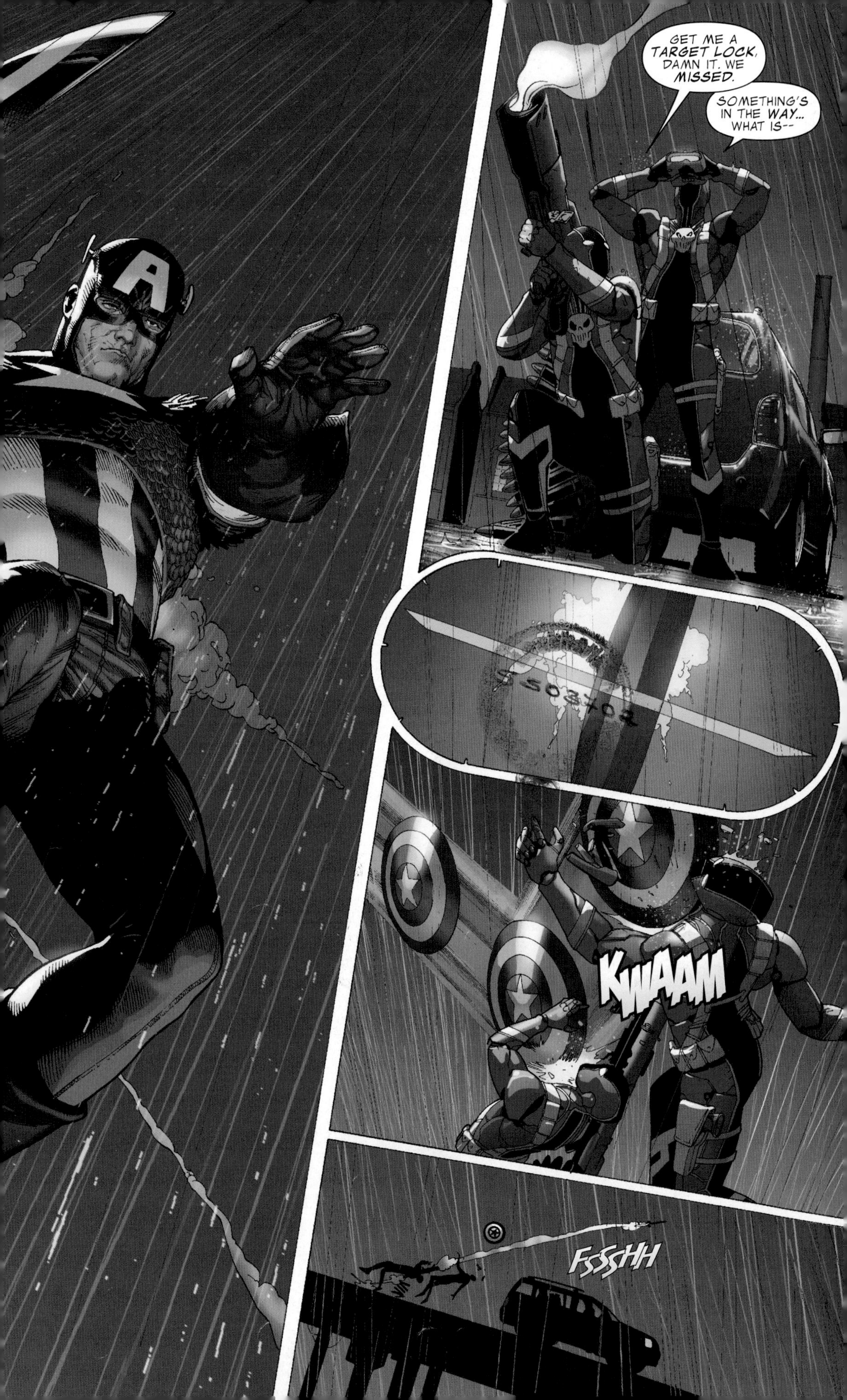
GET ME A TARGET LOCK, DAMN IT. WE MISSED.
SOMETHING'S IN THE WAY... WHAT IS--
KWAAM
FSSSHH

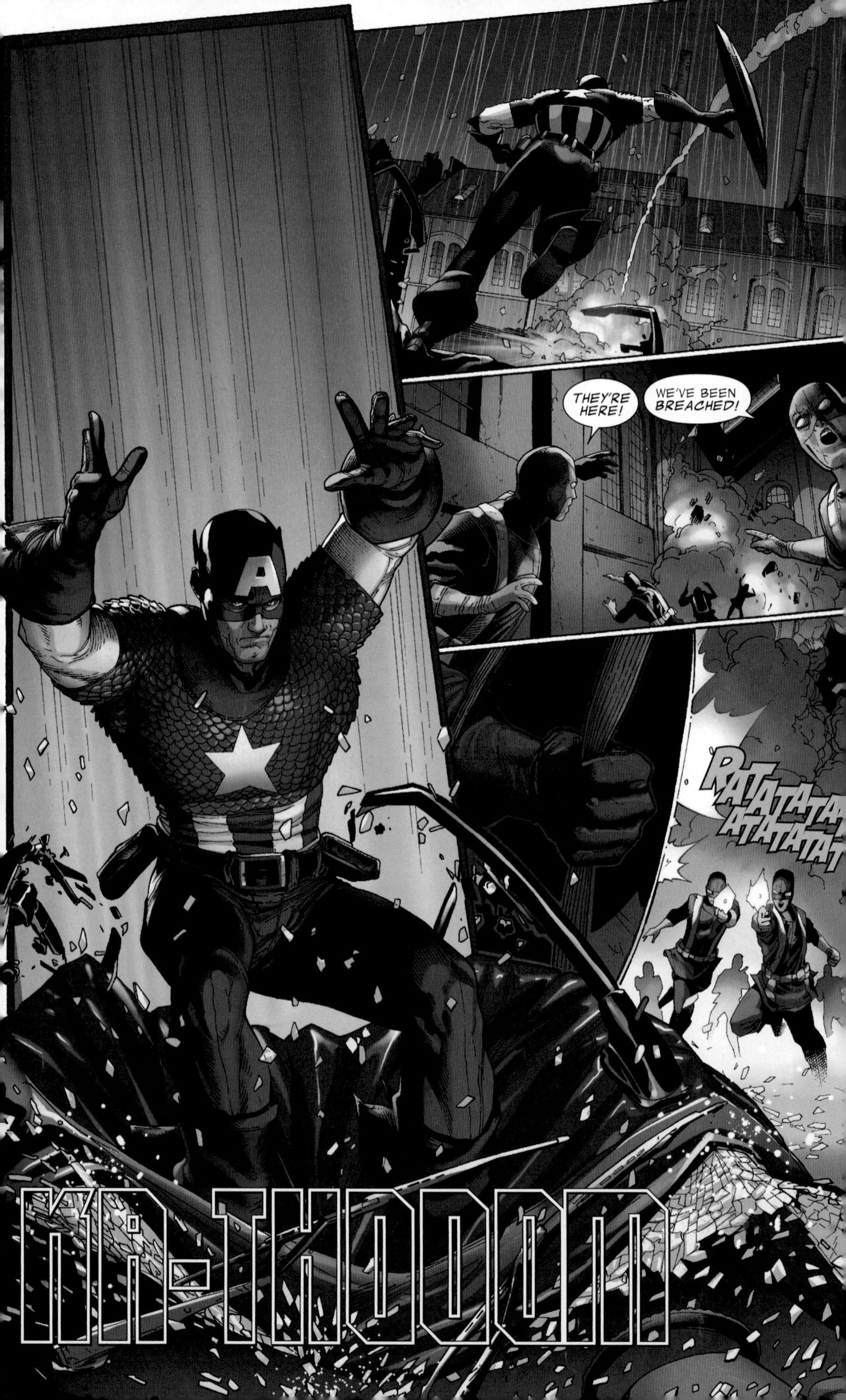
THEY'RE HERE!
WE'VE BEEN BREACHED!
RATATATATATATATAT
KR-THOOOM

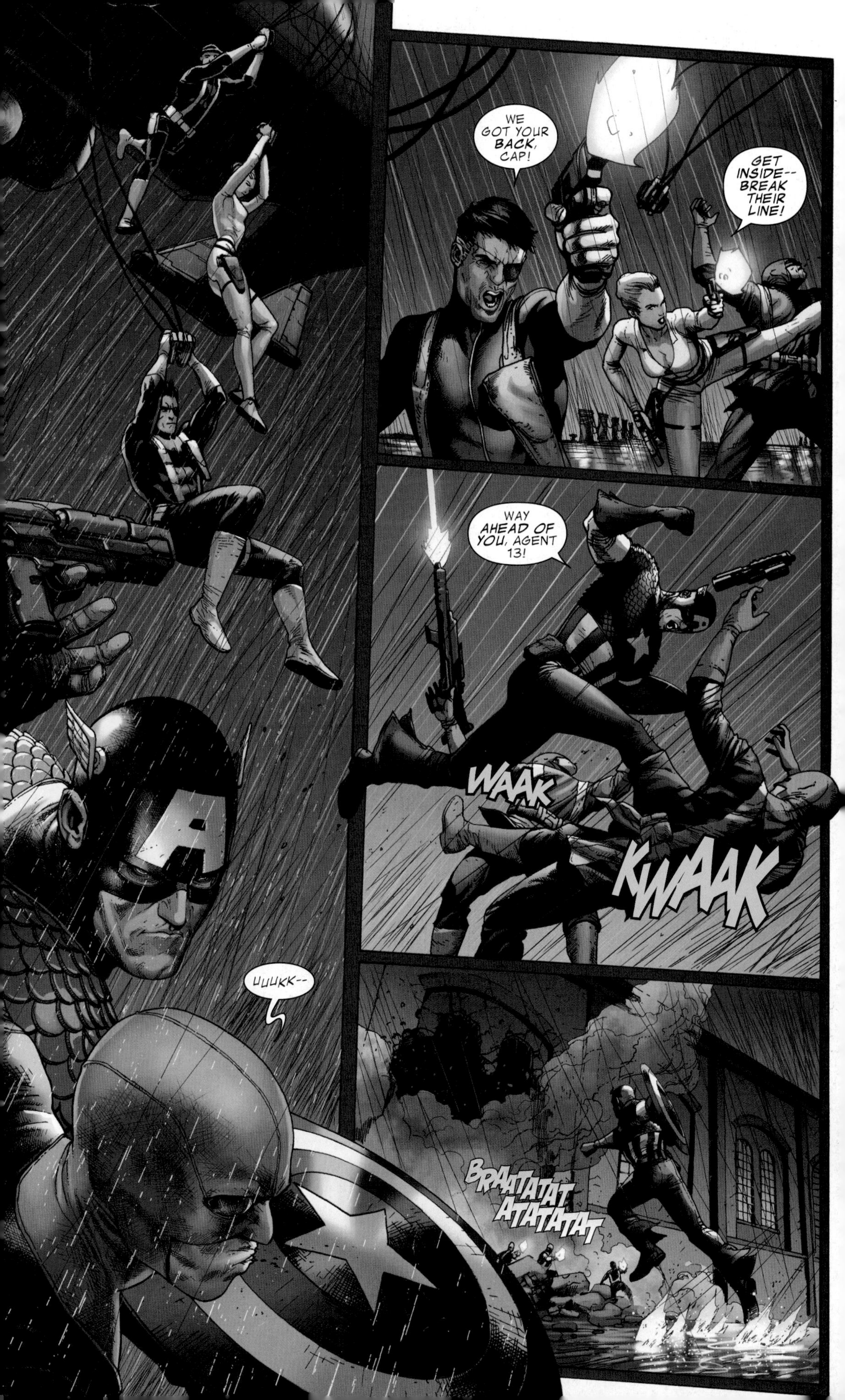
UUUKK--
WE GOT YOUR BACK, CAP!
GET INSIDE-- BREAK THEIR LINE!
WAY AHEAD OF YOU, AGENT 13!
WAAK
KWAAK
BRAATATAT ATATATAT

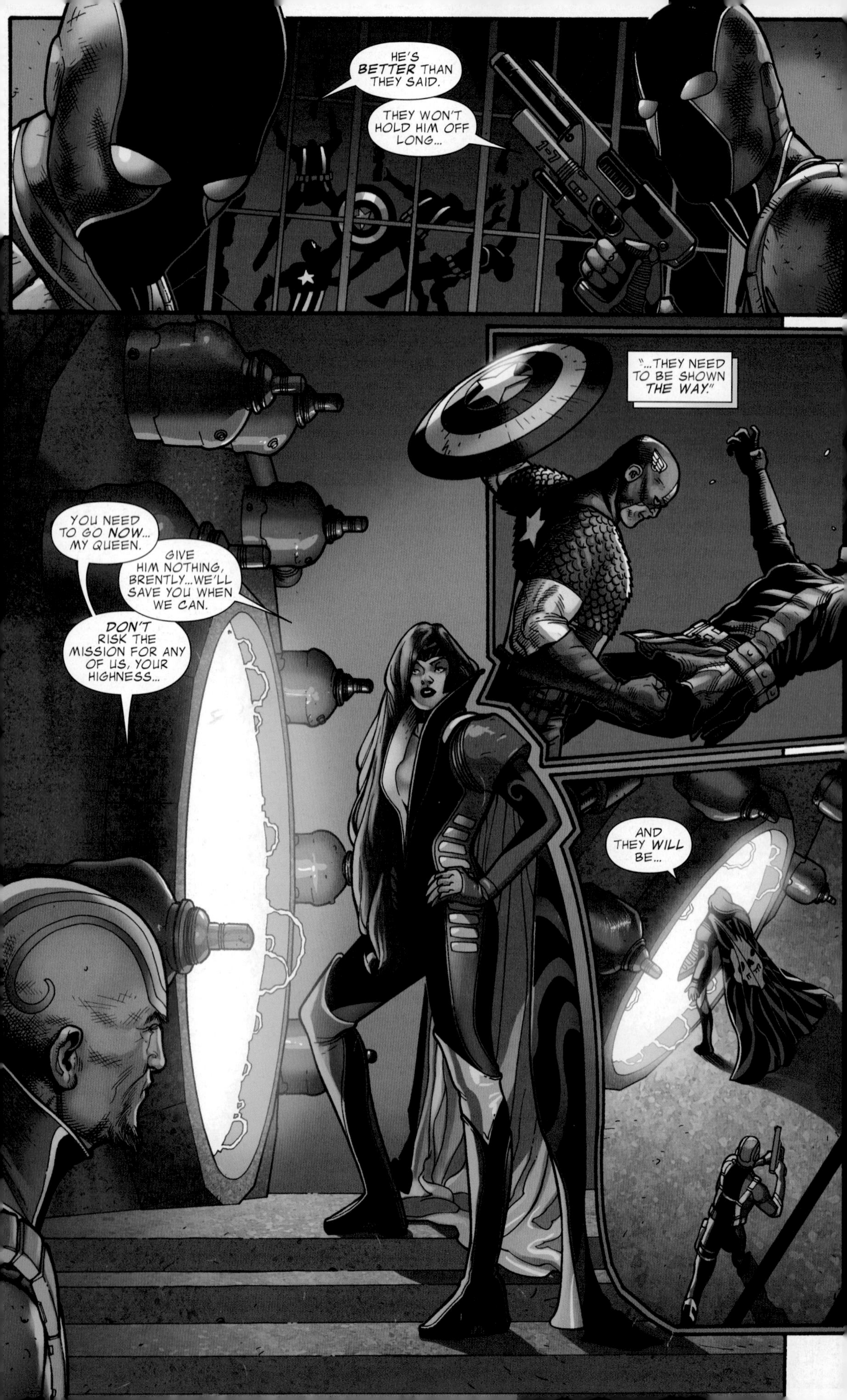
HE'S BETTER THAN THEY SAID.
THEY WON'T HOLD HIM OFF LONG...
"...THEY NEED TO BE SHOWN THE WAY."
YOU NEED TO GO NOW... MY QUEEN.
GIVE HIM NOTHING, BRENTLY...WE'LL SAVE YOU WHEN WE CAN.
DON'T RISK THE MISSION FOR ANY OF US, YOUR HIGHNESS...
AND THEY WILL BE...

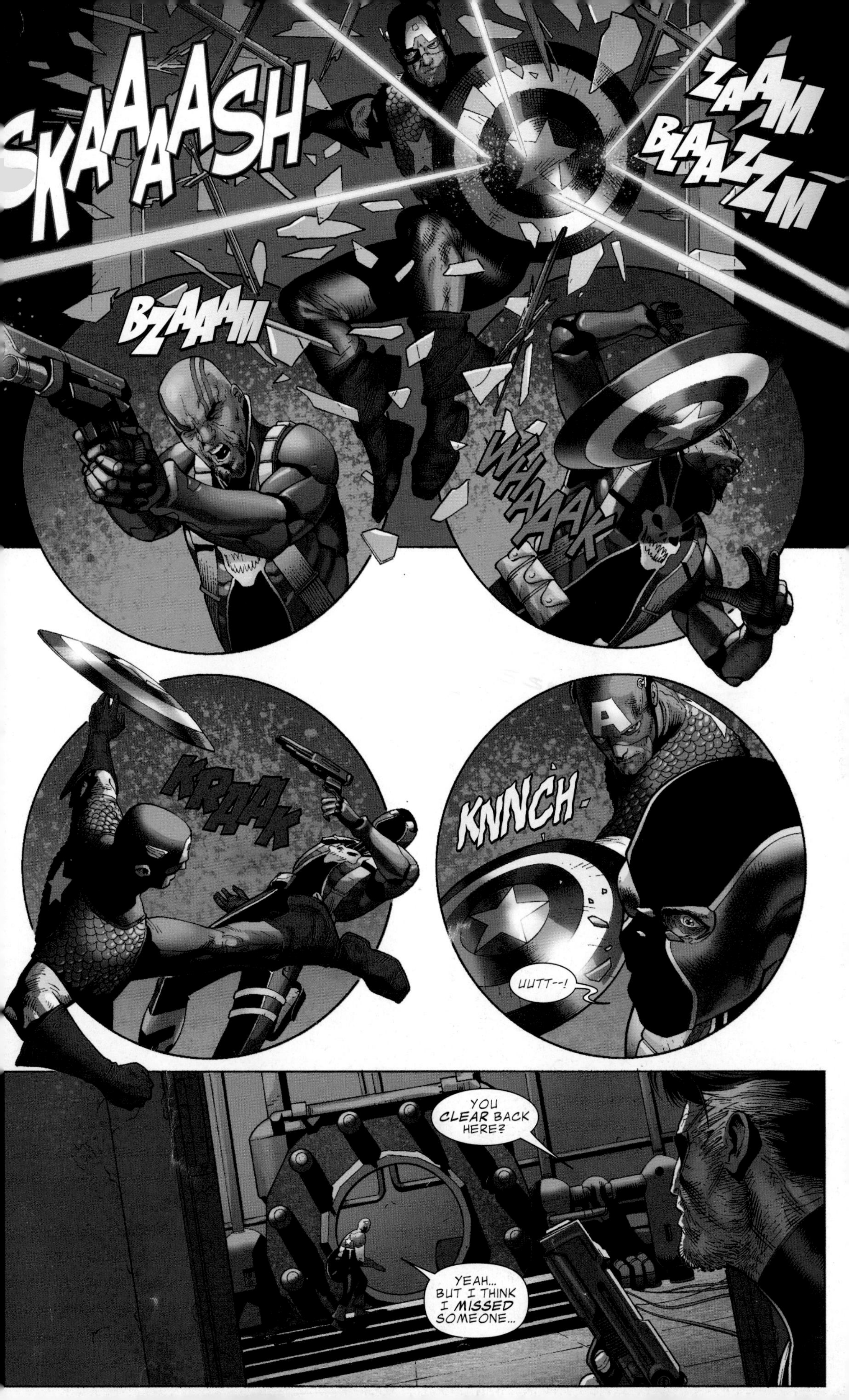
SKAAAASH
ZAAAM
BLAAZZM
BZAAAAM
WHAAAK
KRAAK
KNNCH
UUTT--!
YOU CLEAR BACK HERE?
YEAH... BUT I THINK I MISSED SOMEONE...

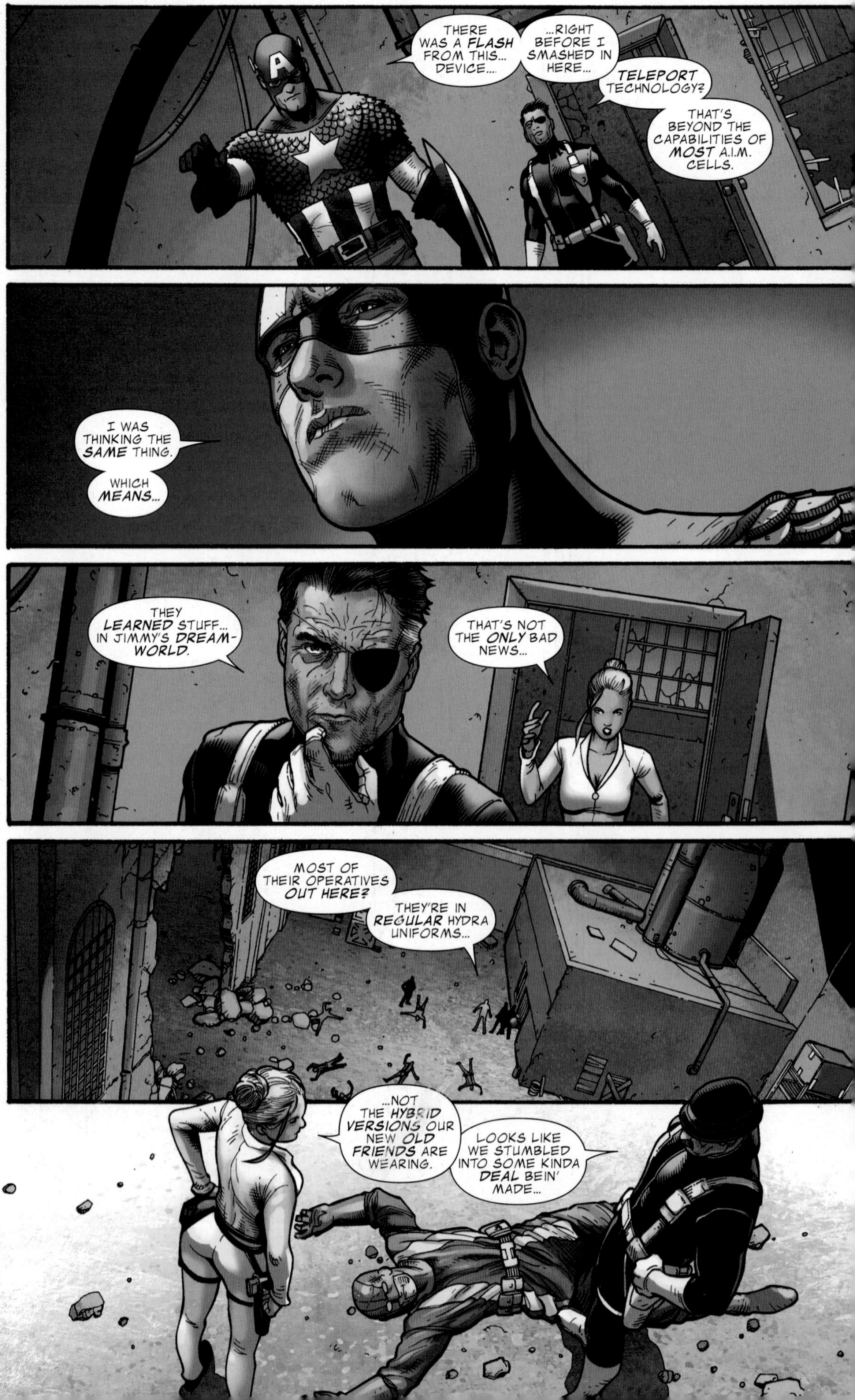
THERE WAS A FLASH FROM THIS... DEVICE....
...RIGHT BEFORE I SMASHED IN HERE...
TELEPORT TECHNOLOGY?
THAT'S BEYOND THE CAPABILITIES OF MOST A.I.M. CELLS.
I WAS THINKING THE SAME THING.
WHICH MEANS...
THEY LEARNED STUFF... IN JIMMY'S DREAM-WORLD.
THAT'S NOT THE ONLY BAD NEWS...
MOST OF THEIR OPERATIVES OUT HERE?
THEY'RE IN REGULAR HYDRA UNIFORMS...
...NOT THE HYBRID VERSIONS OUR NEW OLD FRIENDS ARE WEARING.
LOOKS LIKE WE STUMBLED INTO SOME KINDA DEAL BEIN' MADE...

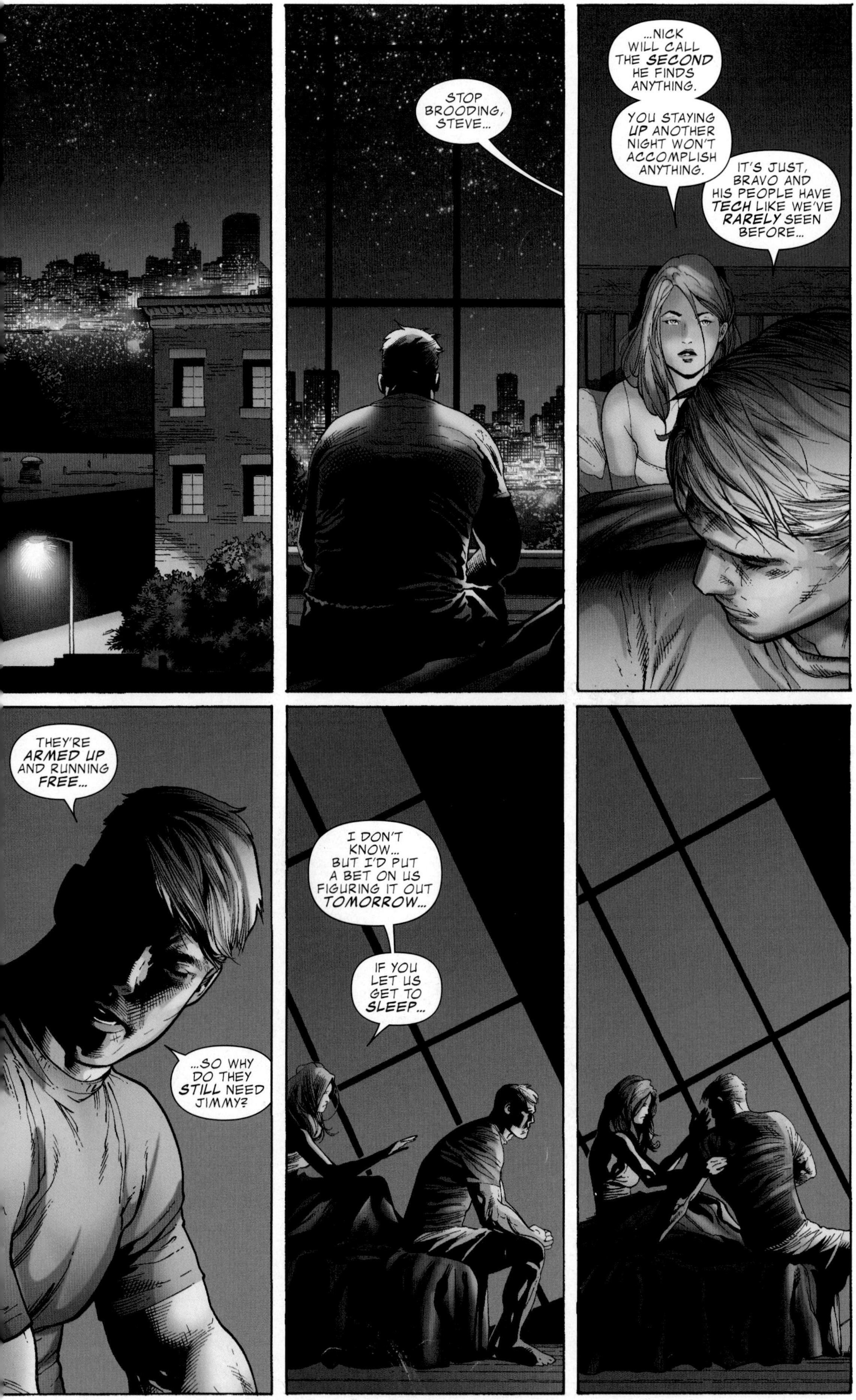
STOP BROODING, STEVE...
...NICK WILL CALL THE SECOND HE FINDS ANYTHING.
YOU STAYING UP ANOTHER NIGHT WON'T ACCOMPLISH ANYTHING.
IT'S JUST, BRAVO AND HIS PEOPLE HAVE TECH LIKE WE'VE RARELY SEEN BEFORE...
THEY'RE ARMED UP AND RUNNING FREE...
...SO WHY DO THEY STILL NEED JIMMY?
I DON'T KNOW... BUT I'D PUT A BET ON US FIGURING IT OUT TOMORROW...
IF YOU LET US GET TO SLEEP...

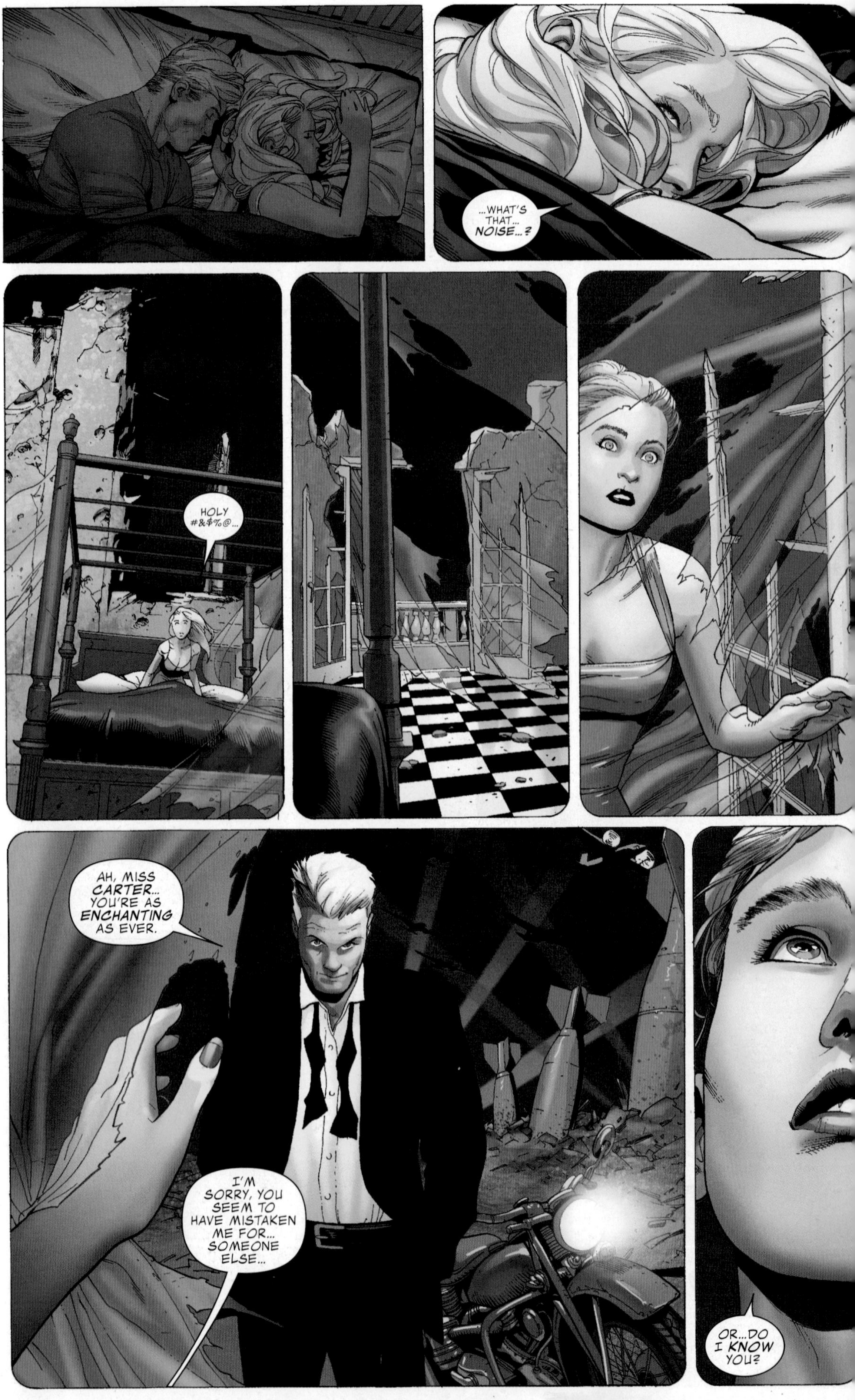
...WHAT'S THAT... NOISE...?
HOLY #&$%@...
AH, MISS CARTER... YOU'RE AS ENCHANTING AS EVER.
I'M SORRY, YOU SEEM TO HAVE MISTAKEN ME FOR... SOMEONE ELSE...
OR...DO I KNOW YOU?

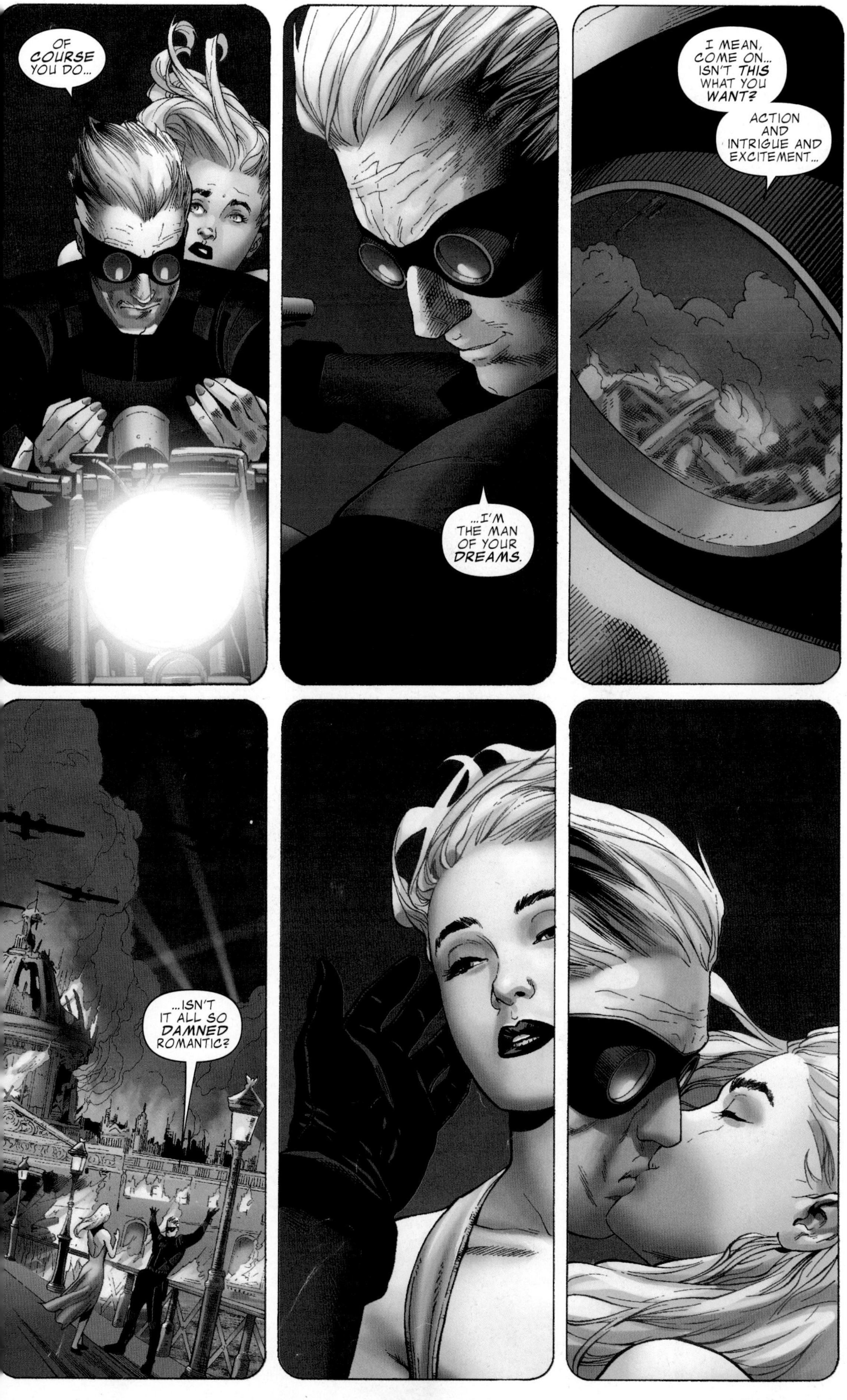
OF COURSE YOU DO...
...I'M THE MAN OF YOUR DREAMS.
I MEAN, COME ON... ISN'T THIS WHAT YOU WANT?
ACTION AND INTRIGUE AND EXCITEMENT...
...ISN'T IT ALL SO DAMNED ROMANTIC?

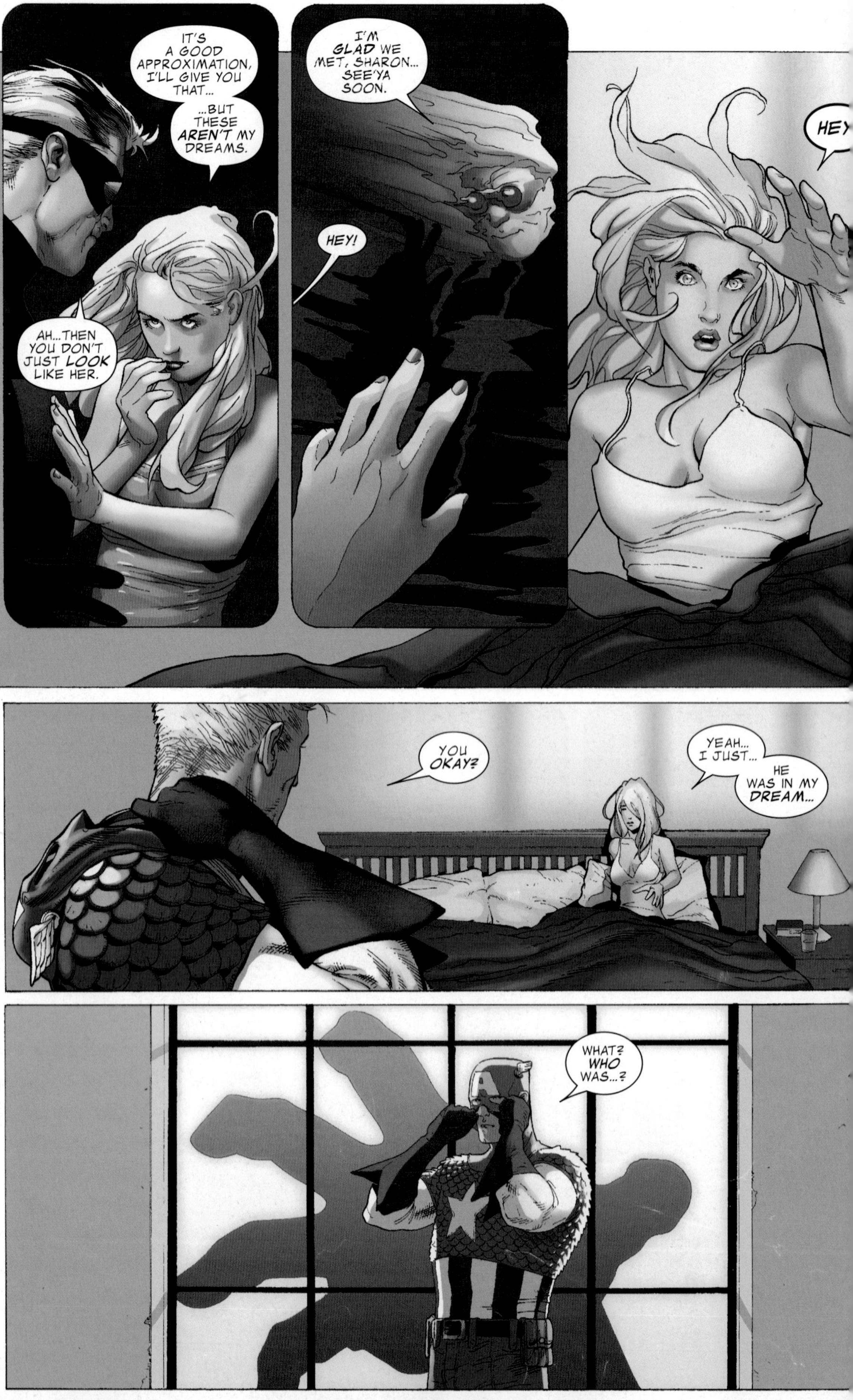
IT'S A GOOD APPROXIMATION, I'LL GIVE YOU THAT...
...BUT THESE AREN'T MY DREAMS.
AH...THEN YOU DON'T JUST LOOK LIKE HER.
I'M GLAD WE MET, SHARON... SEE'YA SOON.
HEY!
HEY
YOU OKAY?
YEAH... I JUST...
HE WAS IN MY DREAM...
WHAT? WHO WAS...?

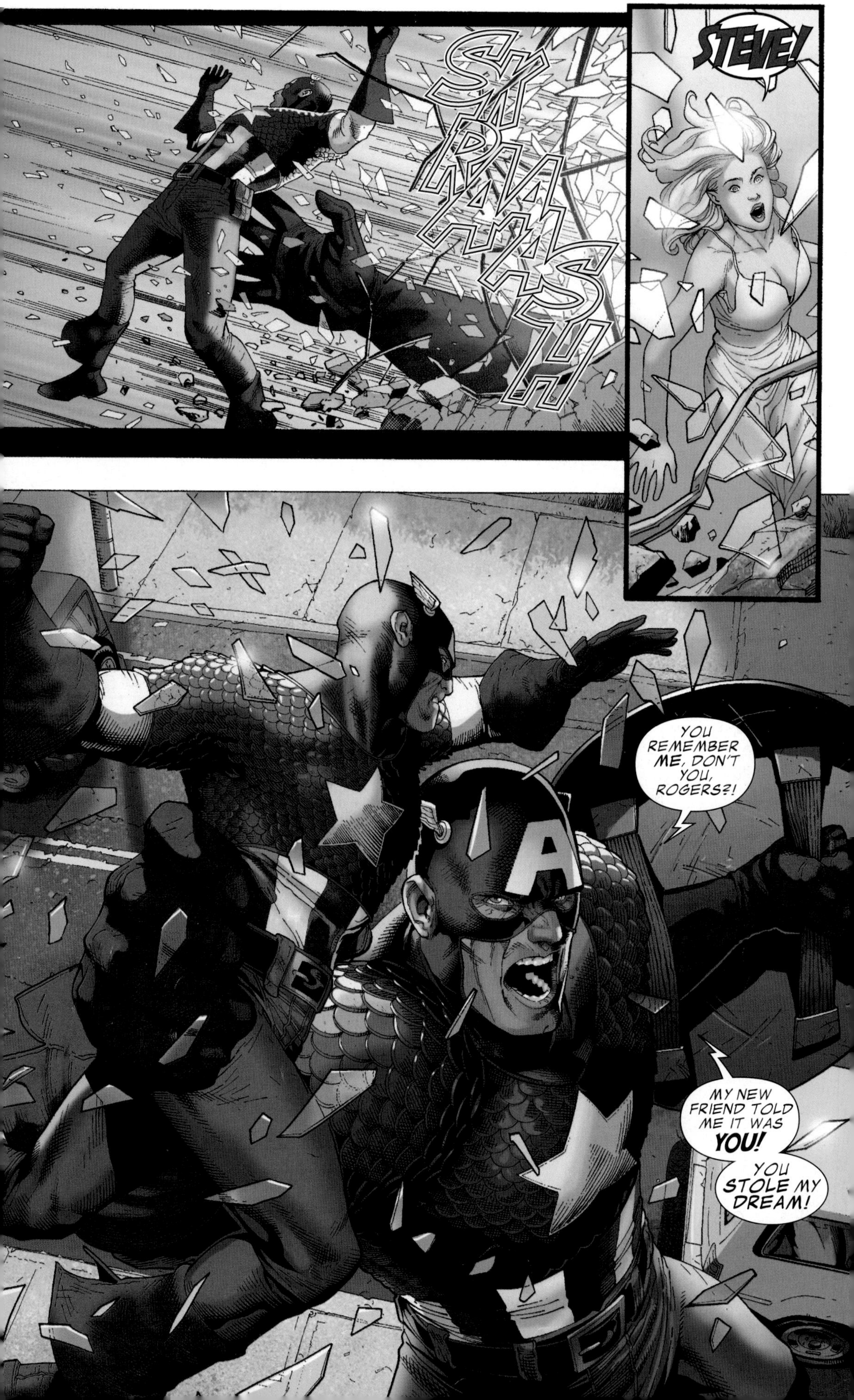
SKRAAASH
STEVE!
YOU REMEMBER ME, DON'T YOU, ROGERS?!
MY NEW FRIEND TOLD ME IT WAS YOU!
YOU STOLE MY DREAM!

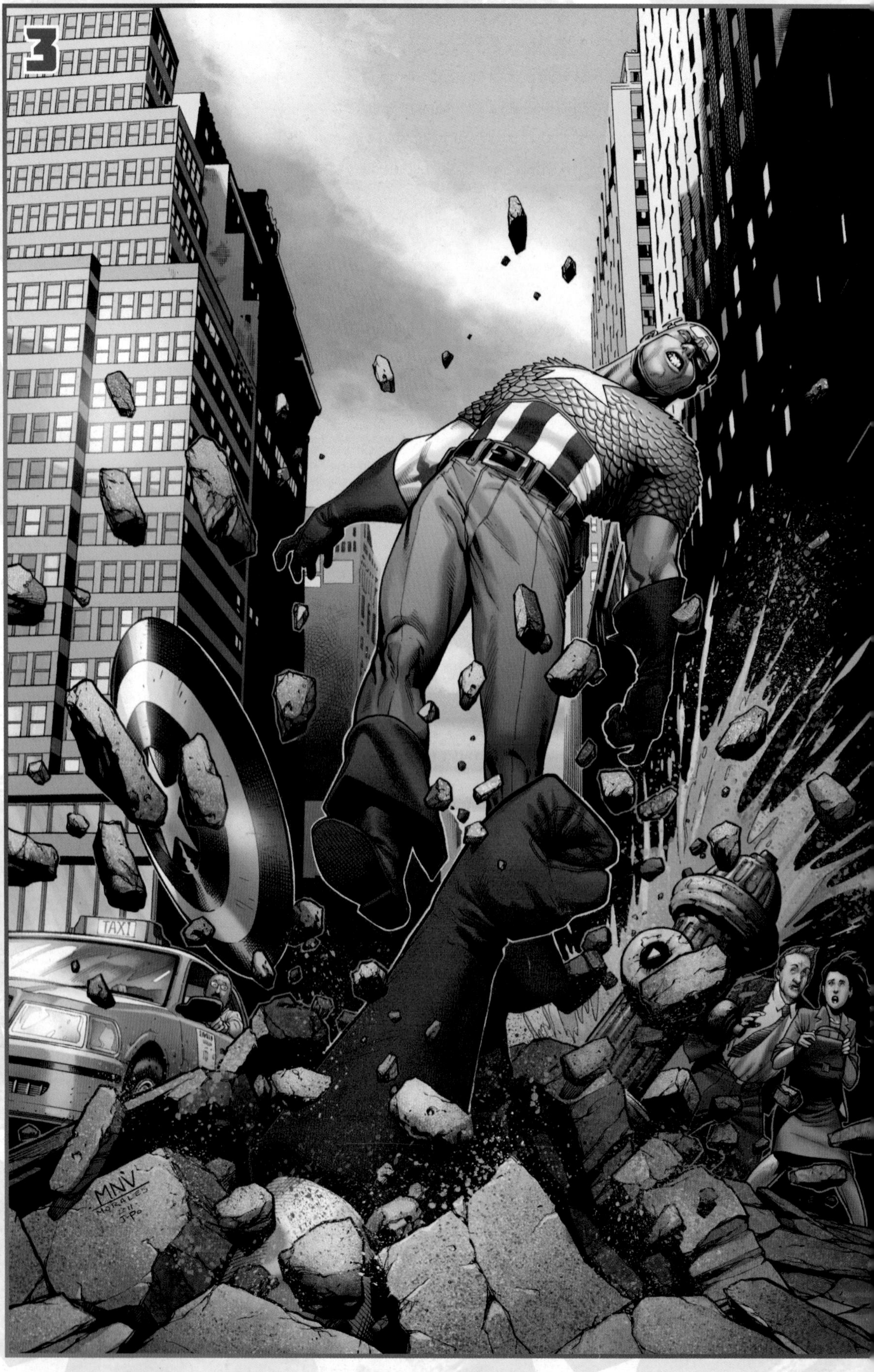
3
TAXI

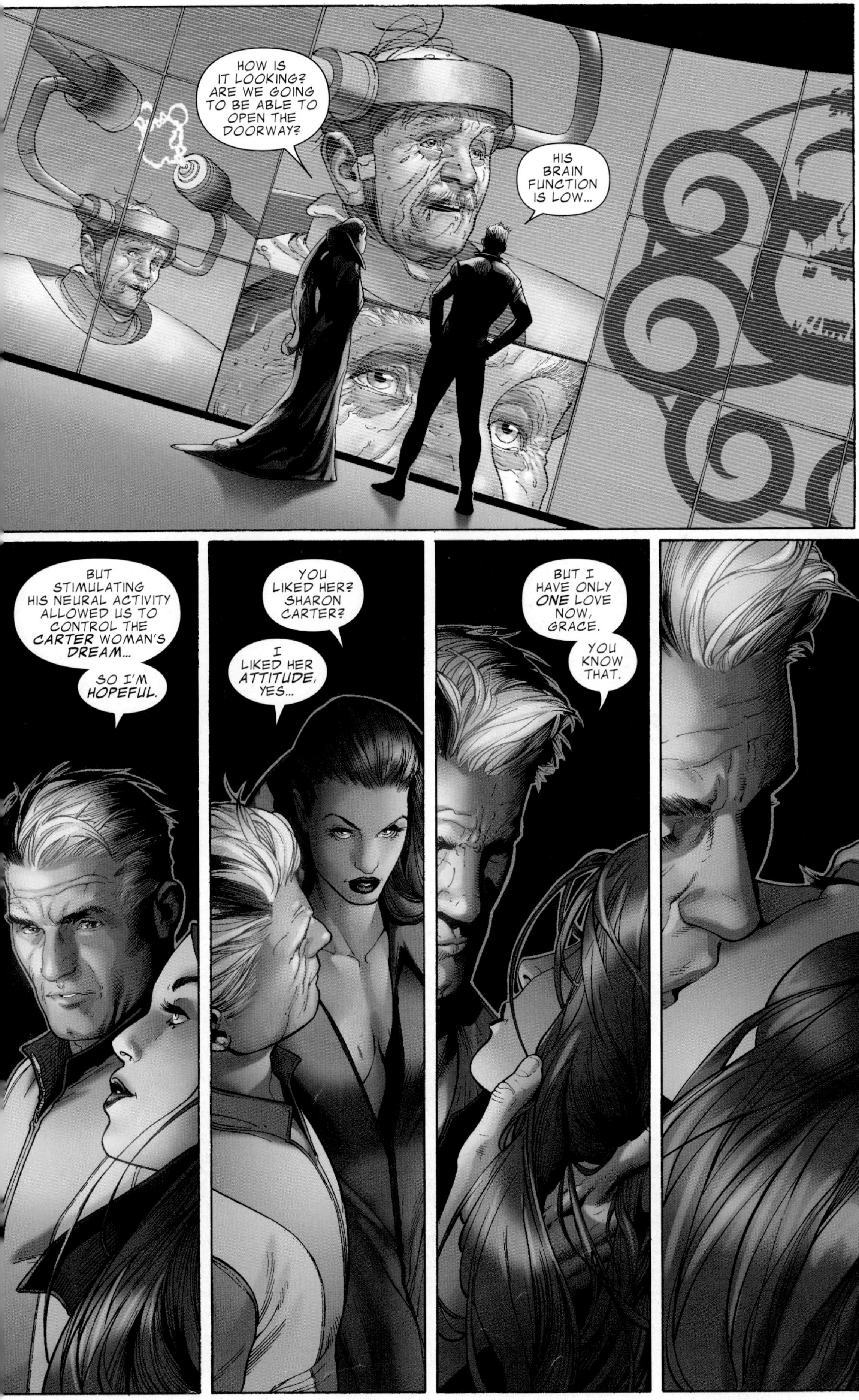
HOW IS IT LOOKING? ARE WE GOING TO BE ABLE TO OPEN THE DOORWAY?
HIS BRAIN FUNCTION IS LOW...
BUT STIMULATING HIS NEURAL ACTIVITY ALLOWED US TO CONTROL THE CARTER WOMAN'S DREAM...
SO I'M HOPEFUL.
YOU LIKED HER? SHARON CARTER?
I LIKED HER ATTITUDE, YES...
BUT I HAVE ONLY ONE LOVE NOW, GRACE.
YOU KNOW THAT.

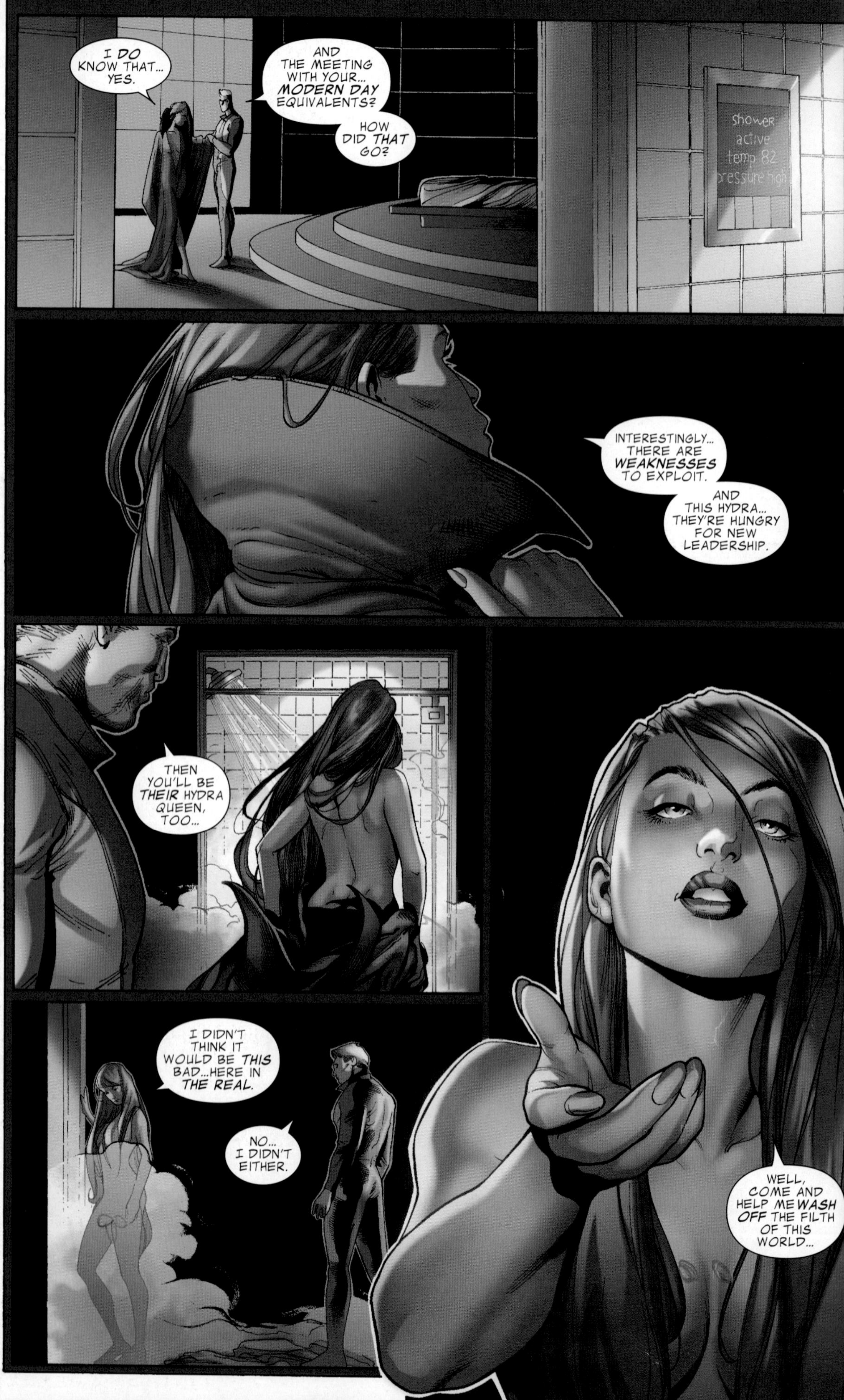
I DO KNOW THAT... YES.
AND THE MEETING WITH YOUR... MODERN DAY EQUIVALENTS?
HOW DID THAT GO?
shower active temp 82 pressure high
INTERESTINGLY... THERE ARE WEAKNESSES TO EXPLOIT.
AND THIS HYDRA... THEY'RE HUNGRY FOR NEW LEADERSHIP.
THEN YOU'LL BE THEIR HYDRA QUEEN, TOO...
I DIDN'T THINK IT WOULD BE THIS BAD...HERE IN THE REAL.
NO... I DIDN'T EITHER.
WELL, COME AND HELP ME WASH OFF THE FILTH OF THIS WORLD...

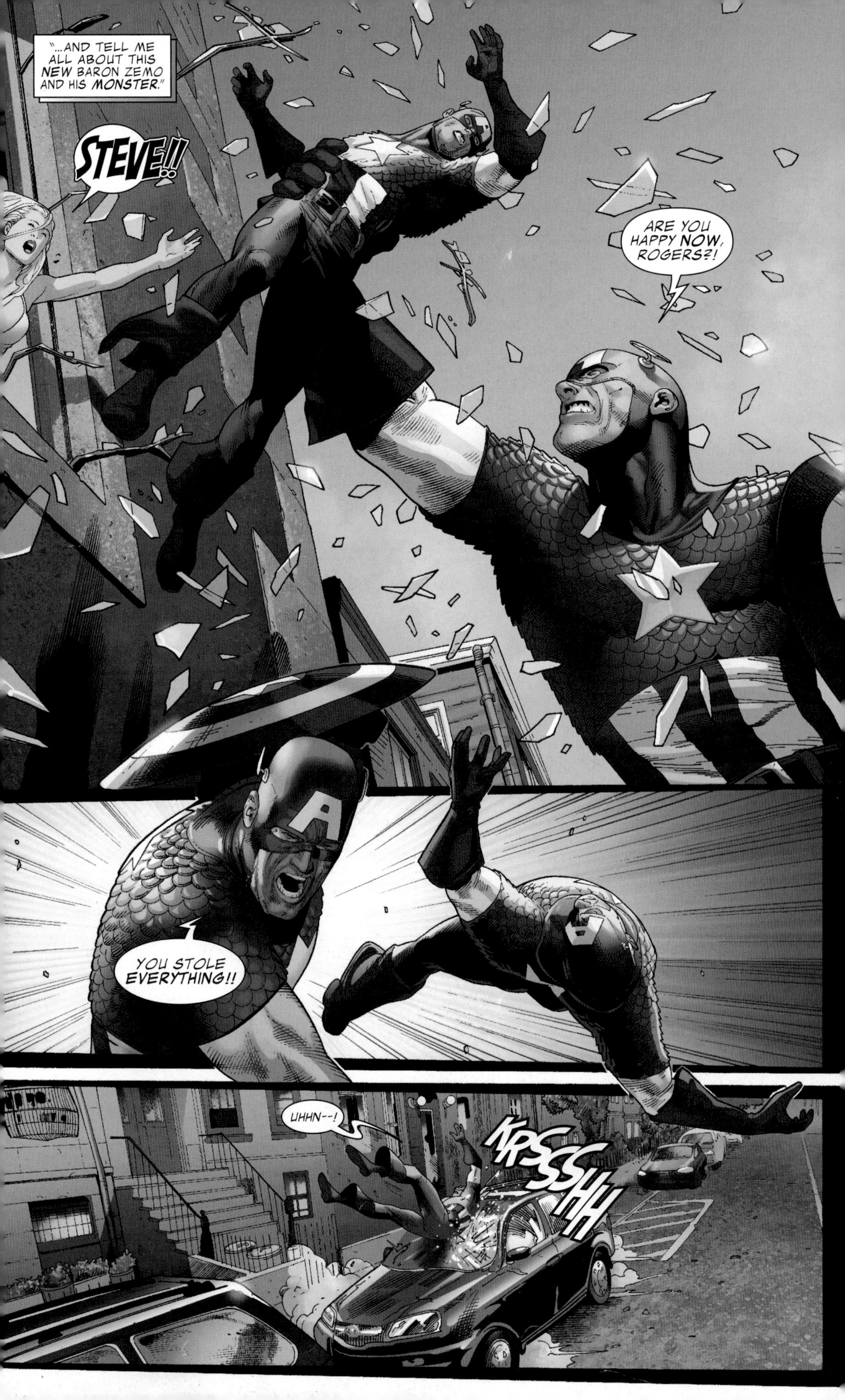
"...AND TELL ME ALL ABOUT THIS NEW BARON ZEMO AND HIS MONSTER."
STEVE!!
ARE YOU HAPPY NOW, ROGERS?!
YOU STOLE EVERYTHING!!
UHHN--!
KRSSSHH

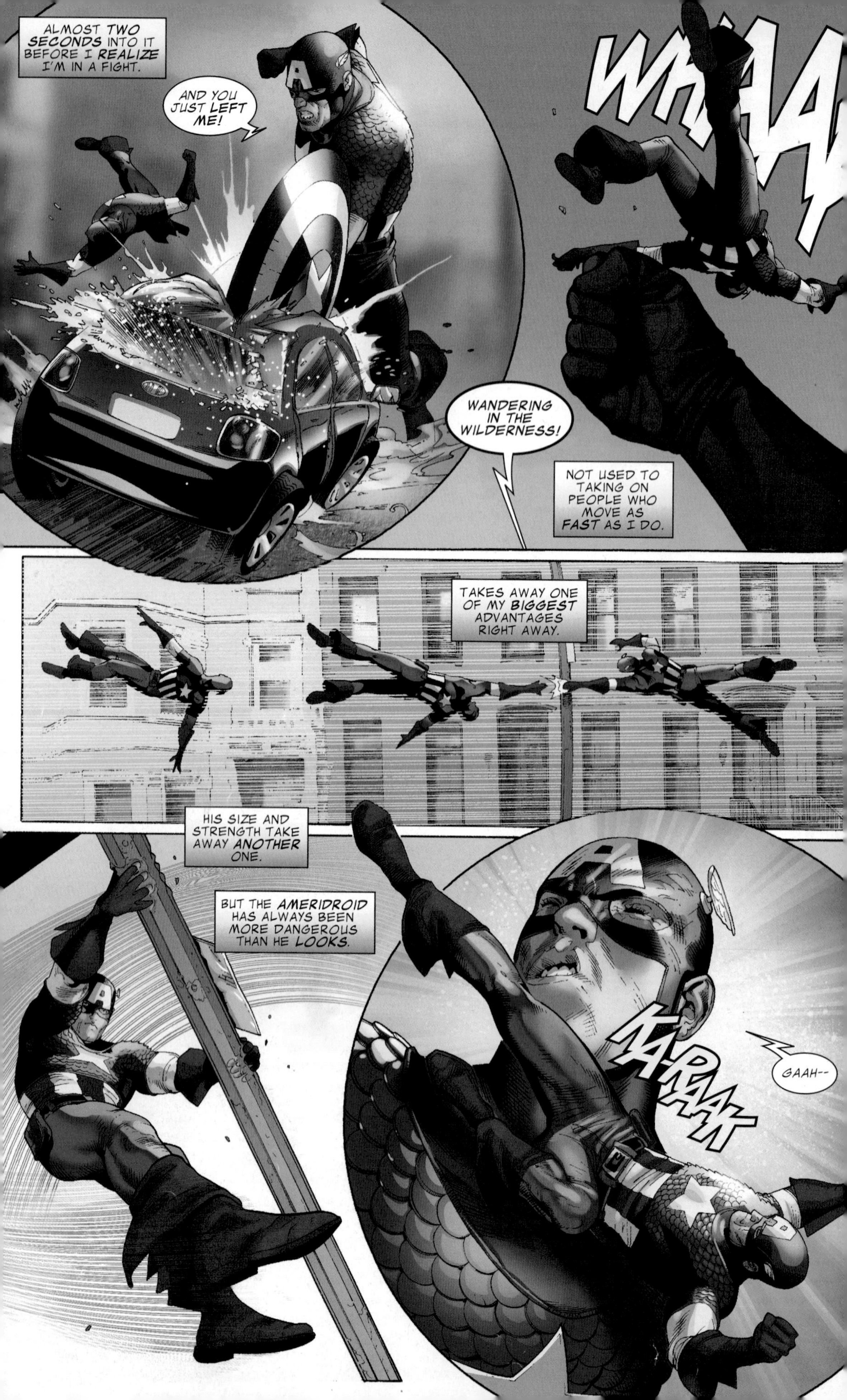
ALMOST TWO SECONDS INTO IT BEFORE I REALIZE I'M IN A FIGHT.
AND YOU JUST LEFT ME!
WHAA
WANDERING IN THE WILDERNESS!
NOT USED TO TAKING ON PEOPLE WHO MOVE AS FAST AS I DO.
TAKES AWAY ONE OF MY BIGGEST ADVANTAGES RIGHT AWAY.
HIS SIZE AND STRENGTH TAKE AWAY ANOTHER ONE.
BUT THE AMERIDROID HAS ALWAYS BEEN MORE DANGEROUS THAN HE LOOKS.
KA-RAK
GAAH--

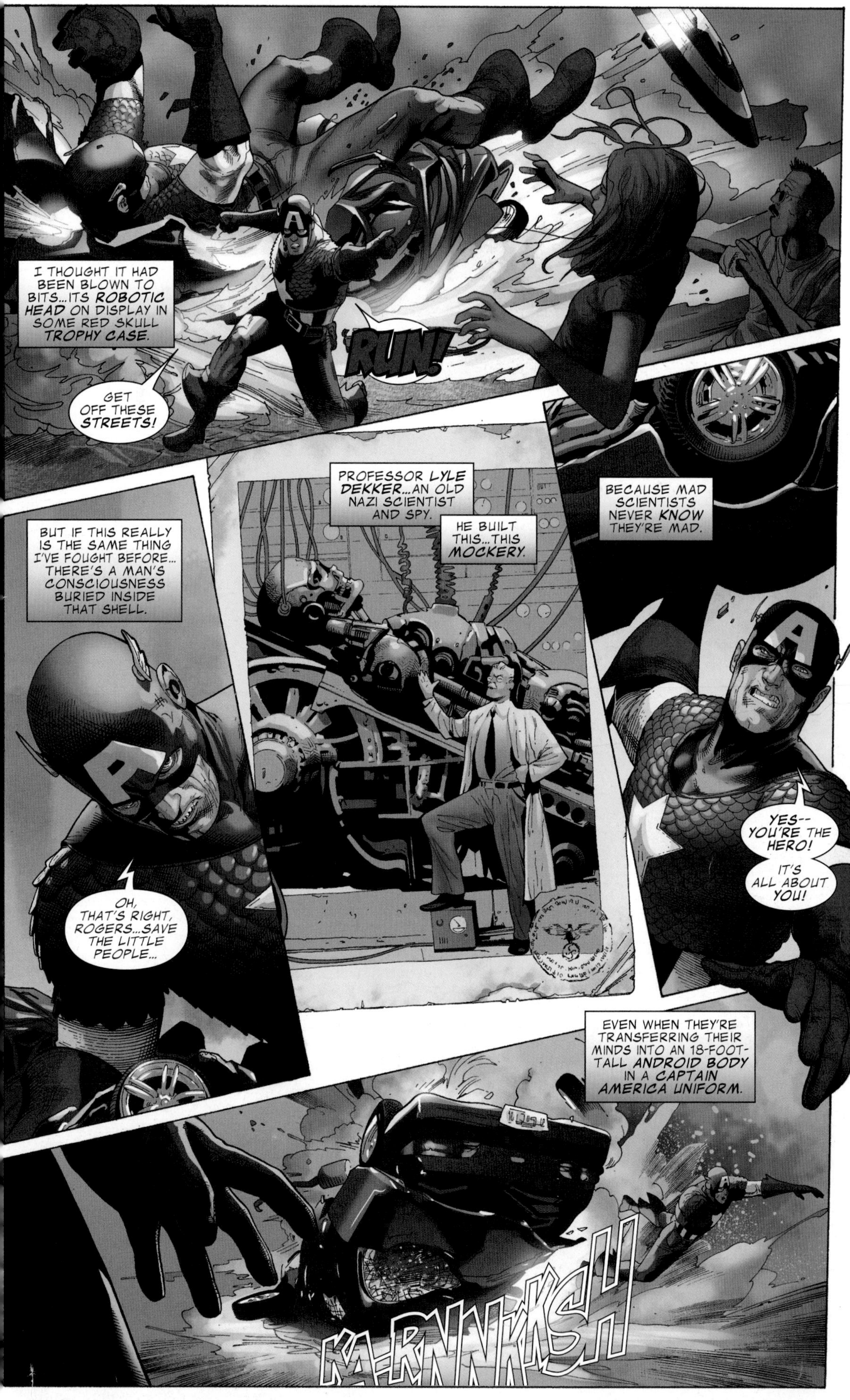
I THOUGHT IT HAD BEEN BLOWN TO BITS...ITS ROBOTIC HEAD ON DISPLAY IN SOME RED SKULL TROPHY CASE.
RUN!
GET OFF THESE STREETS!
PROFESSOR LYLE DEKKER...AN OLD NAZI SCIENTIST AND SPY.
HE BUILT THIS...THIS MOCKERY.
BECAUSE MAD SCIENTISTS NEVER KNOW THEY'RE MAD.
BUT IF THIS REALLY IS THE SAME THING I'VE FOUGHT BEFORE... THERE'S A MAN'S CONSCIOUSNESS BURIED INSIDE THAT SHELL.
OH, THAT'S RIGHT, ROGERS...SAVE THE LITTLE PEOPLE...
YES-- YOU'RE THE HERO!
IT'S ALL ABOUT YOU!
EVEN WHEN THEY'RE TRANSFERRING THEIR MINDS INTO AN 18-FOOT-TALL ANDROID BODY IN A CAPTAIN AMERICA UNIFORM.
KA-RNNKKSH

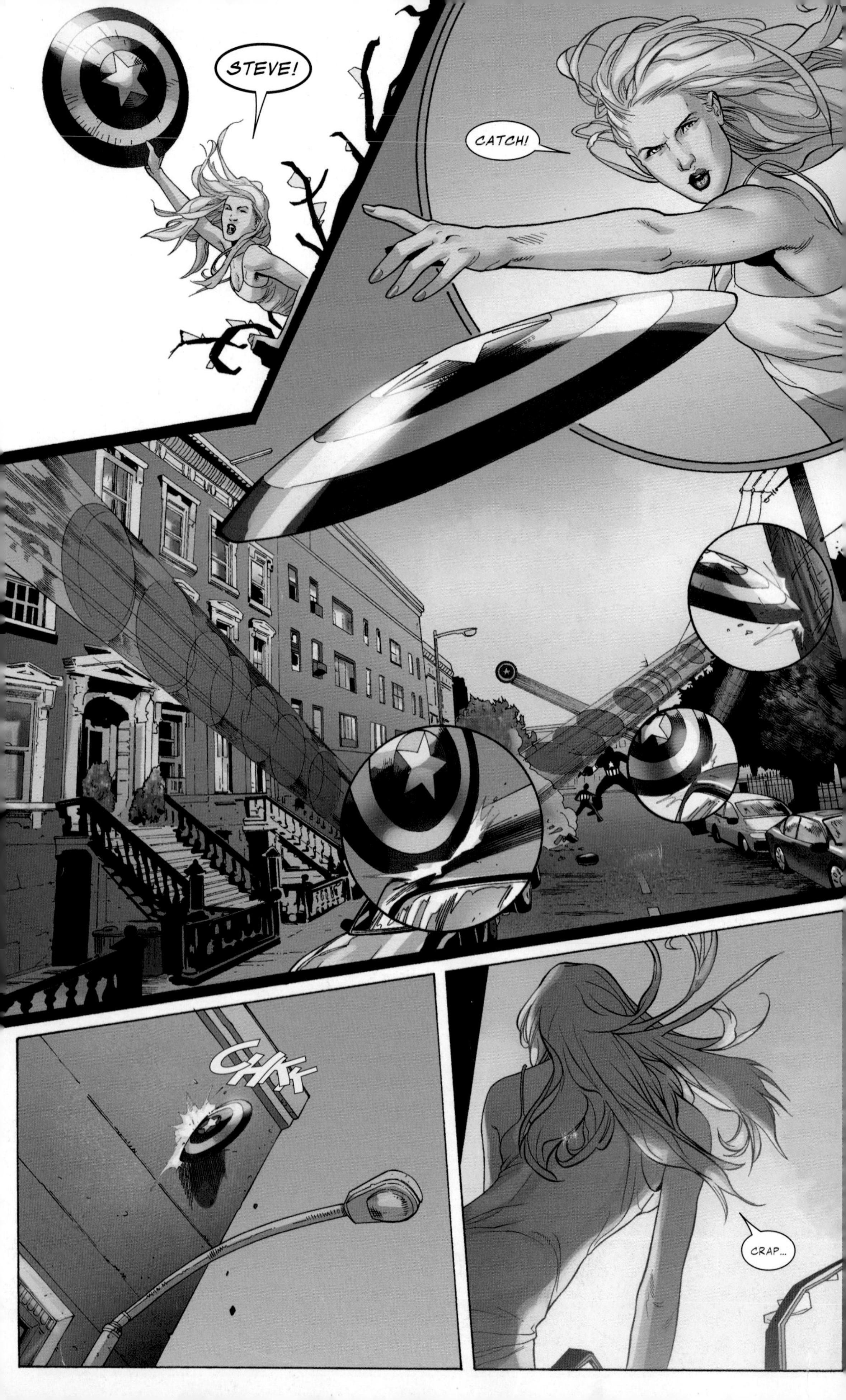
STEVE!
CATCH!
CHKK
CRAP...

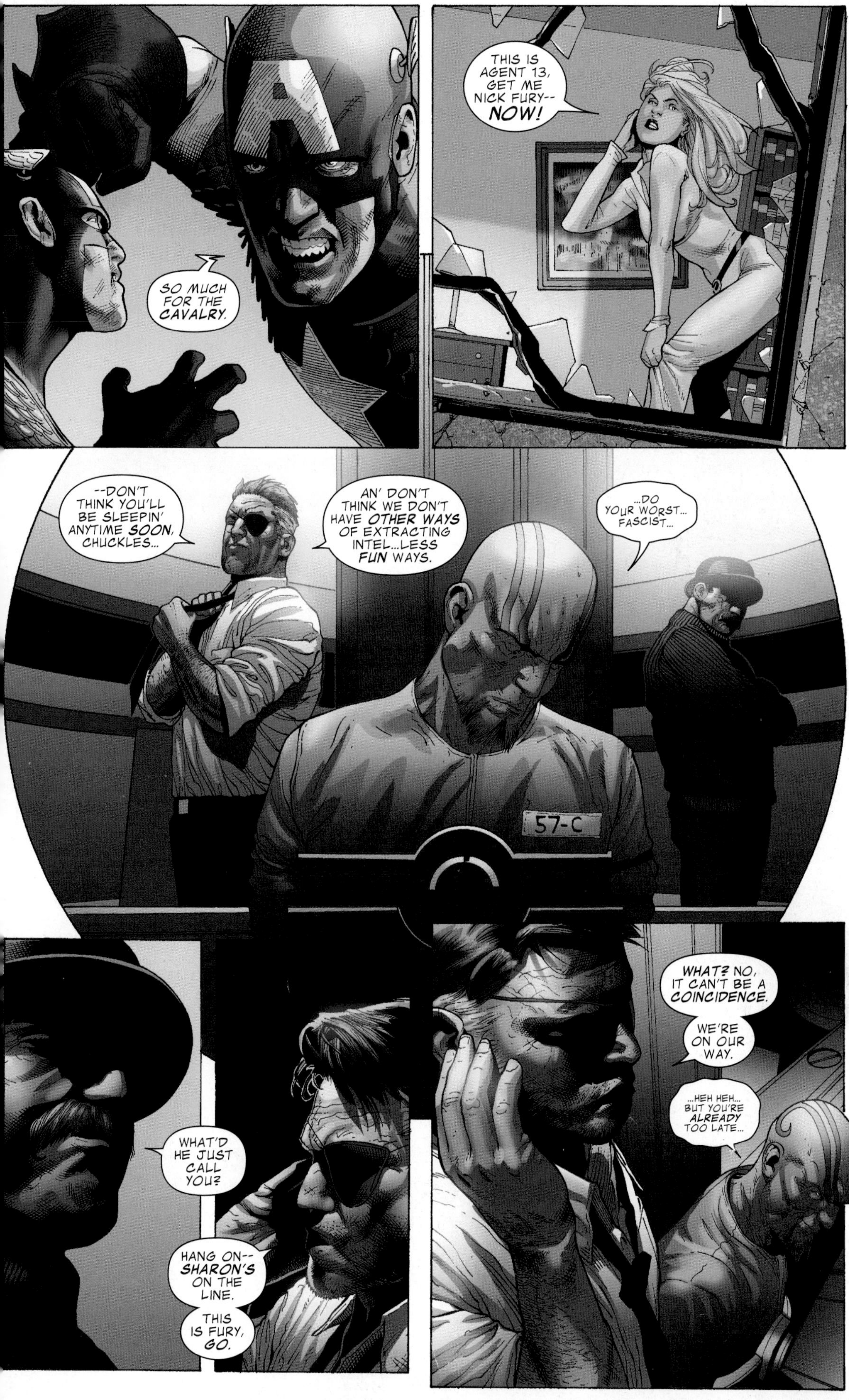
SO MUCH FOR THE CAVALRY.
THIS IS AGENT 13, GET ME NICK FURY-- NOW!
--DON'T THINK YOU'LL BE SLEEPIN' ANYTIME SOON, CHUCKLES...
AN' DON'T THINK WE DON'T HAVE OTHER WAYS OF EXTRACTING INTEL...LESS FUN WAYS.
...DO YOUR WORST... FASCIST...
57-C
WHAT'D HE JUST CALL YOU?
HANG ON-- SHARON'S ON THE LINE.
THIS IS FURY, GO.
WHAT? NO, IT CAN'T BE A COINCIDENCE.
WE'RE ON OUR WAY.
...HEH HEH... BUT YOU'RE ALREADY TOO LATE...

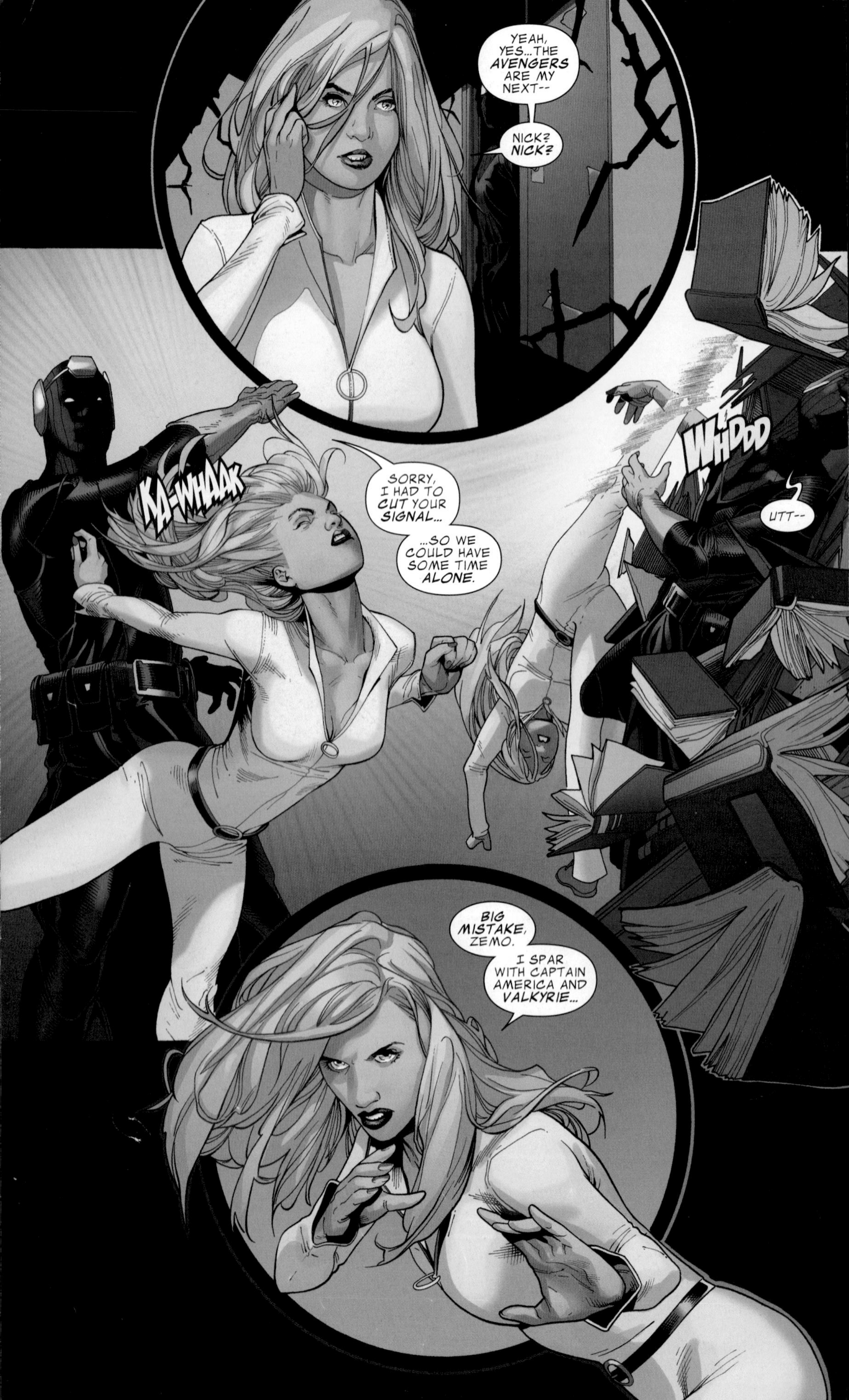
YEAH, YES...THE AVENGERS ARE MY NEXT--
NICK? NICK?
KA-WHAAK
SORRY, I HAD TO CUT YOUR SIGNAL...
...SO WE COULD HAVE SOME TIME ALONE.
WHDDD
UTT--
BIG MISTAKE, ZEMO.
I SPAR WITH CAPTAIN AMERICA AND VALKYRIE...

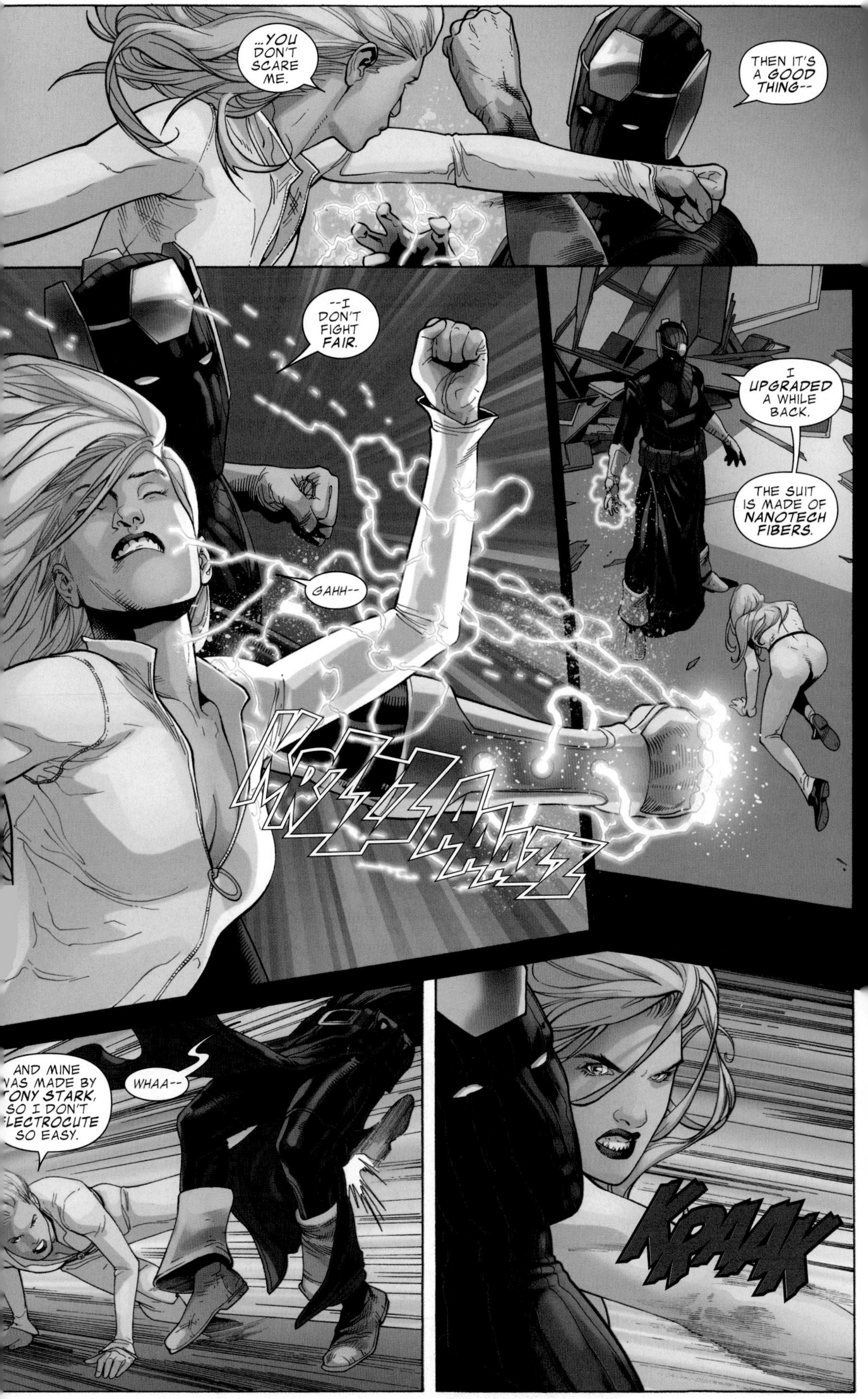

...YOU DON'T SCARE ME.
THEN IT'S A GOOD THING--
--I DON'T FIGHT FAIR.
GAHH--
I UPGRADED A WHILE BACK.
THE SUIT IS MADE OF NANOTECH FIBERS.
AND MINE WAS MADE BY TONY STARK, SO I DON'T ELECTROCUTE SO EASY.
WHAA--
KRAAK

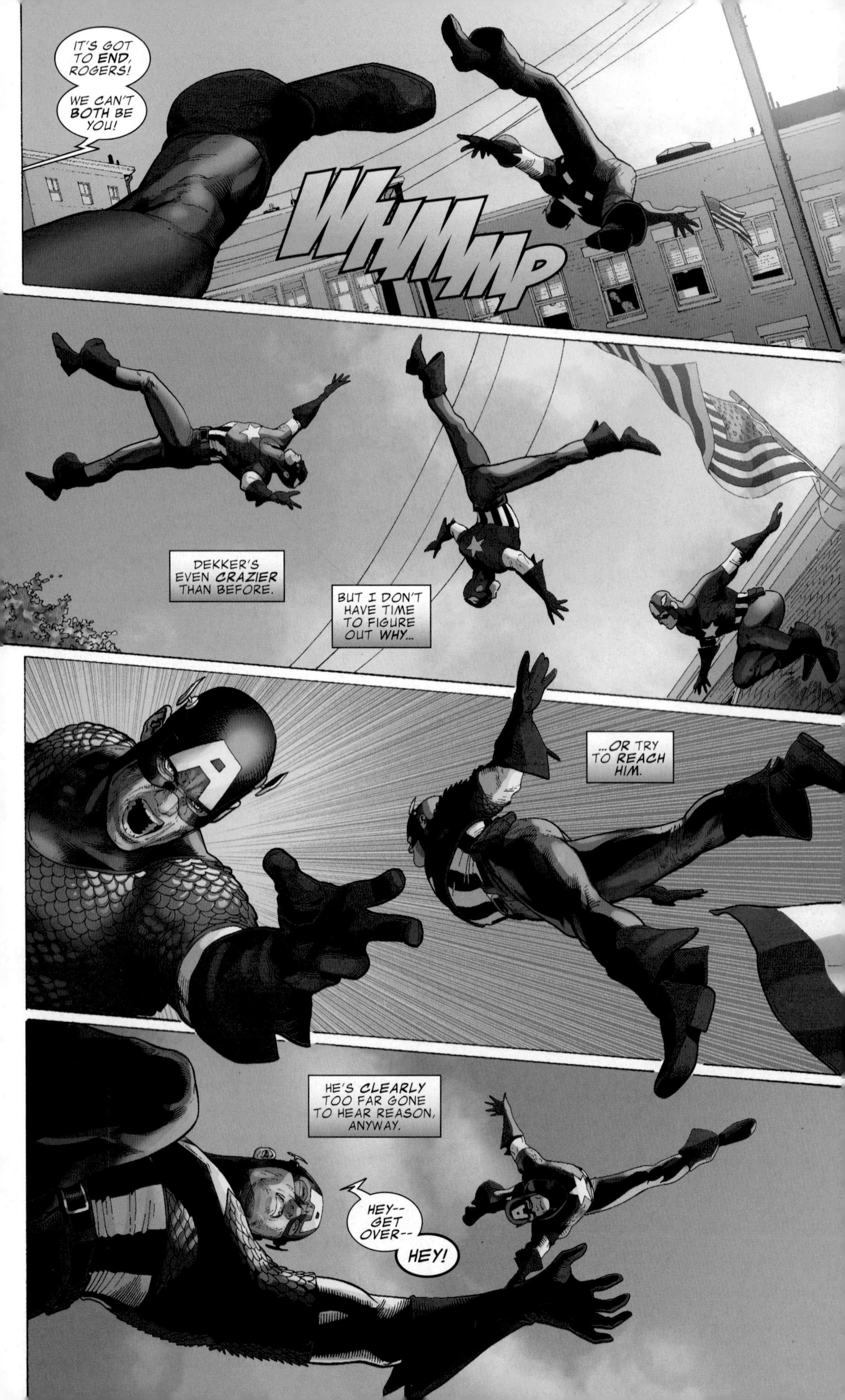
IT'S GOT TO END, ROGERS!
WE CAN'T BOTH BE YOU!
WHMMMP
DEKKER'S EVEN CRAZIER THAN BEFORE.
BUT I DON'T HAVE TIME TO FIGURE OUT WHY...
...OR TRY TO REACH HIM.
HE'S CLEARLY TOO FAR GONE TO HEAR REASON, ANYWAY.
HEY-- GET OVER--
HEY!

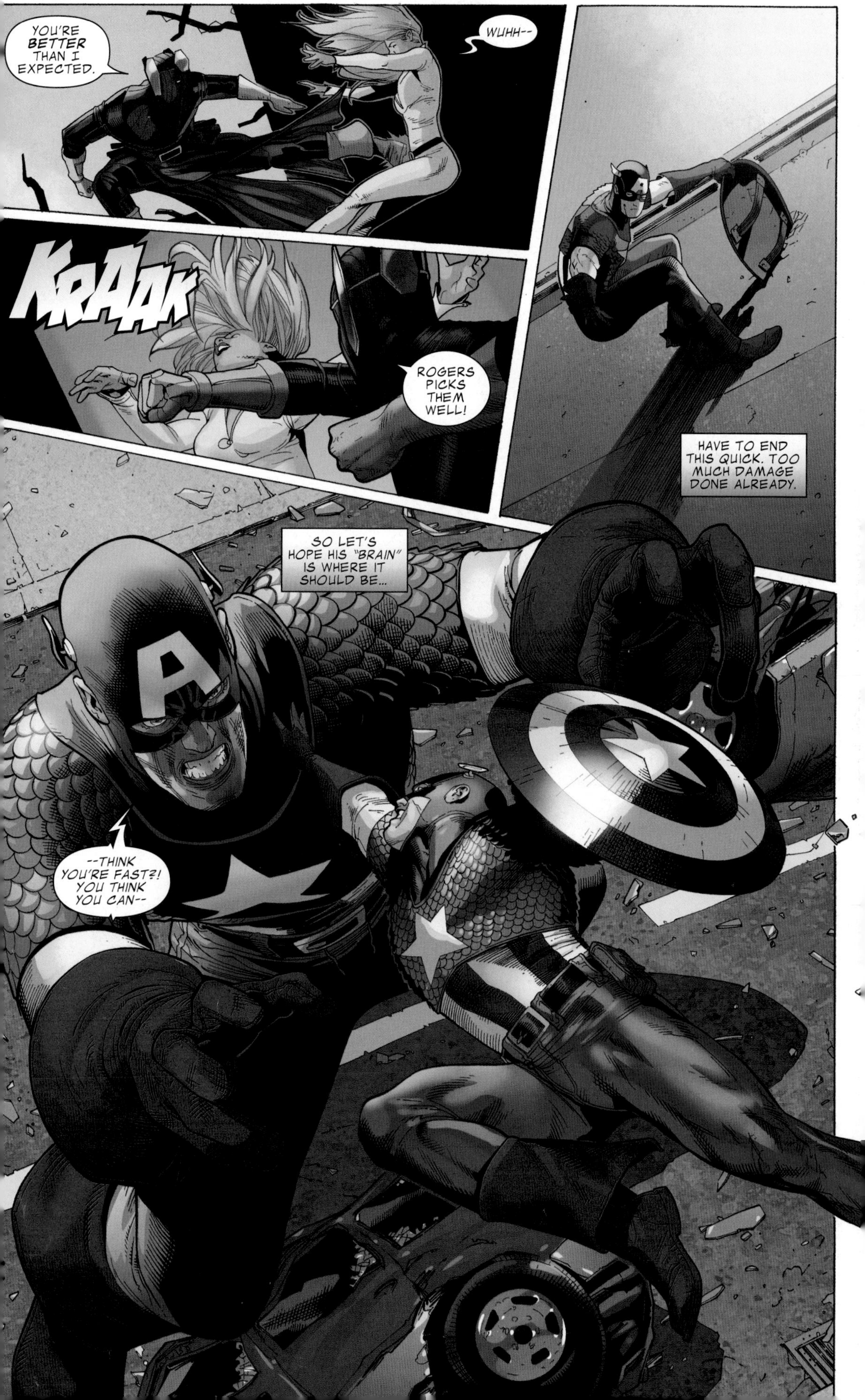
YOU'RE BETTER THAN I EXPECTED.
WUHH--
KRAAK
ROGERS PICKS THEM WELL!
HAVE TO END THIS QUICK. TOO MUCH DAMAGE DONE ALREADY.
SO LET'S HOPE HIS "BRAIN" IS WHERE IT SHOULD BE...
--THINK YOU'RE FAST?! YOU THINK YOU CAN--

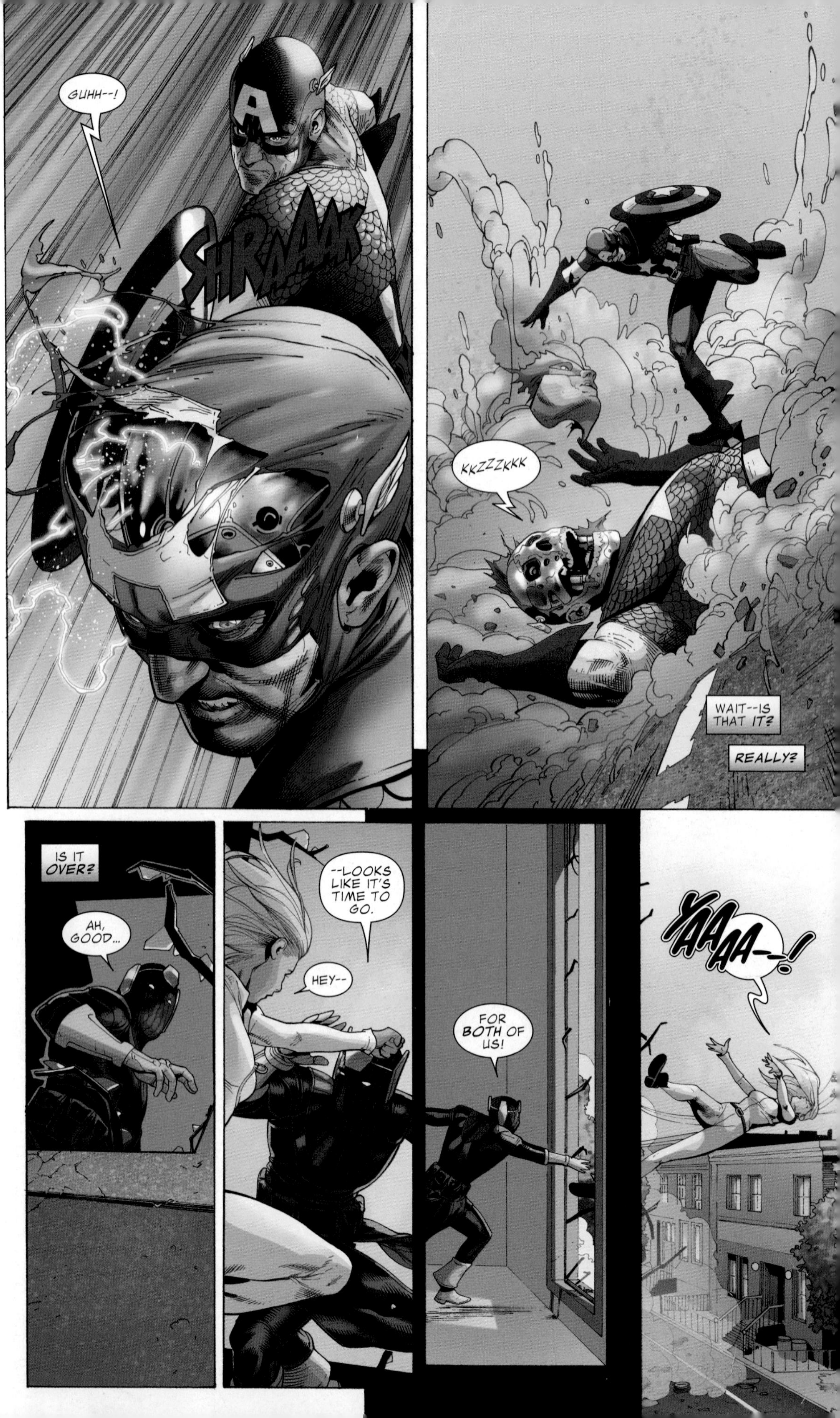
GUHH--!
SHRAAAK
KKZZZKKK
WAIT--IS THAT IT?
REALLY?
IS IT OVER?
AH, GOOD...
--LOOKS LIKE IT'S TIME TO GO.
HEY--
FOR BOTH OF US!
YAAAAA--!

SHARON!!

HUPP--!

KRRSSSH

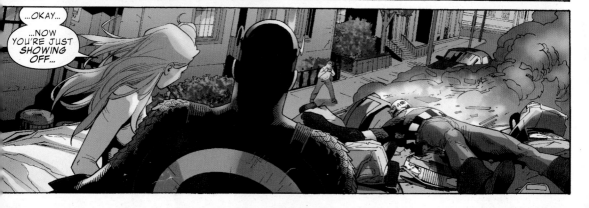

...OKAY...
...NOW YOU'RE JUST SHOWING OFF...

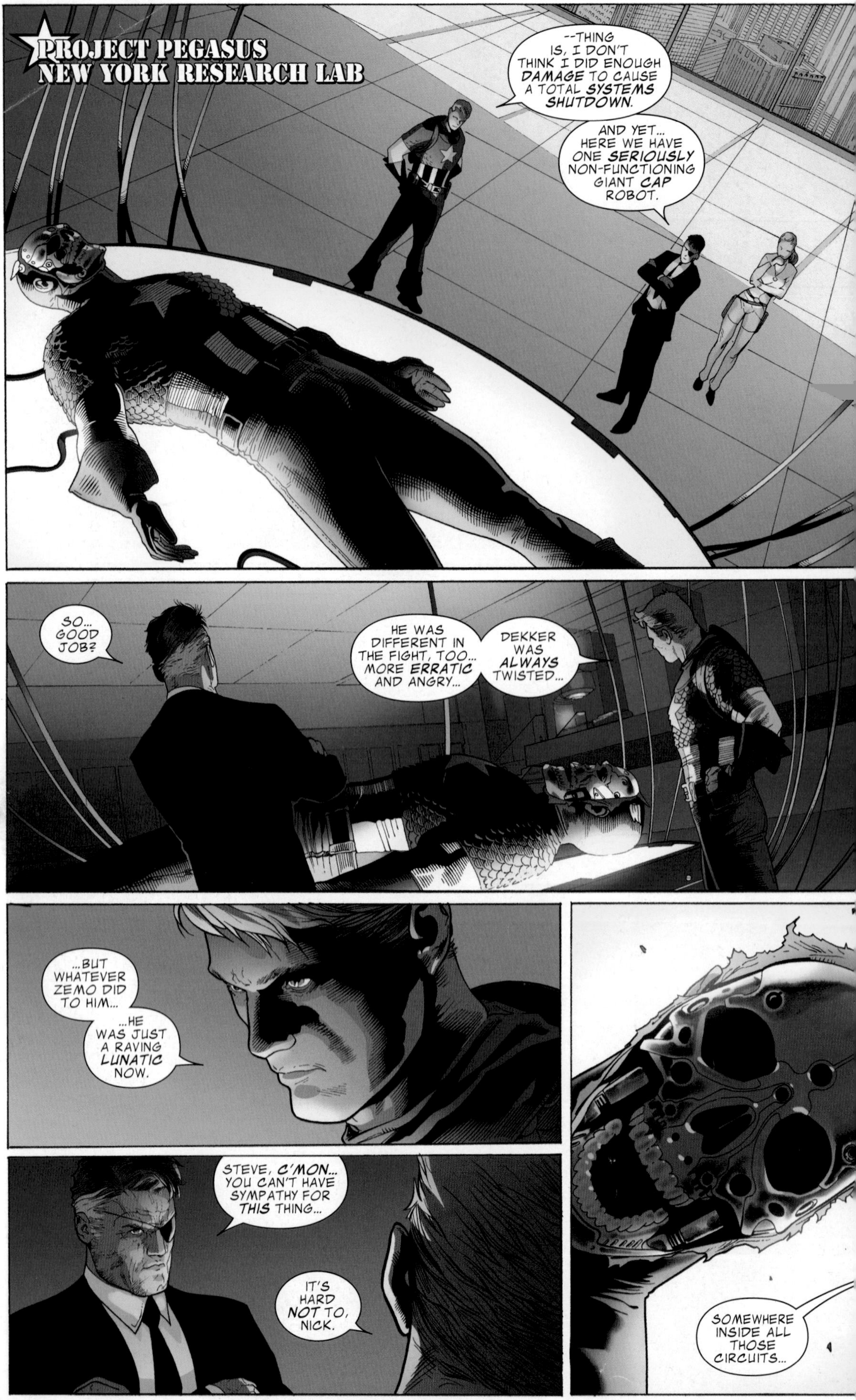
PROJECT PEGASUS
NEW YORK RESEARCH LAB
--THING IS, I DON'T THINK I DID ENOUGH DAMAGE TO CAUSE A TOTAL SYSTEMS SHUTDOWN.
AND YET... HERE WE HAVE ONE SERIOUSLY NON-FUNCTIONING GIANT CAP ROBOT.
SO... GOOD JOB?
HE WAS DIFFERENT IN THE FIGHT, TOO... MORE ERRATIC AND ANGRY...
DEKKER WAS ALWAYS TWISTED...
...BUT WHATEVER ZEMO DID TO HIM...
...HE WAS JUST A RAVING LUNATIC NOW.
STEVE, C'MON... YOU CAN'T HAVE SYMPATHY FOR THIS THING...
IT'S HARD NOT TO, NICK.
SOMEWHERE INSIDE ALL THOSE CIRCUITS...

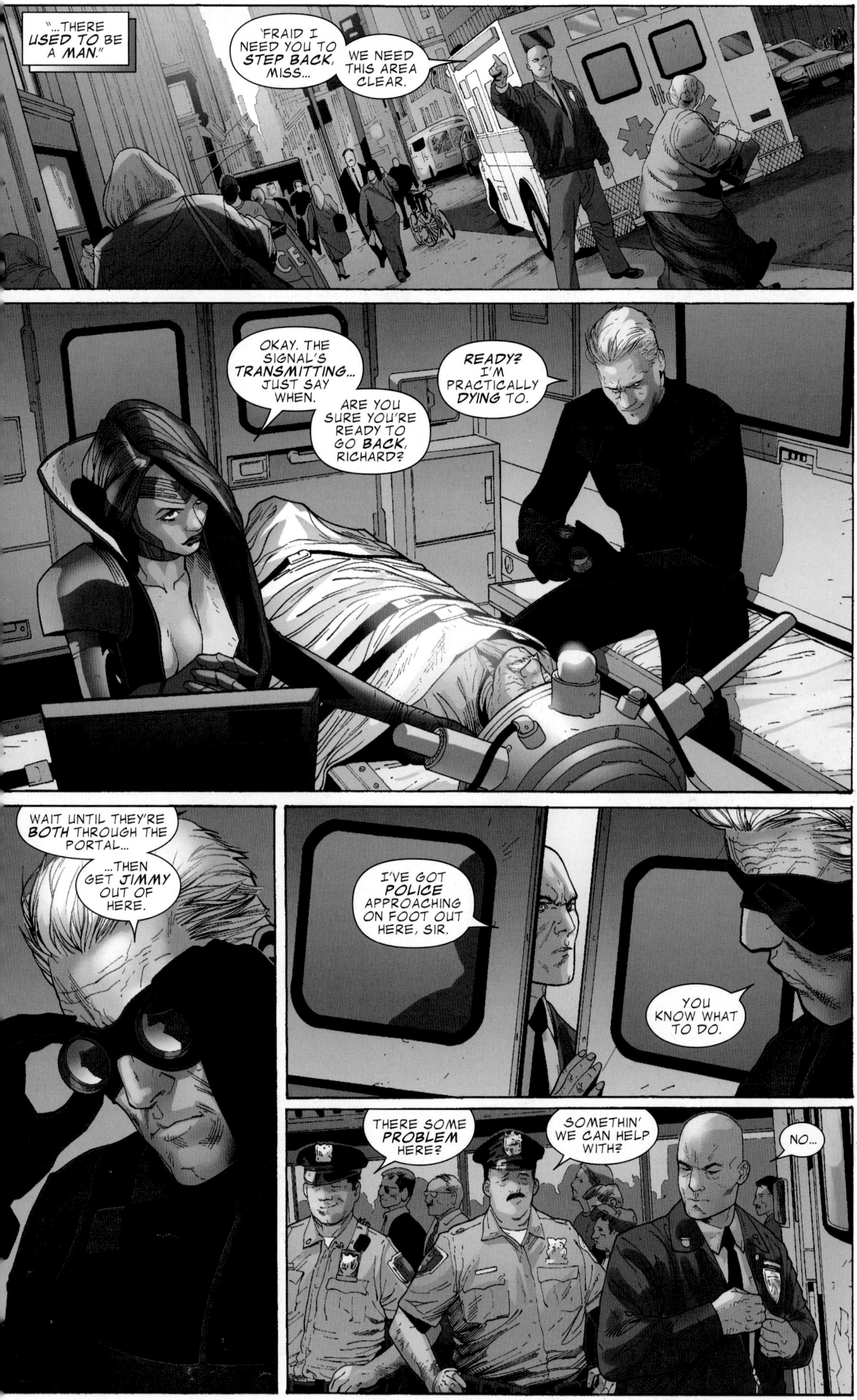
"...THERE USED TO BE A MAN."
'FRAID I NEED YOU TO STEP BACK, MISS...
WE NEED THIS AREA CLEAR.
OKAY. THE SIGNAL'S TRANSMITTING... JUST SAY WHEN.
ARE YOU SURE YOU'RE READY TO GO BACK, RICHARD?
READY? I'M PRACTICALLY DYING TO.
WAIT UNTIL THEY'RE BOTH THROUGH THE PORTAL...
...THEN GET JIMMY OUT OF HERE.
I'VE GOT POLICE APPROACHING ON FOOT OUT HERE, SIR.
YOU KNOW WHAT TO DO.
THERE SOME PROBLEM HERE?
SOMETHIN' WE CAN HELP WITH?
NO...

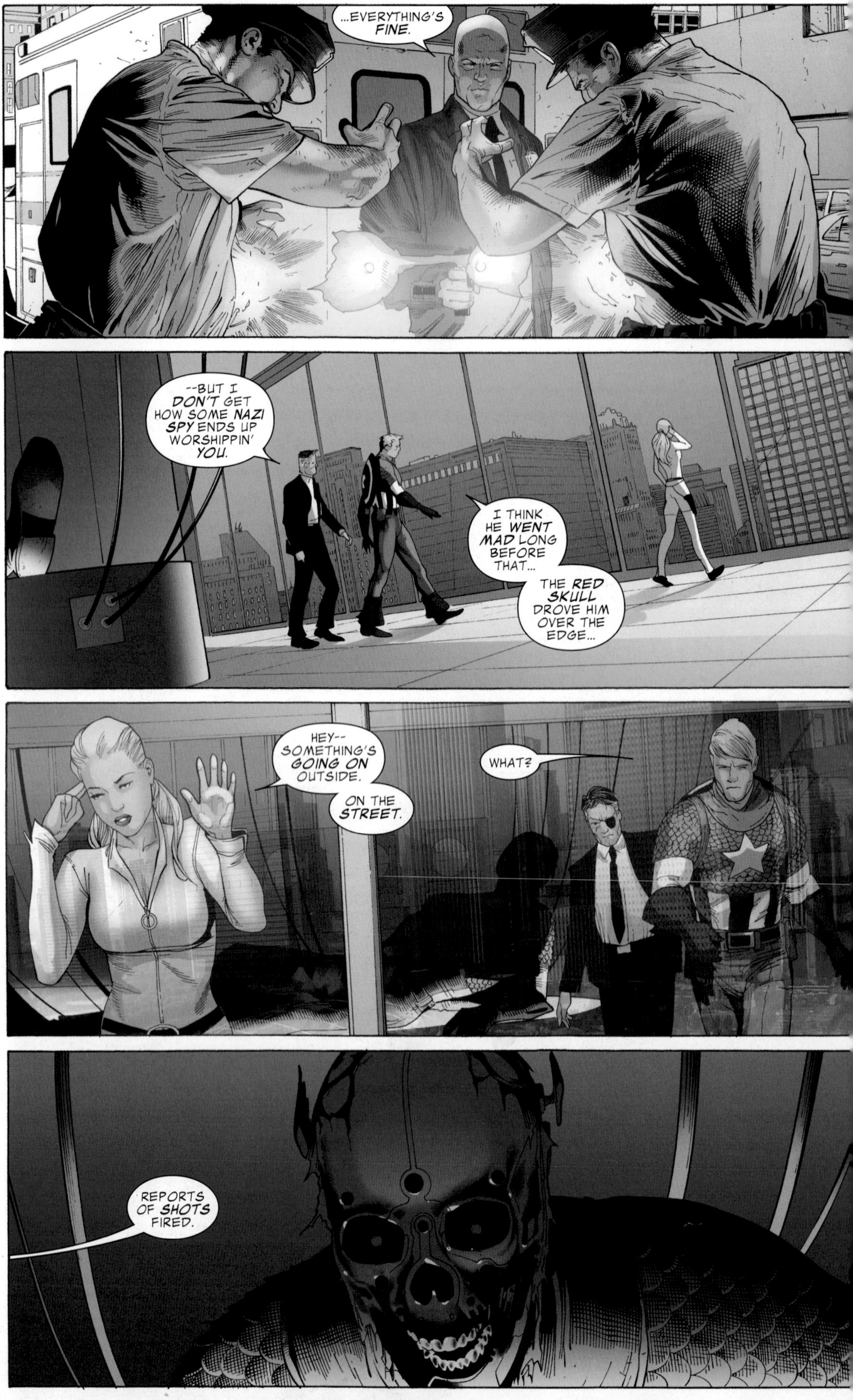
...EVERYTHING'S FINE.
--BUT I DON'T GET HOW SOME NAZI SPY ENDS UP WORSHIPPIN' YOU.
I THINK HE WENT MAD LONG BEFORE THAT...
THE RED SKULL DROVE HIM OVER THE EDGE...
HEY-- SOMETHING'S GOING ON OUTSIDE.
ON THE STREET.
WHAT?
REPORTS OF SHOTS FIRED.

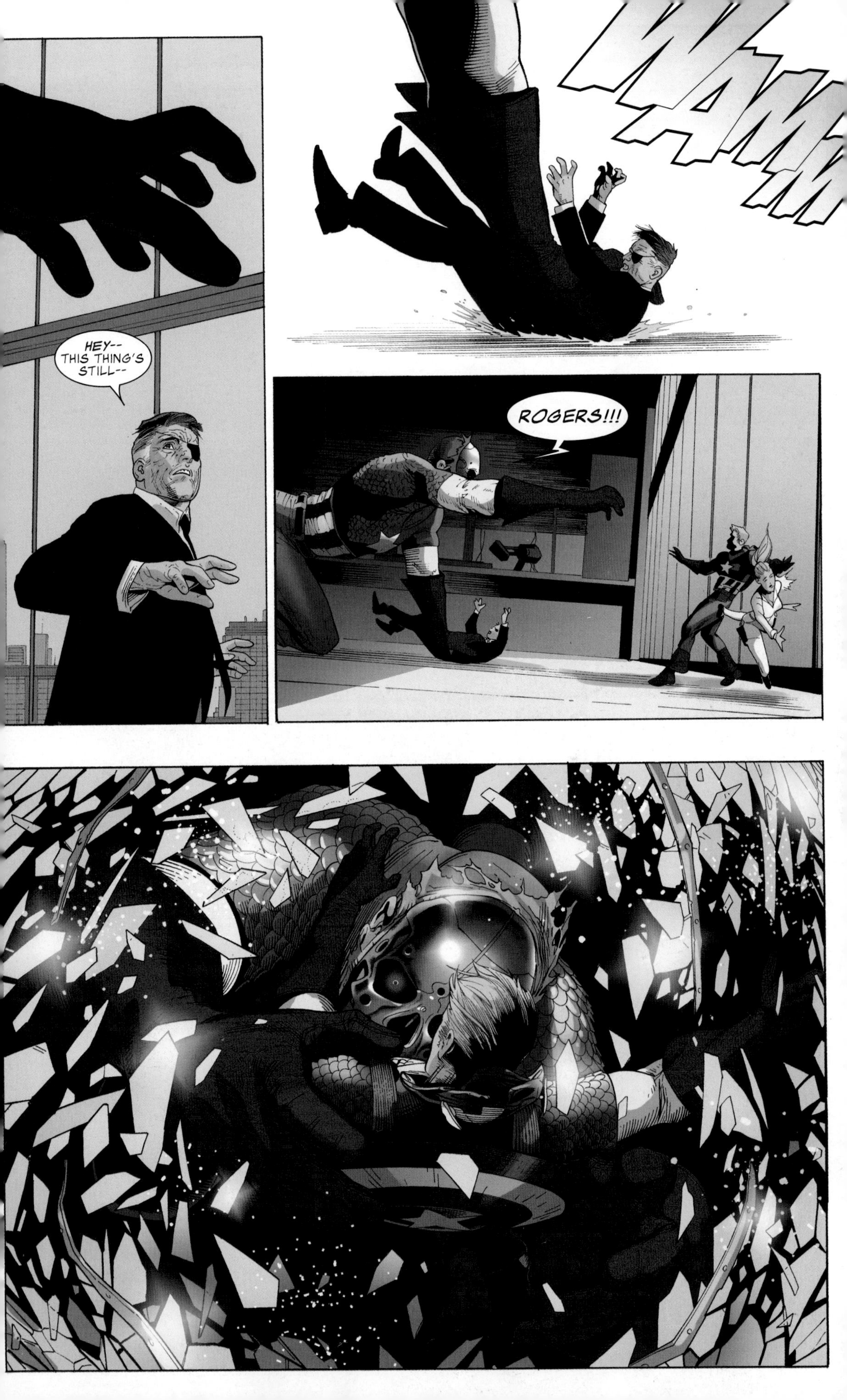
WAMM
HEY-- THIS THING'S STILL--
ROGERS!!!

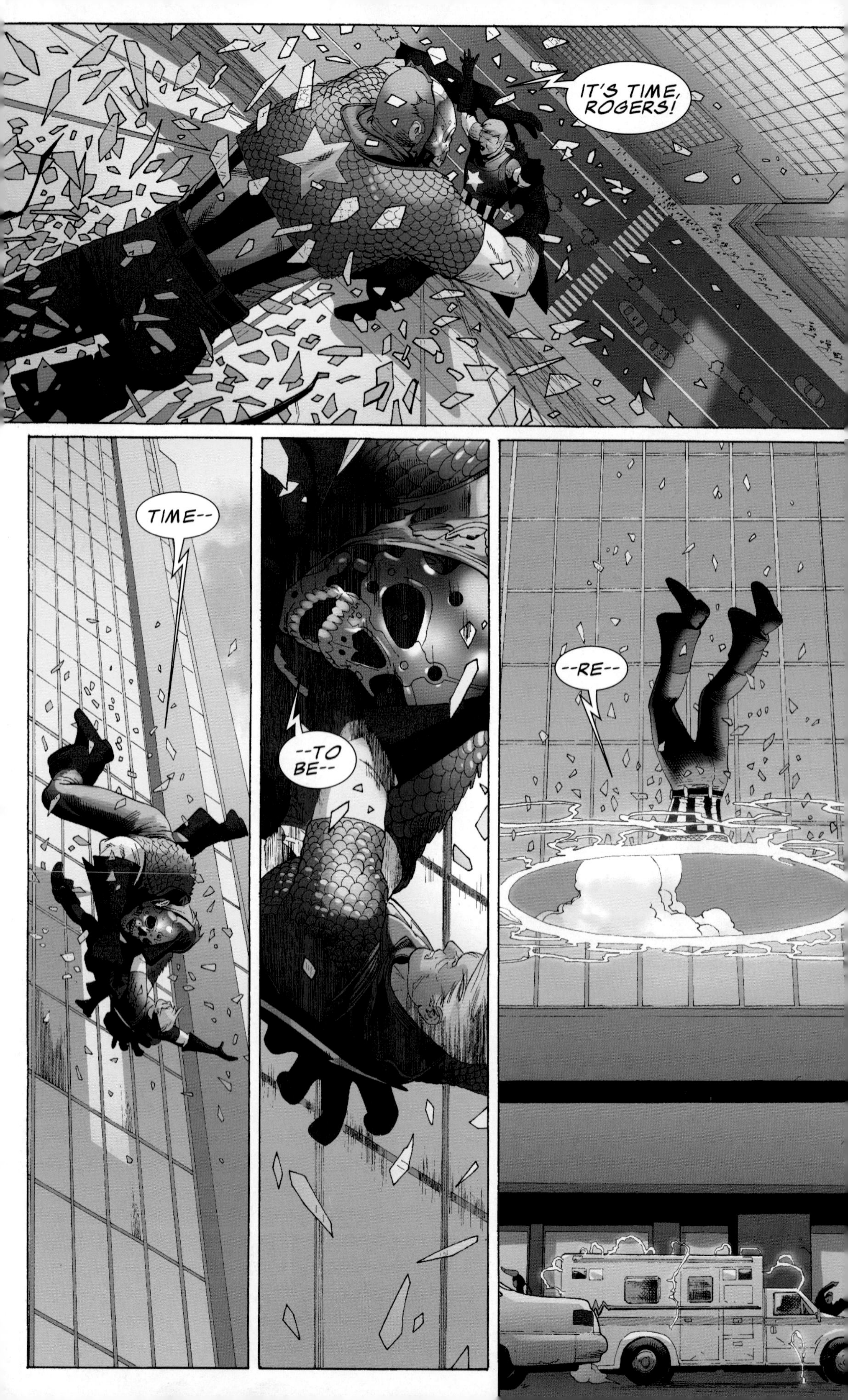
IT'S TIME, ROGERS!
TIME--
--TO BE--
--RE--

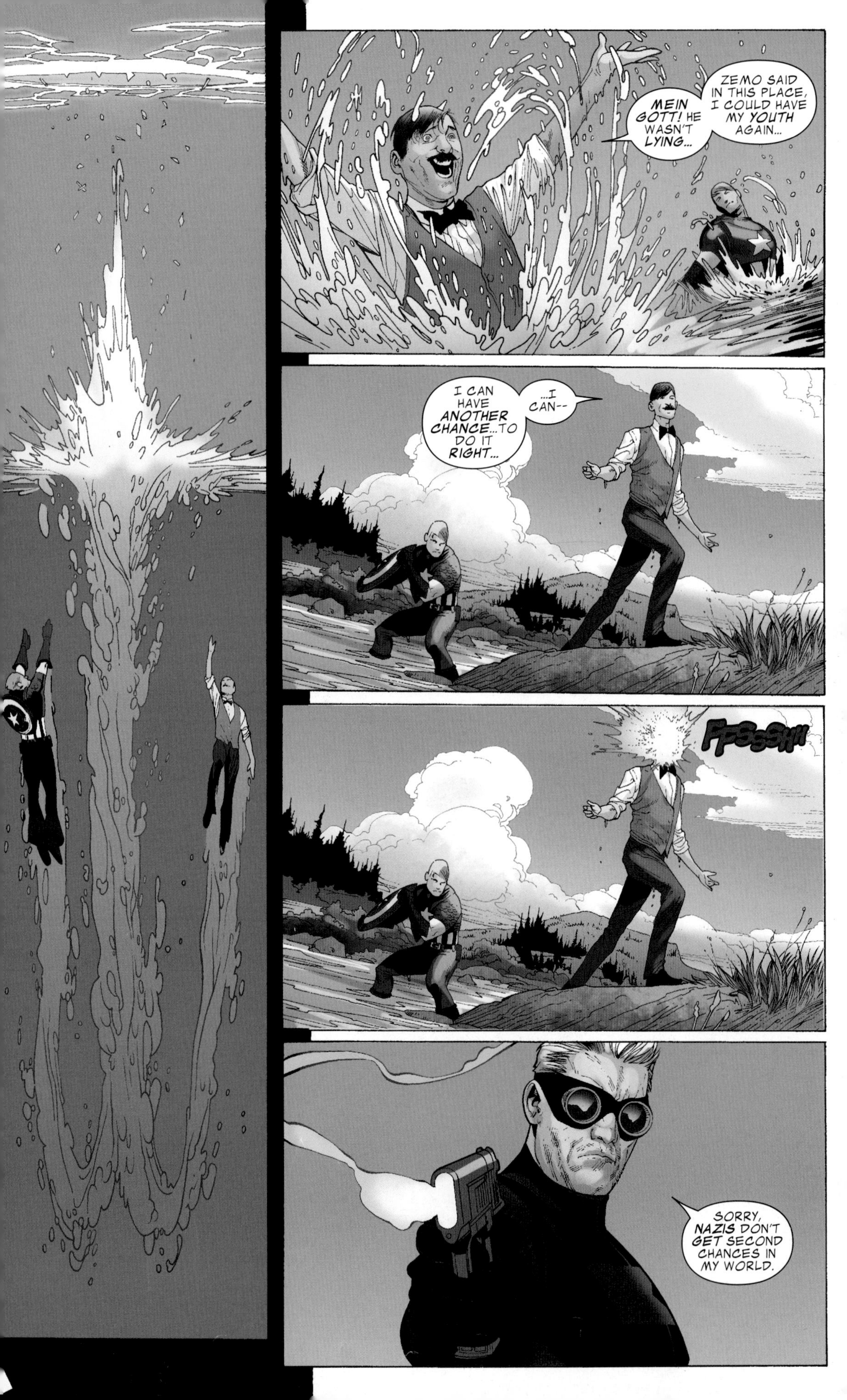
MEIN GOTT! HE WASN'T LYING...
ZEMO SAID IN THIS PLACE, I COULD HAVE MY YOUTH AGAIN...
I CAN HAVE ANOTHER CHANCE...TO DO IT RIGHT...
...I CAN--
SORRY, NAZIS DON'T GET SECOND CHANCES IN MY WORLD.

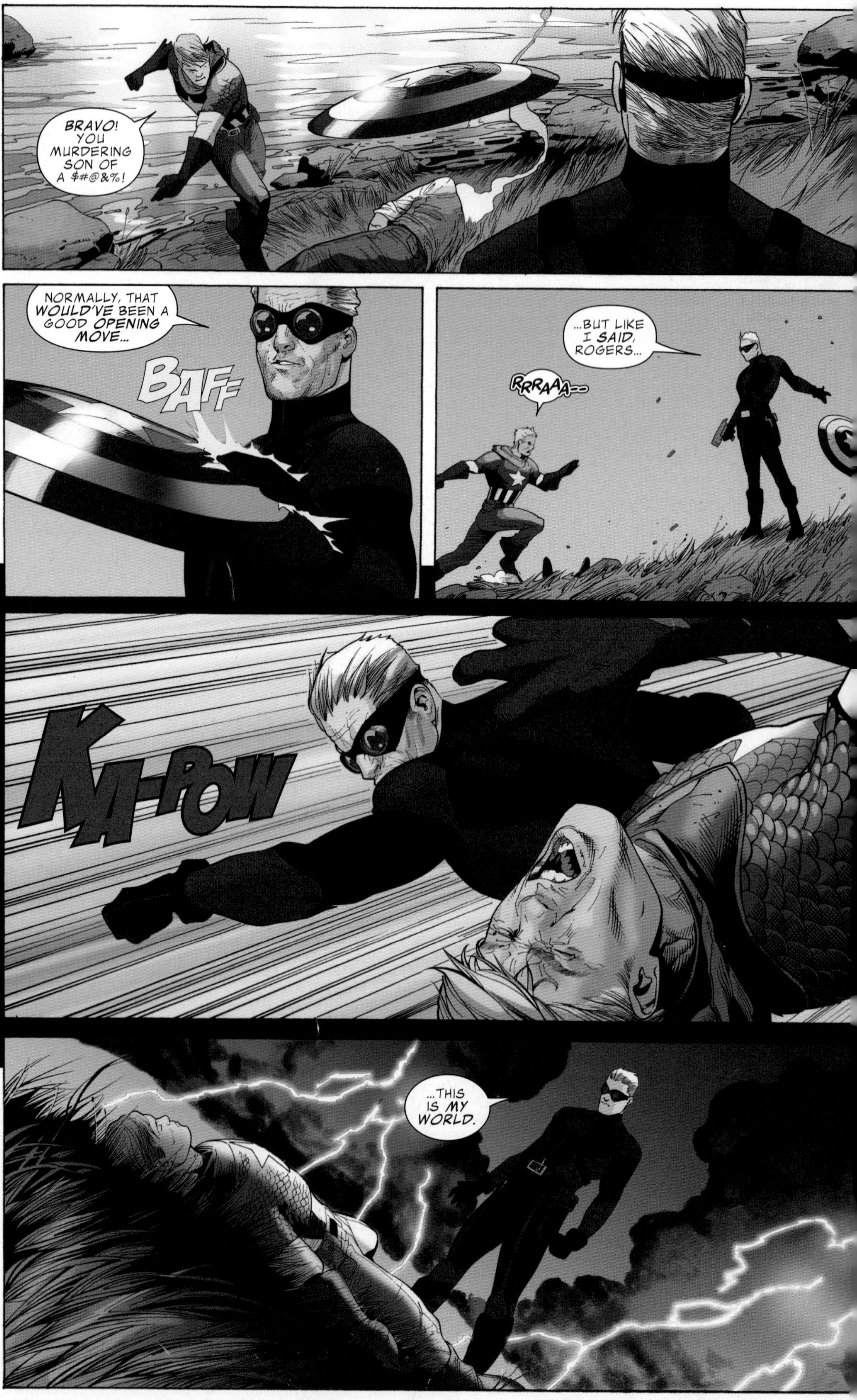
BRAVO! YOU MURDERING SON OF A $#@&%!
NORMALLY, THAT WOULD'VE BEEN A GOOD OPENING MOVE...
BAFF
...BUT LIKE I SAID, ROGERS...
RRRAAA--
KA-POW
...THIS IS MY WORLD.

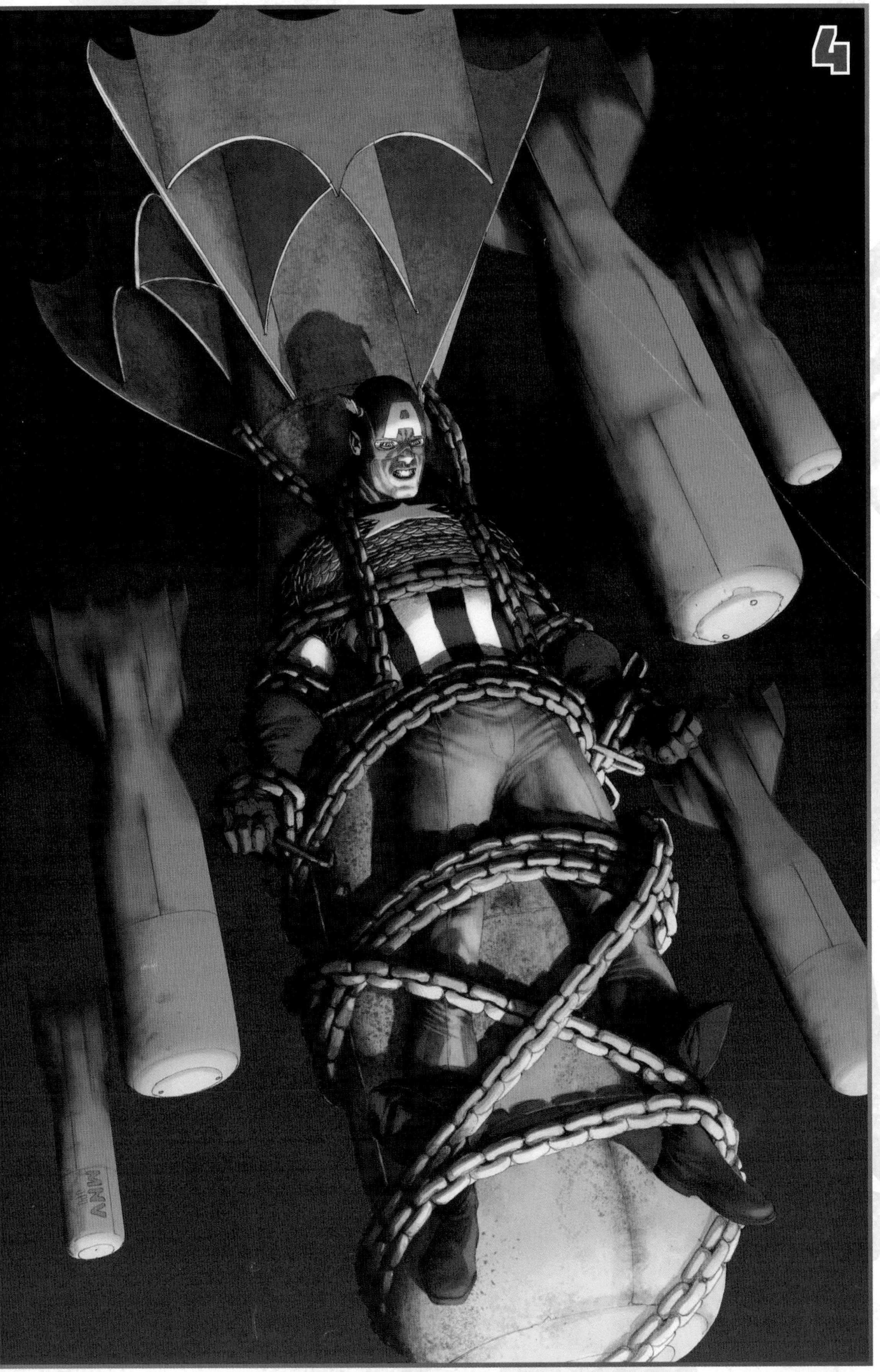
4

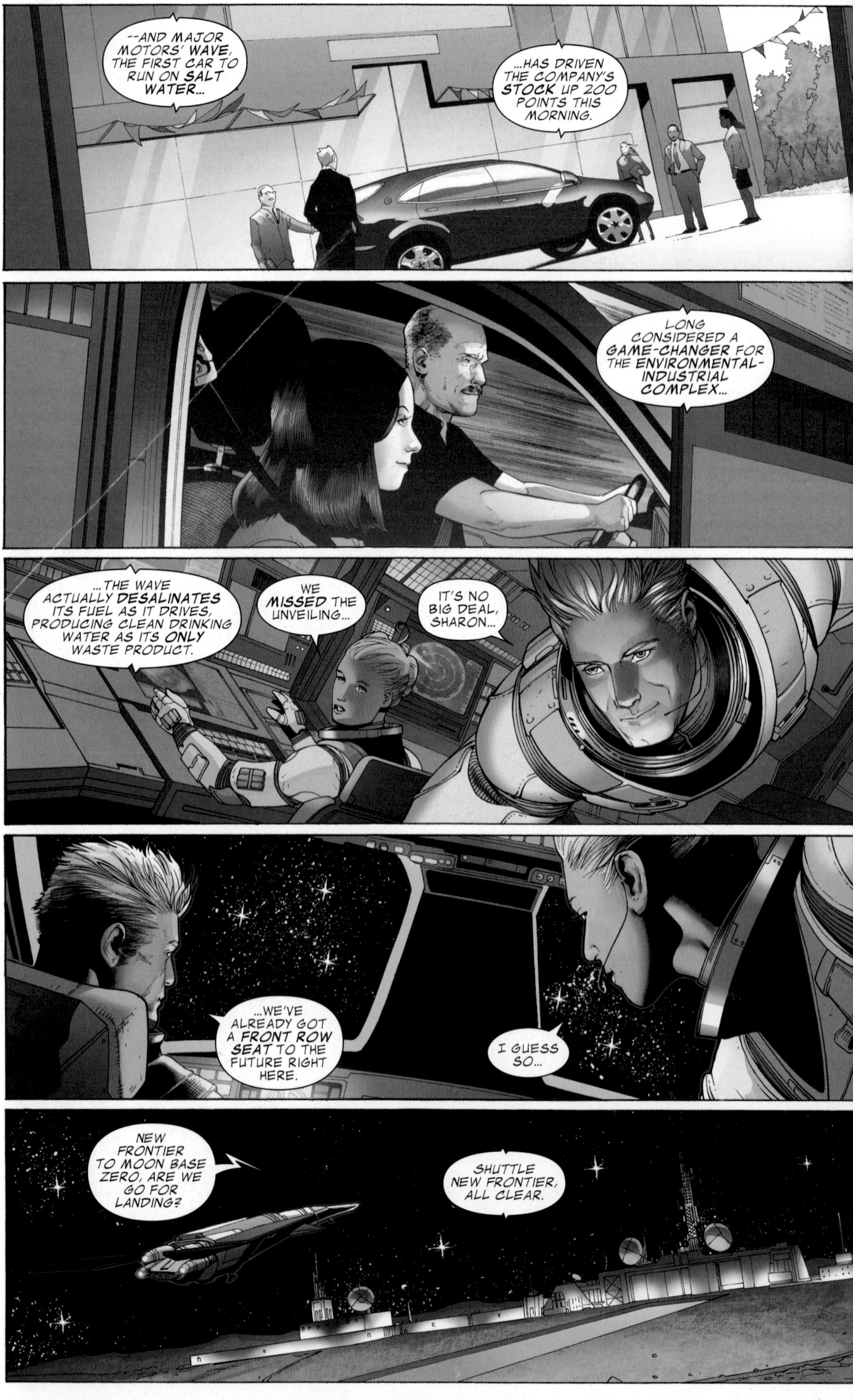
--AND MAJOR MOTORS' WAVE, THE FIRST CAR TO RUN ON SALT WATER...
...HAS DRIVEN THE COMPANY'S STOCK UP 200 POINTS THIS MORNING.
LONG CONSIDERED A GAME-CHANGER FOR THE ENVIRONMENTAL-INDUSTRIAL COMPLEX...
...THE WAVE ACTUALLY DESALINATES ITS FUEL AS IT DRIVES, PRODUCING CLEAN DRINKING WATER AS ITS ONLY WASTE PRODUCT.
WE MISSED THE UNVEILING...
IT'S NO BIG DEAL, SHARON...
...WE'VE ALREADY GOT A FRONT ROW SEAT TO THE FUTURE RIGHT HERE.
I GUESS SO...
NEW FRONTIER TO MOON BASE ZERO, ARE WE GO FOR LANDING?
SHUTTLE NEW FRONTIER, ALL CLEAR.

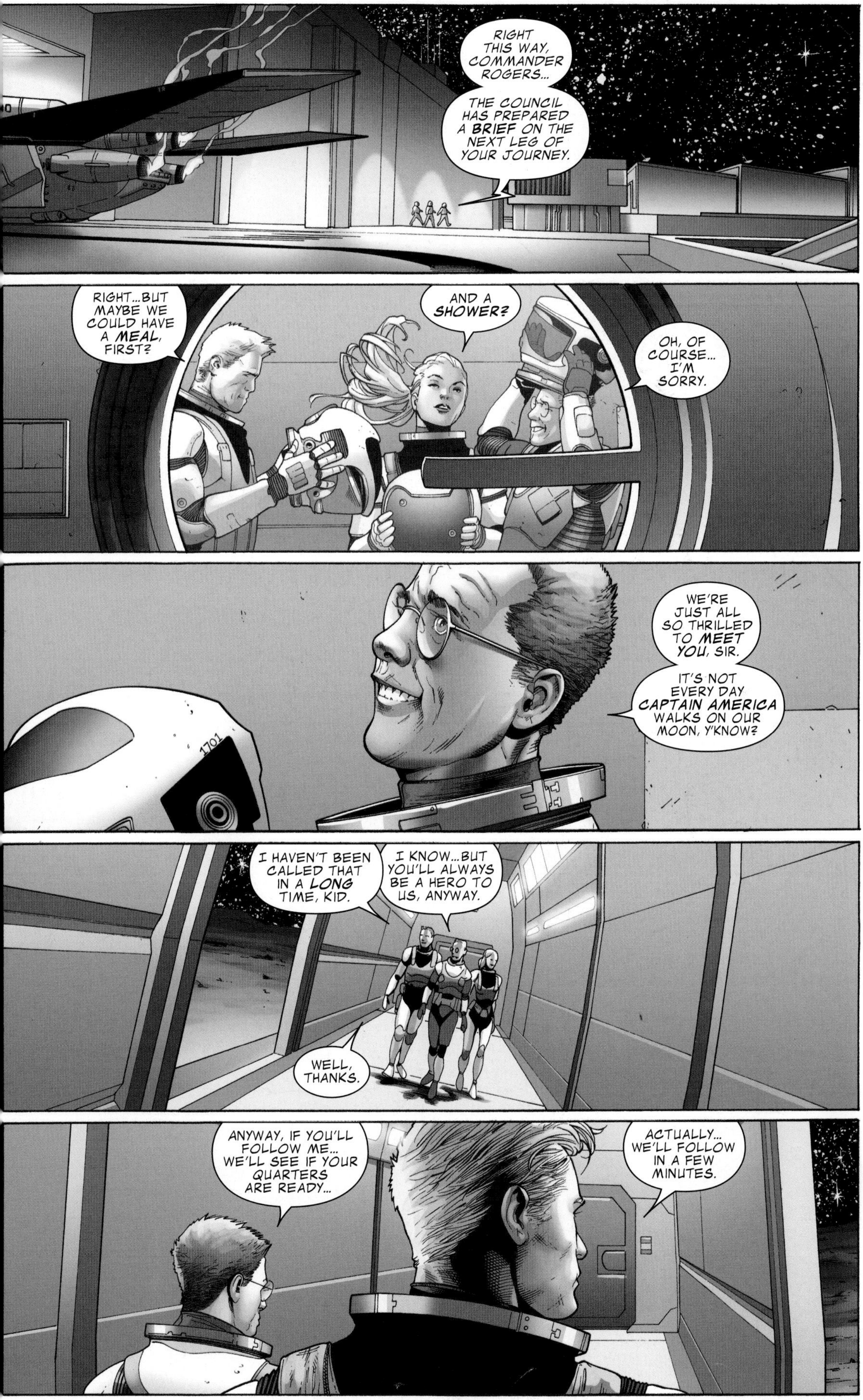
RIGHT THIS WAY, COMMANDER ROGERS...
THE COUNCIL HAS PREPARED A BRIEF ON THE NEXT LEG OF YOUR JOURNEY.
RIGHT...BUT MAYBE WE COULD HAVE A MEAL, FIRST?
AND A SHOWER?
OH, OF COURSE... I'M SORRY.
1701
WE'RE JUST ALL SO THRILLED TO MEET YOU, SIR.
IT'S NOT EVERY DAY CAPTAIN AMERICA WALKS ON OUR MOON, Y'KNOW?
I HAVEN'T BEEN CALLED THAT IN A LONG TIME, KID.
I KNOW...BUT YOU'LL ALWAYS BE A HERO TO US, ANYWAY.
WELL, THANKS.
ANYWAY, IF YOU'LL FOLLOW ME... WE'LL SEE IF YOUR QUARTERS ARE READY...
ACTUALLY... WE'LL FOLLOW IN A FEW MINUTES.

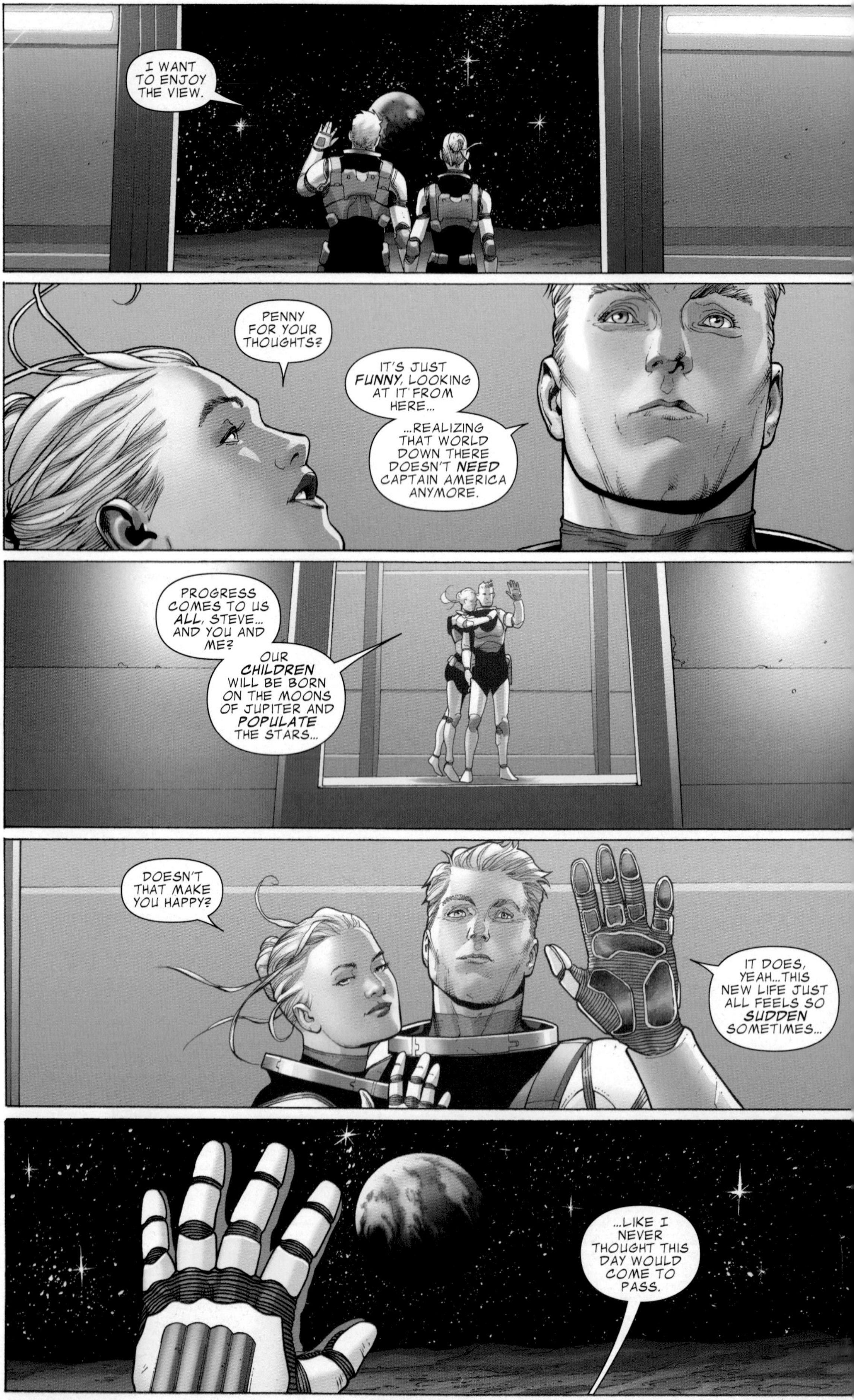
I WANT TO ENJOY THE VIEW.
PENNY FOR YOUR THOUGHTS?
IT'S JUST FUNNY, LOOKING AT IT FROM HERE...
...REALIZING THAT WORLD DOWN THERE DOESN'T NEED CAPTAIN AMERICA ANYMORE.
PROGRESS COMES TO US ALL, STEVE... AND YOU AND ME?
OUR CHILDREN WILL BE BORN ON THE MOONS OF JUPITER AND POPULATE THE STARS...
DOESN'T THAT MAKE YOU HAPPY?
IT DOES, YEAH...THIS NEW LIFE JUST ALL FEELS SO SUDDEN SOMETIMES...
...LIKE I NEVER THOUGHT THIS DAY WOULD COME TO PASS.

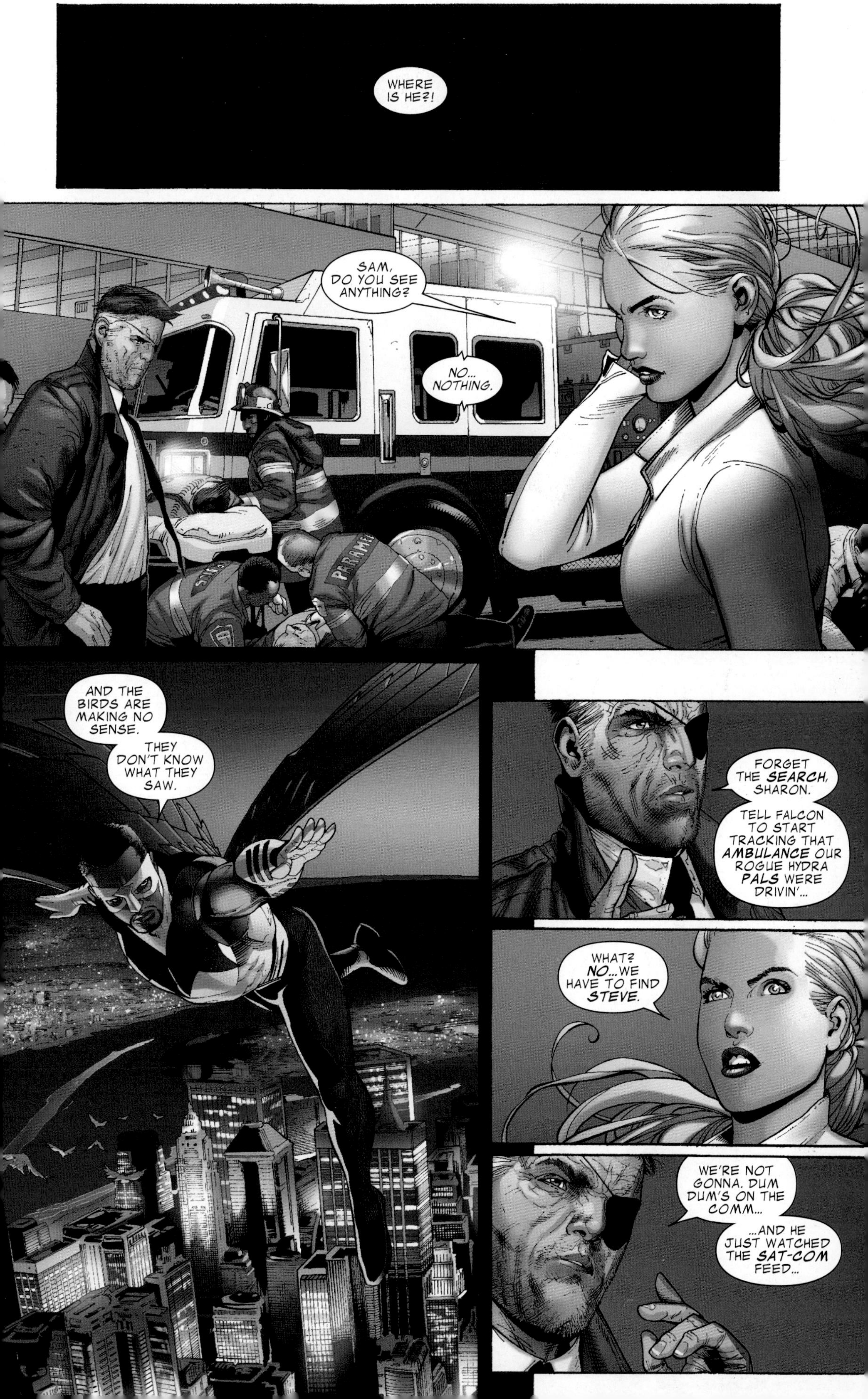
WHERE IS HE?!
SAM, DO YOU SEE ANYTHING?
NO... NOTHING.
AND THE BIRDS ARE MAKING NO SENSE.
THEY DON'T KNOW WHAT THEY SAW.
FORGET THE SEARCH, SHARON.
TELL FALCON TO START TRACKING THAT AMBULANCE OUR ROGUE HYDRA PALS WERE DRIVIN'...
WHAT? NO...WE HAVE TO FIND STEVE.
WE'RE NOT GONNA. DUM DUM'S ON THE COMM...
...AND HE JUST WATCHED THE SAT-COM FEED...

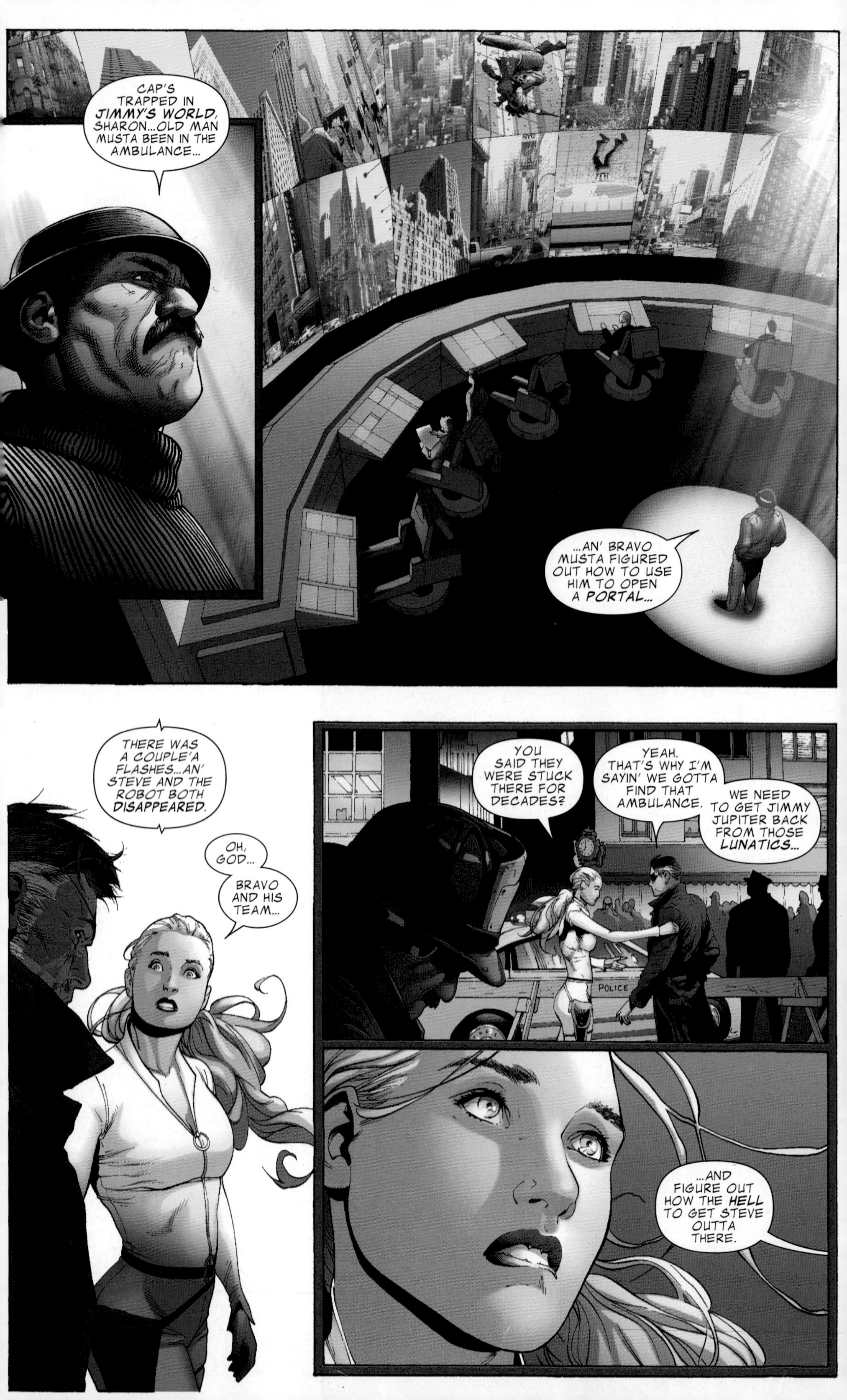
CAP'S TRAPPED IN JIMMY'S WORLD, SHARON...OLD MAN MUSTA BEEN IN THE AMBULANCE...
...AN' BRAVO MUSTA FIGURED OUT HOW TO USE HIM TO OPEN A PORTAL...
THERE WAS A COUPLE'A FLASHES...AN' STEVE AND THE ROBOT BOTH DISAPPEARED.
OH, GOD...
BRAVO AND HIS TEAM...
YOU SAID THEY WERE STUCK THERE FOR DECADES?
YEAH. THAT'S WHY I'M SAYIN' WE GOTTA FIND THAT AMBULANCE.
WE NEED TO GET JIMMY JUPITER BACK FROM THOSE LUNATICS...
...AND FIGURE OUT HOW THE HELL TO GET STEVE OUTTA THERE.
POLICE

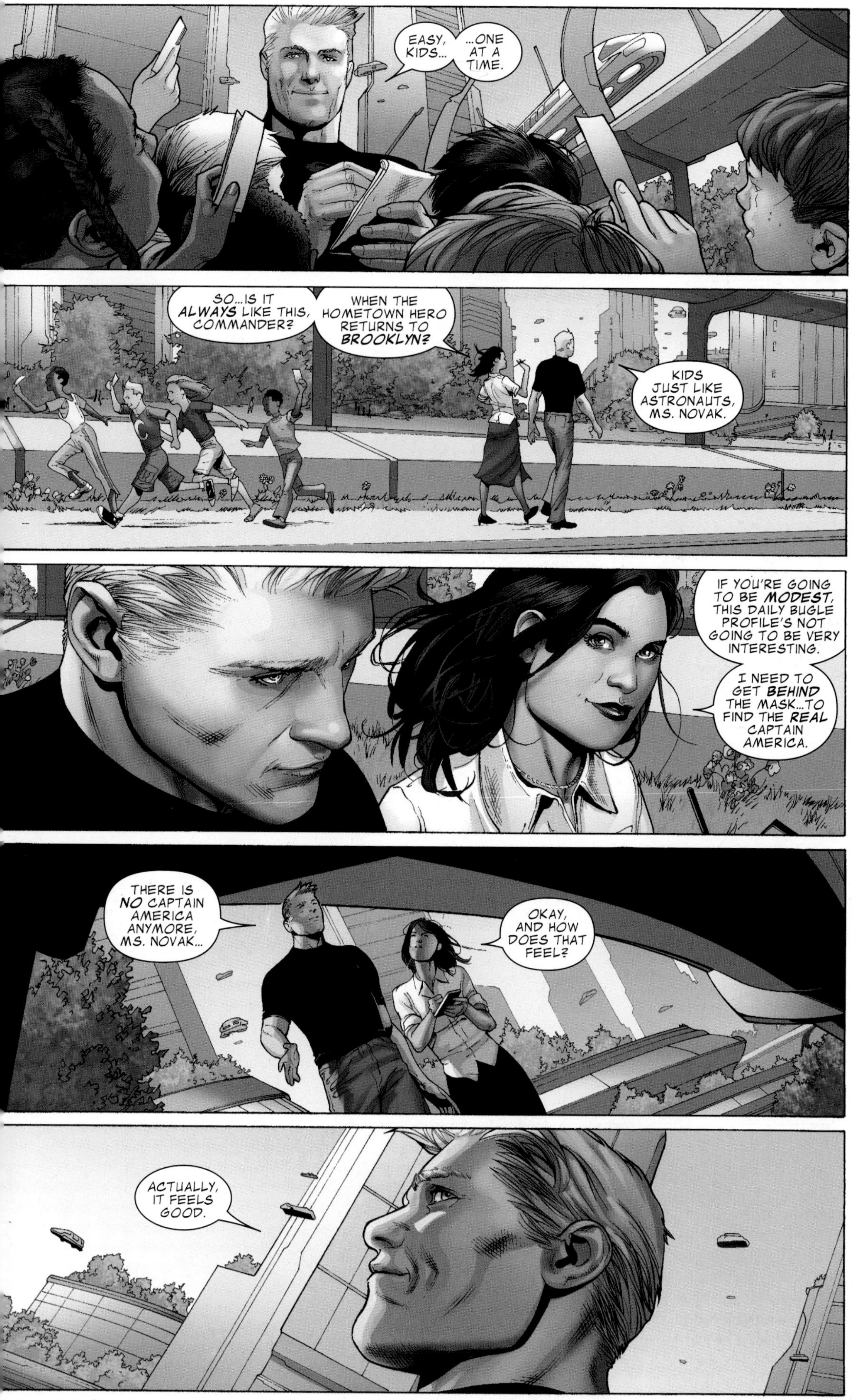
EASY, KIDS...
...ONE AT A TIME.
SO...IS IT ALWAYS LIKE THIS, COMMANDER?
WHEN THE HOMETOWN HERO RETURNS TO BROOKLYN?
KIDS JUST LIKE ASTRONAUTS, MS. NOVAK.
IF YOU'RE GOING TO BE MODEST, THIS DAILY BUGLE PROFILE'S NOT GOING TO BE VERY INTERESTING.
I NEED TO GET BEHIND THE MASK...TO FIND THE REAL CAPTAIN AMERICA.
THERE IS NO CAPTAIN AMERICA ANYMORE, MS. NOVAK...
OKAY, AND HOW DOES THAT FEEL?
ACTUALLY, IT FEELS GOOD.

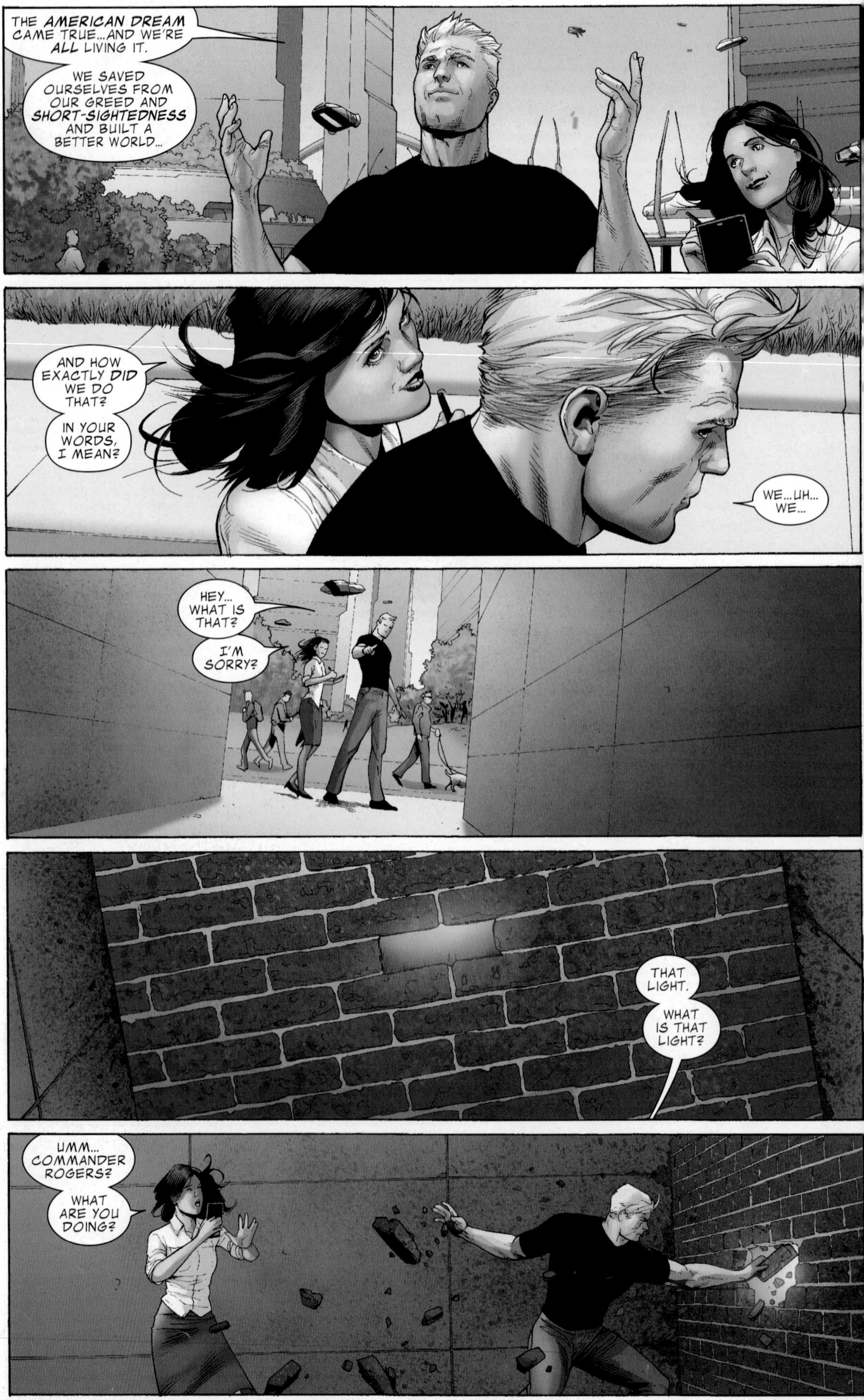
THE AMERICAN DREAM CAME TRUE...AND WE'RE ALL LIVING IT.
WE SAVED OURSELVES FROM OUR GREED AND SHORT-SIGHTEDNESS AND BUILT A BETTER WORLD...
AND HOW EXACTLY DID WE DO THAT?
IN YOUR WORDS, I MEAN?
WE...UH... WE...
HEY... WHAT IS THAT?
I'M SORRY?
THAT LIGHT.
WHAT IS THAT LIGHT?
UMM... COMMANDER ROGERS?
WHAT ARE YOU DOING?

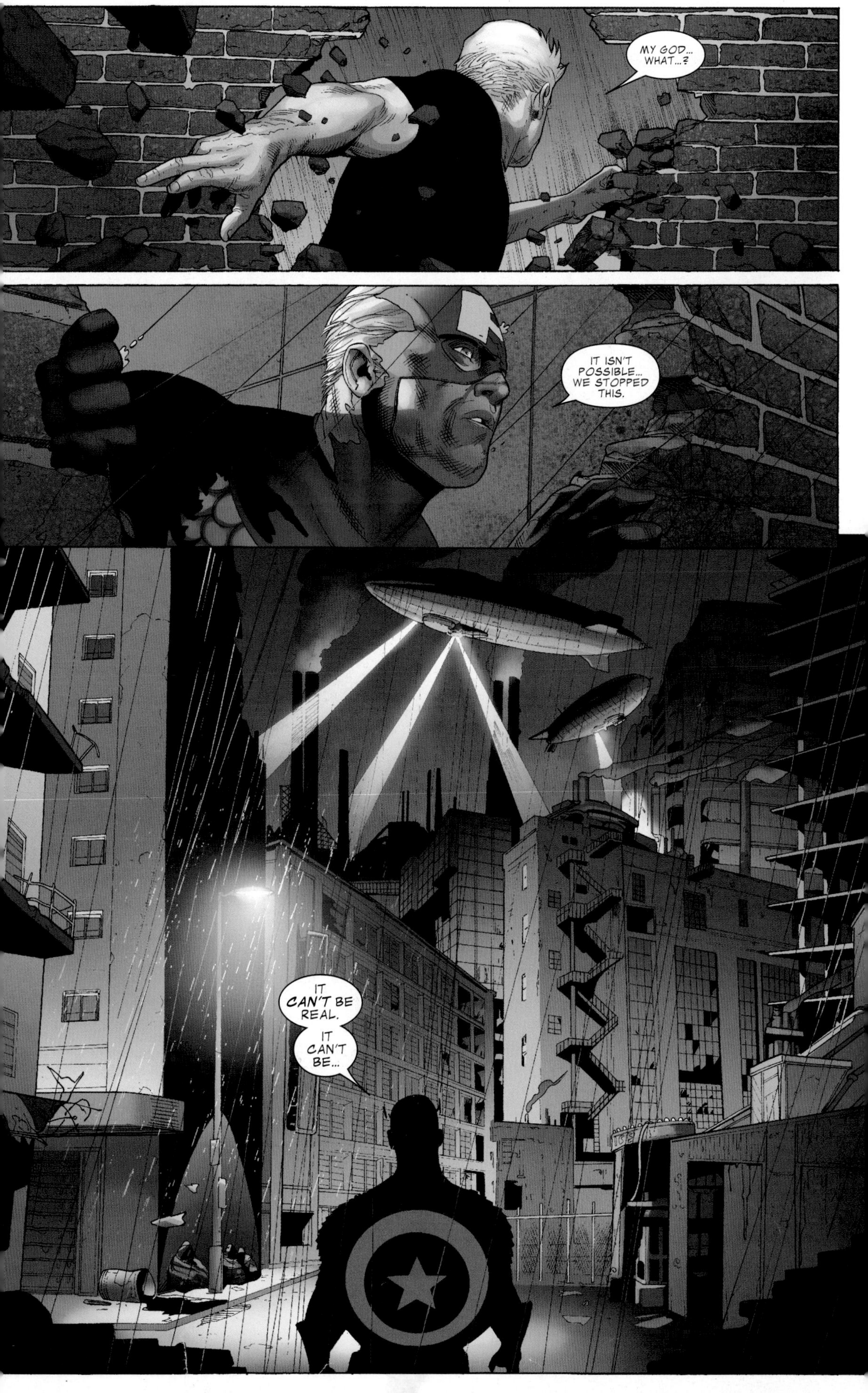
MY GOD... WHAT...?
IT ISN'T POSSIBLE... WE STOPPED THIS.
IT CAN'T BE REAL.
IT CAN'T BE...

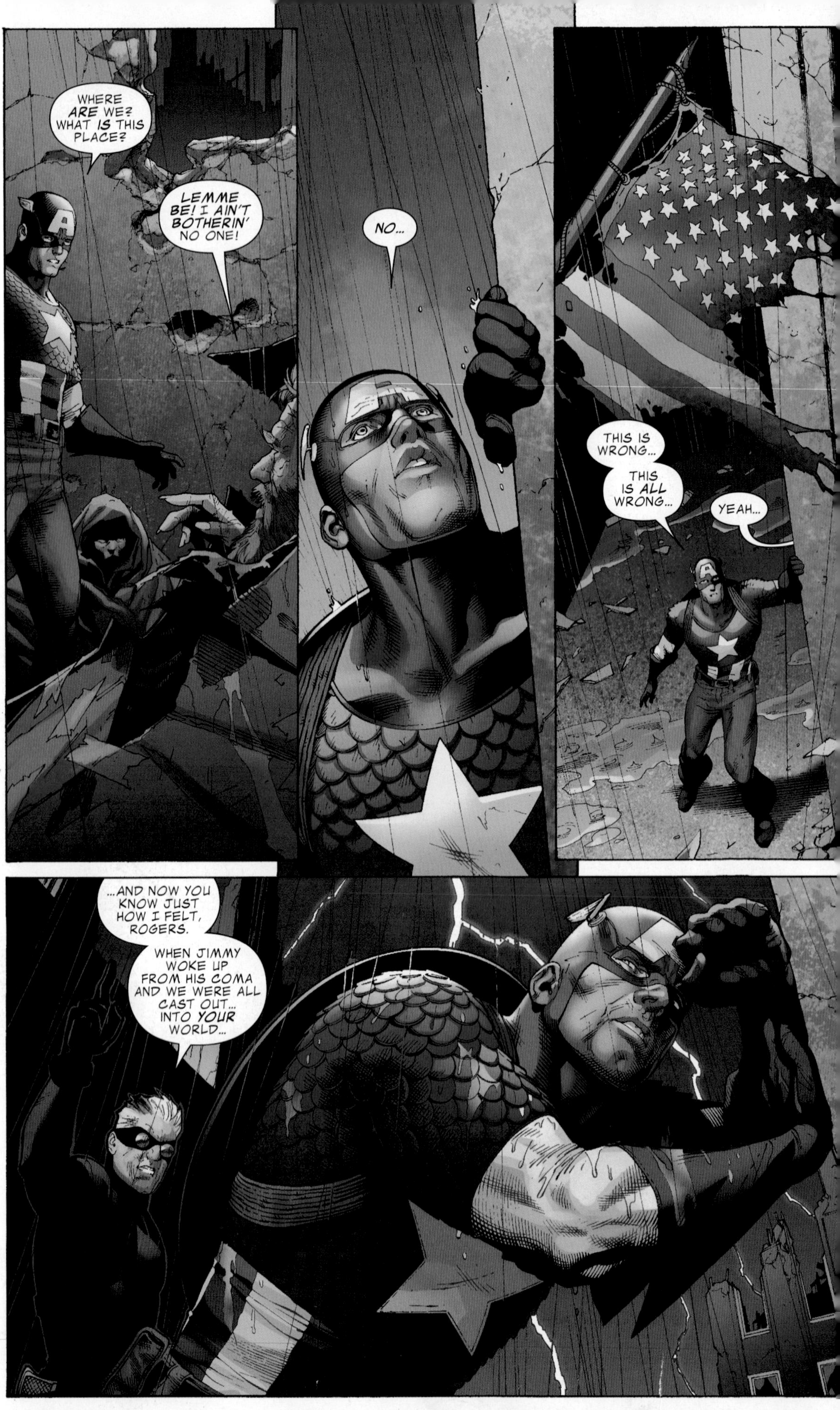
WHERE ARE WE? WHAT IS THIS PLACE?
LEMME BE! I AIN'T BOTHERIN' NO ONE!
NO...
THIS IS WRONG...
THIS IS ALL WRONG...
YEAH...
...AND NOW YOU KNOW JUST HOW I FELT, ROGERS.
WHEN JIMMY WOKE UP FROM HIS COMA AND WE WERE ALL CAST OUT... INTO YOUR WORLD...

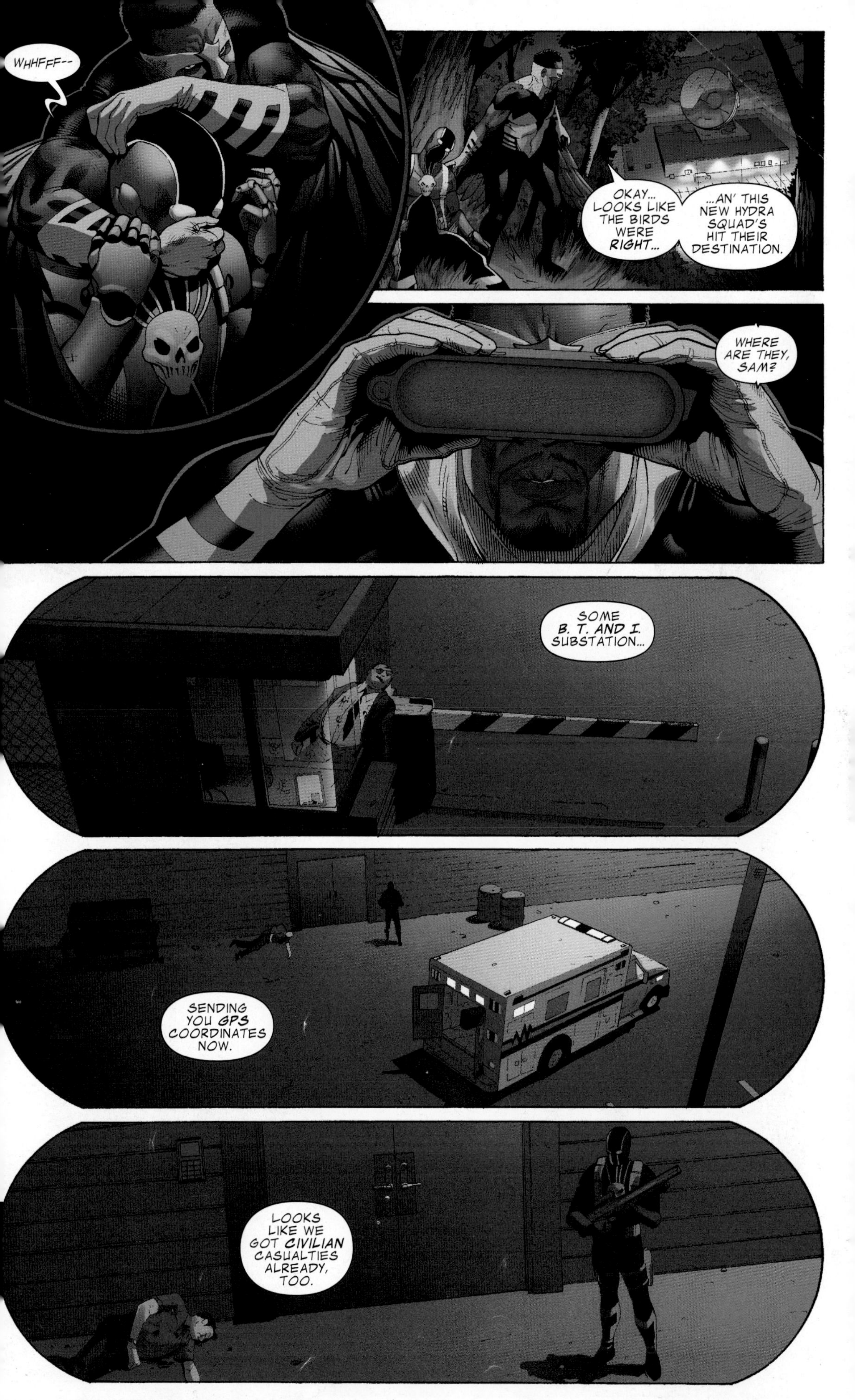
WHHFFF--
OKAY... LOOKS LIKE THE BIRDS WERE RIGHT...
...AN' THIS NEW HYDRA SQUAD'S HIT THEIR DESTINATION.
WHERE ARE THEY, SAM?
SOME B. T. AND I. SUBSTATION...
SENDING YOU GPS COORDINATES NOW.
LOOKS LIKE WE GOT CIVILIAN CASUALTIES ALREADY, TOO.

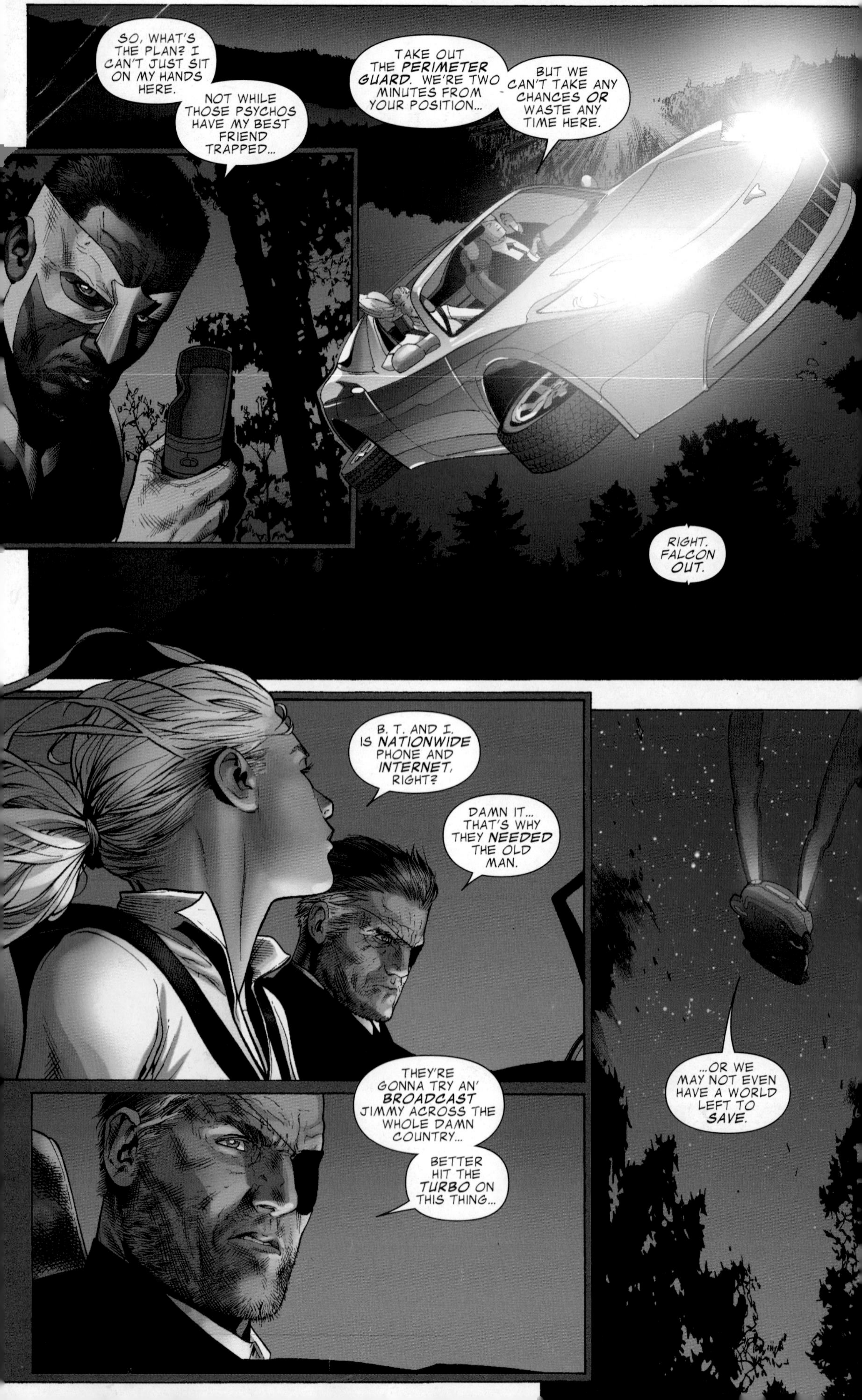
SO, WHAT'S THE PLAN? I CAN'T JUST SIT ON MY HANDS HERE.
NOT WHILE THOSE PSYCHOS HAVE MY BEST FRIEND TRAPPED...
TAKE OUT THE PERIMETER GUARD. WE'RE TWO MINUTES FROM YOUR POSITION...
BUT WE CAN'T TAKE ANY CHANCES OR WASTE ANY TIME HERE.
RIGHT. FALCON OUT.
B. T. AND I. IS NATIONWIDE PHONE AND INTERNET, RIGHT?
DAMN IT... THAT'S WHY THEY NEEDED THE OLD MAN.
THEY'RE GONNA TRY AN' BROADCAST JIMMY ACROSS THE WHOLE DAMN COUNTRY...
BETTER HIT THE TURBO ON THIS THING...
...OR WE MAY NOT EVEN HAVE A WORLD LEFT TO SAVE.

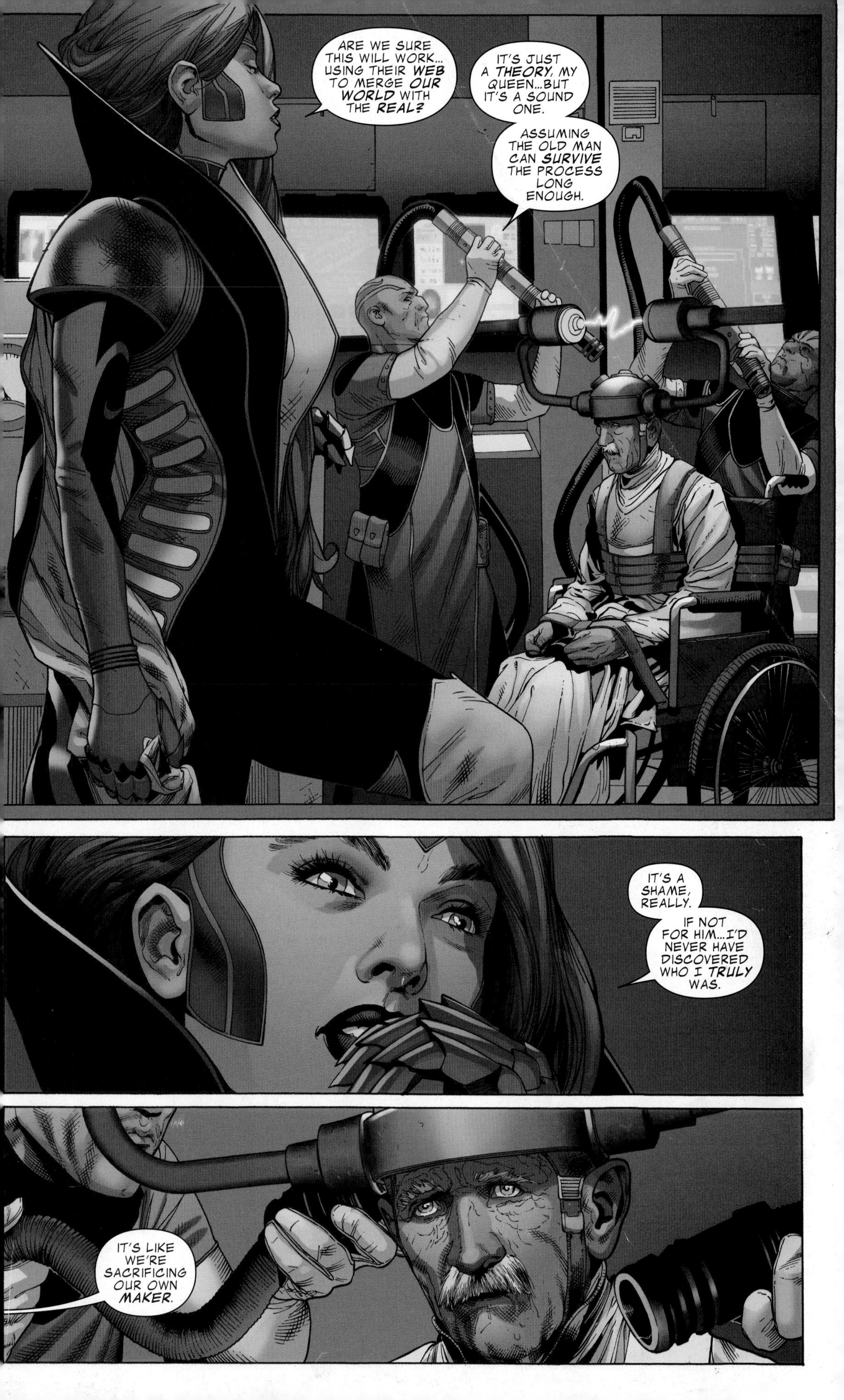
ARE WE SURE THIS WILL WORK... USING THEIR WEB TO MERGE OUR WORLD WITH THE REAL?
IT'S JUST A THEORY, MY QUEEN...BUT IT'S A SOUND ONE.
ASSUMING THE OLD MAN CAN SURVIVE THE PROCESS LONG ENOUGH.
IT'S A SHAME, REALLY.
IF NOT FOR HIM...I'D NEVER HAVE DISCOVERED WHO I TRULY WAS.
IT'S LIKE WE'RE SACRIFICING OUR OWN MAKER.

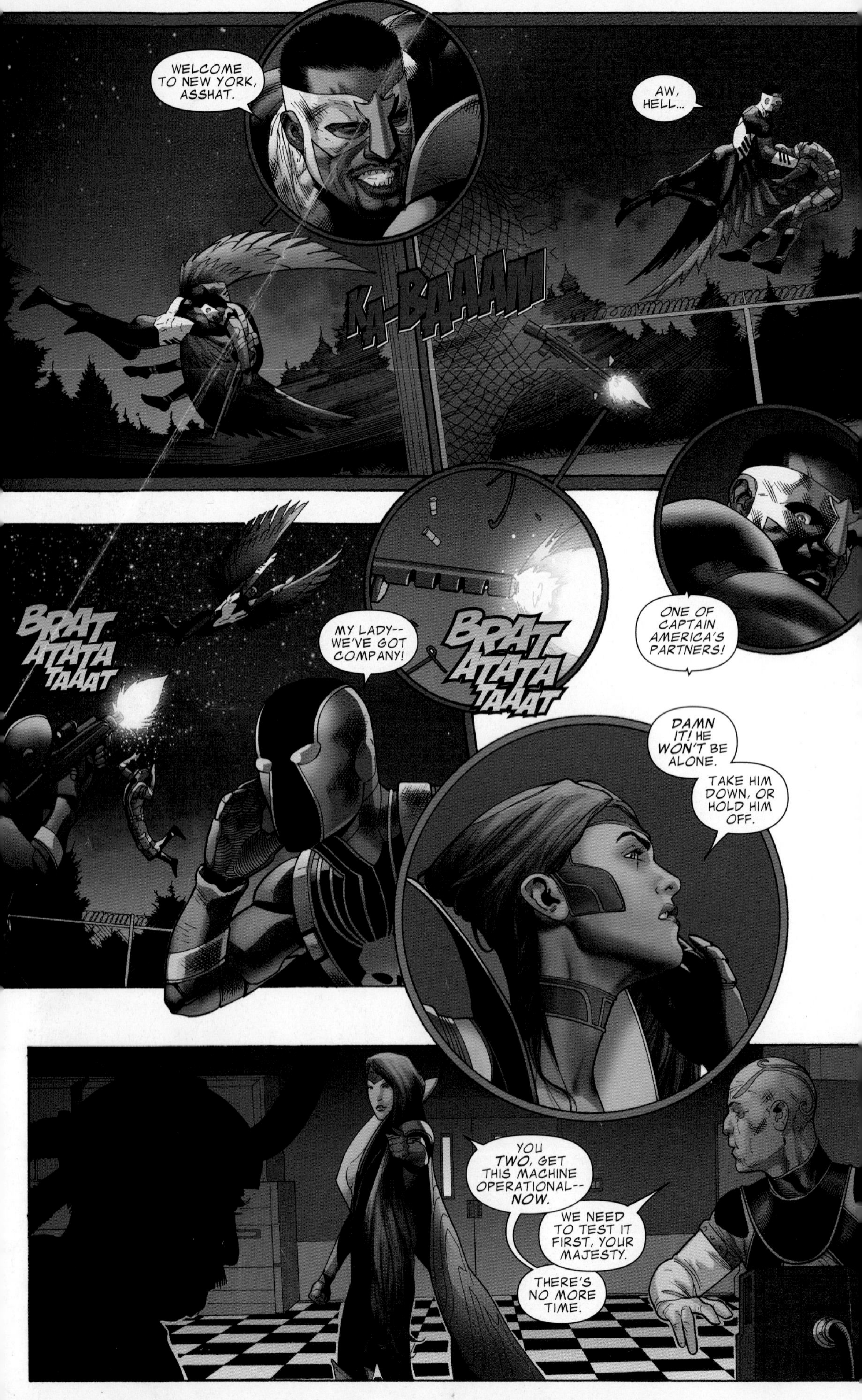
WELCOME TO NEW YORK, ASSHAT.
AW, HELL...
KA-BAAAM
BRAT ATATA TAAAT
MY LADY-- WE'VE GOT COMPANY!
BRAT ATATA TAAAT
ONE OF CAPTAIN AMERICA'S PARTNERS!
DAMN IT! HE WON'T BE ALONE.
TAKE HIM DOWN, OR HOLD HIM OFF.
YOU TWO, GET THIS MACHINE OPERATIONAL-- NOW.
WE NEED TO TEST IT FIRST, YOUR MAJESTY.
THERE'S NO MORE TIME.

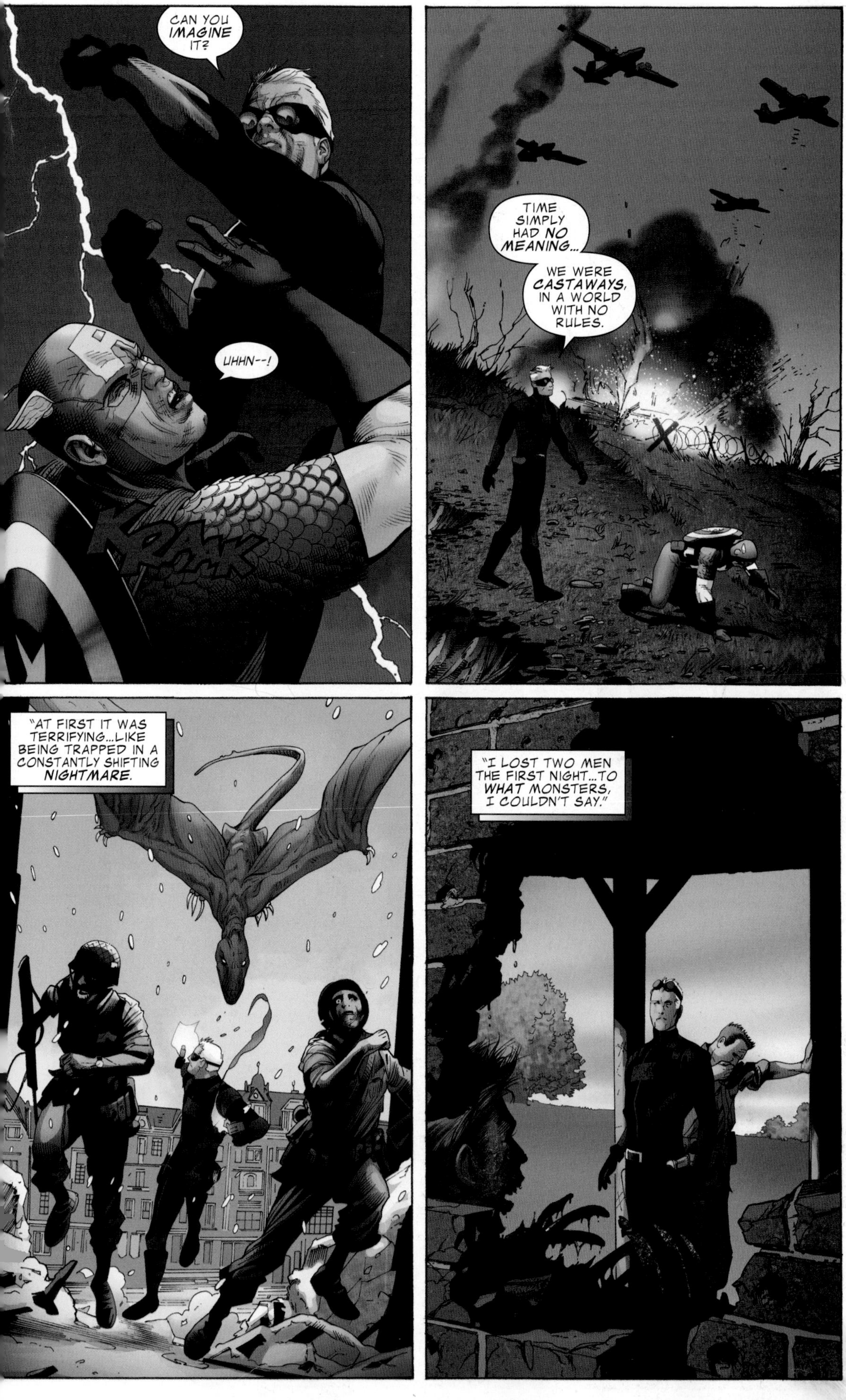
CAN YOU IMAGINE IT?
UHHN--!
TIME SIMPLY HAD NO MEANING...
WE WERE CASTAWAYS, IN A WORLD WITH NO RULES.
"AT FIRST IT WAS TERRIFYING...LIKE BEING TRAPPED IN A CONSTANTLY SHIFTING NIGHTMARE.
"I LOST TWO MEN THE FIRST NIGHT...TO WHAT MONSTERS, I COULDN'T SAY."

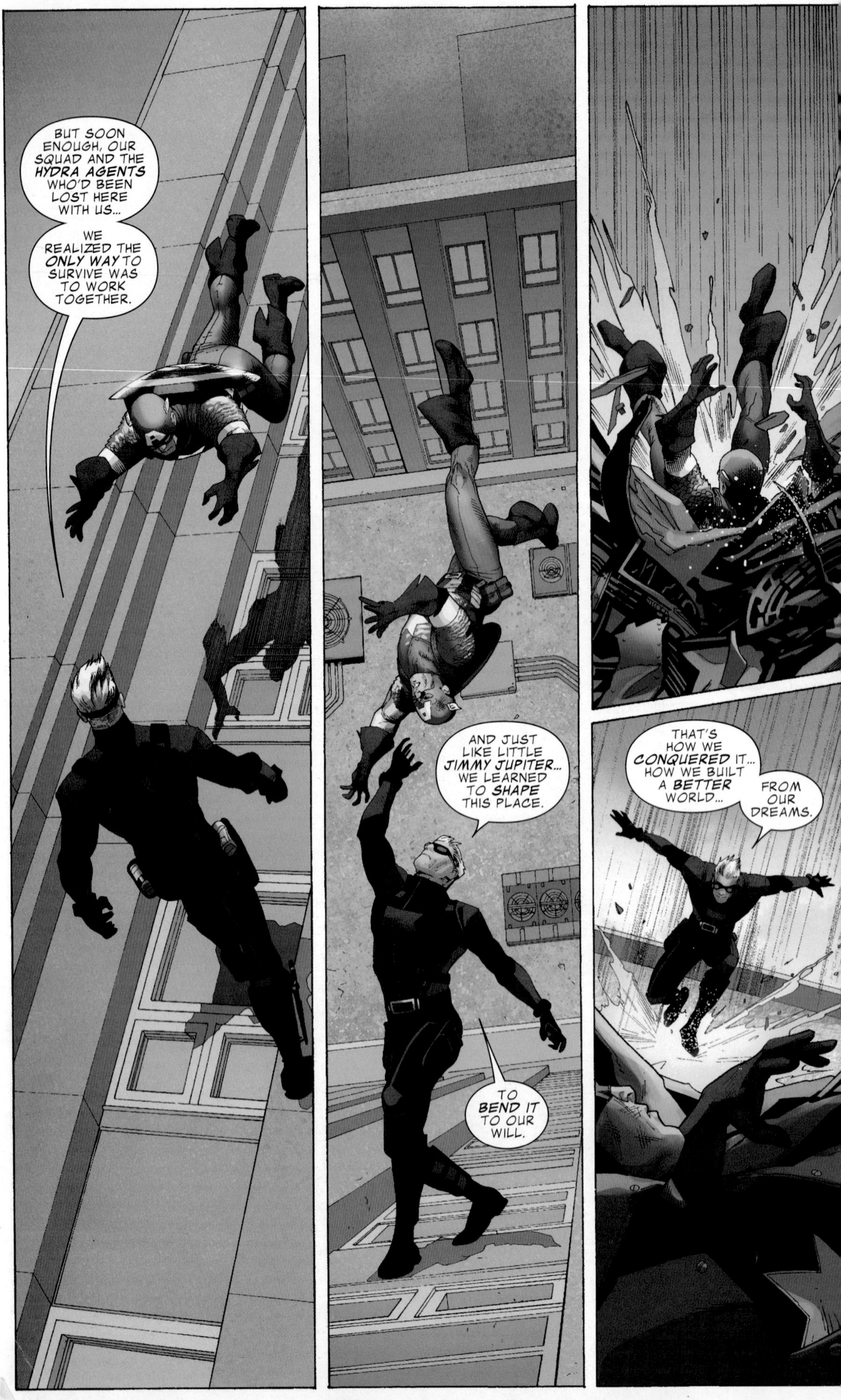
BUT SOON ENOUGH, OUR SQUAD AND THE **HYDRA AGENTS** WHO'D BEEN LOST HERE WITH US...
WE REALIZED THE **ONLY WAY** TO SURVIVE WAS TO WORK TOGETHER.
AND JUST LIKE LITTLE **JIMMY JUPITER**... WE LEARNED TO **SHAPE** THIS PLACE.
TO **BEND IT** TO OUR WILL.
THAT'S HOW WE **CONQUERED** IT... HOW WE BUILT A **BETTER** WORLD...
FROM OUR DREAMS.

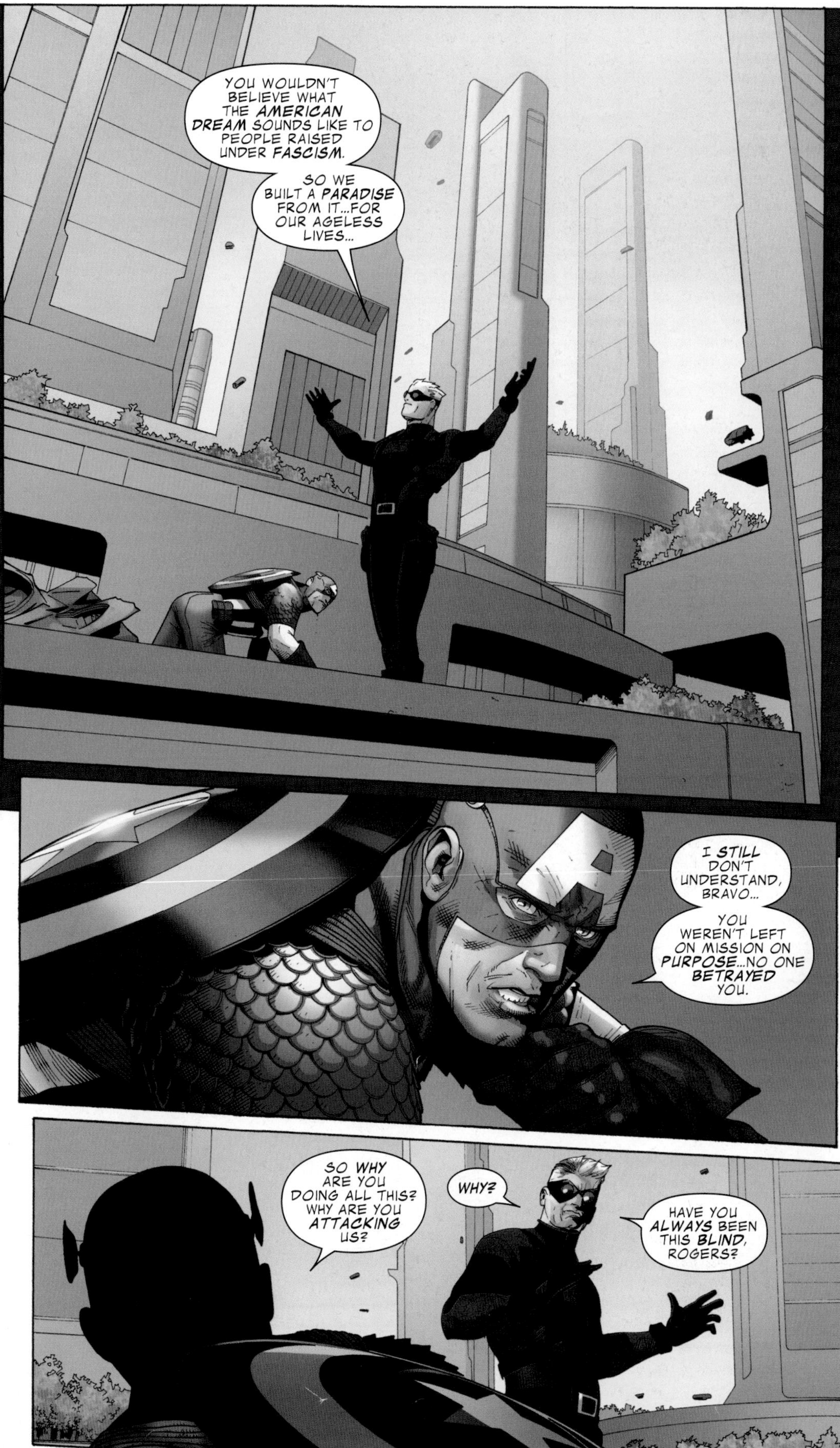
YOU WOULDN'T BELIEVE WHAT THE AMERICAN DREAM SOUNDS LIKE TO PEOPLE RAISED UNDER FASCISM.
SO WE BUILT A PARADISE FROM IT...FOR OUR AGELESS LIVES...
I STILL DON'T UNDERSTAND, BRAVO...
YOU WEREN'T LEFT ON MISSION ON PURPOSE...NO ONE BETRAYED YOU.
SO WHY ARE YOU DOING ALL THIS? WHY ARE YOU ATTACKING US?
WHY?
HAVE YOU ALWAYS BEEN THIS BLIND, ROGERS?

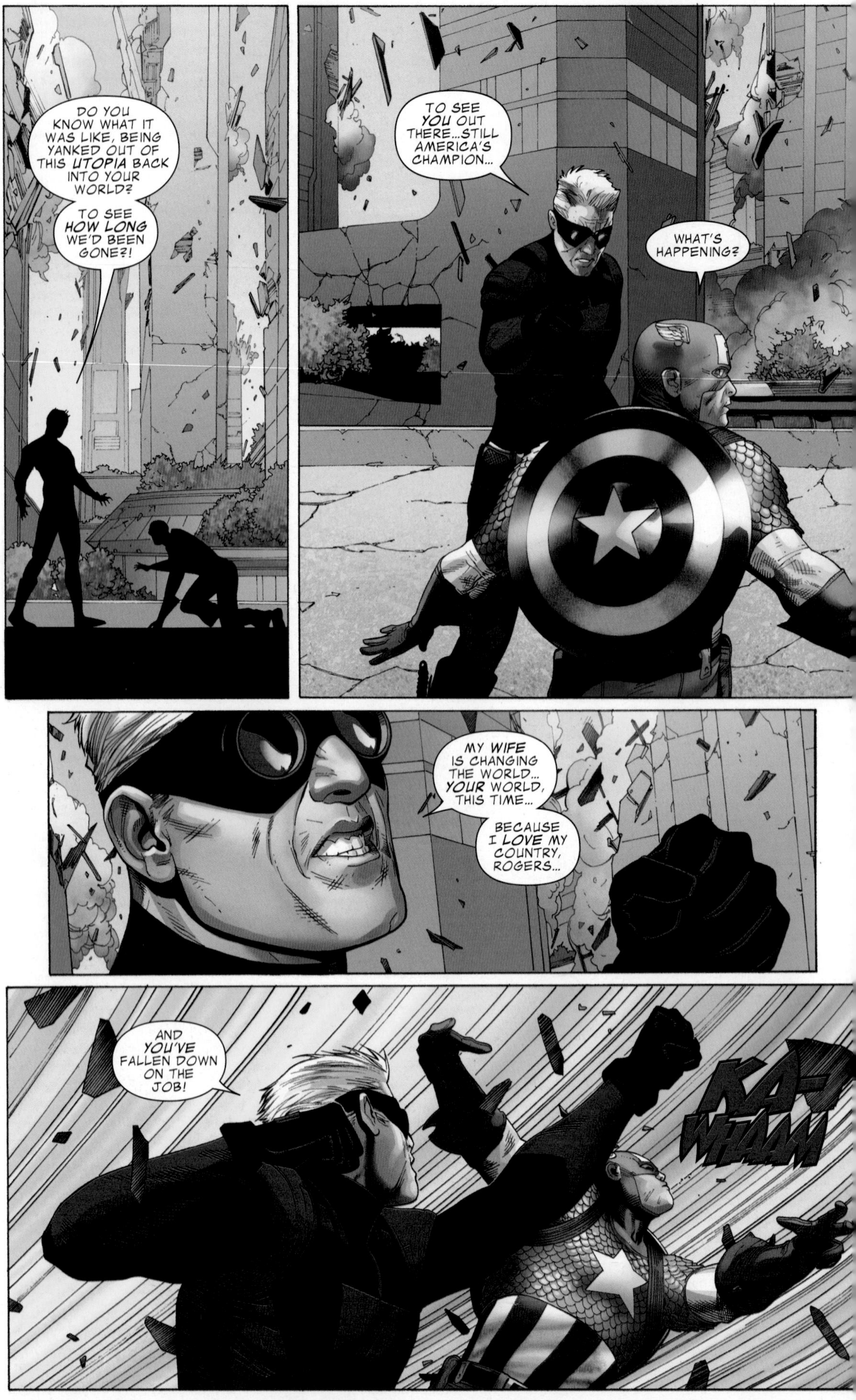
DO YOU KNOW WHAT IT WAS LIKE, BEING YANKED OUT OF THIS UTOPIA BACK INTO YOUR WORLD?
TO SEE HOW LONG WE'D BEEN GONE?!
TO SEE YOU OUT THERE...STILL AMERICA'S CHAMPION...
WHAT'S HAPPENING?
MY WIFE IS CHANGING THE WORLD... YOUR WORLD, THIS TIME...
BECAUSE I LOVE MY COUNTRY, ROGERS...
AND YOU'VE FALLEN DOWN ON THE JOB!
KA-WHAAM

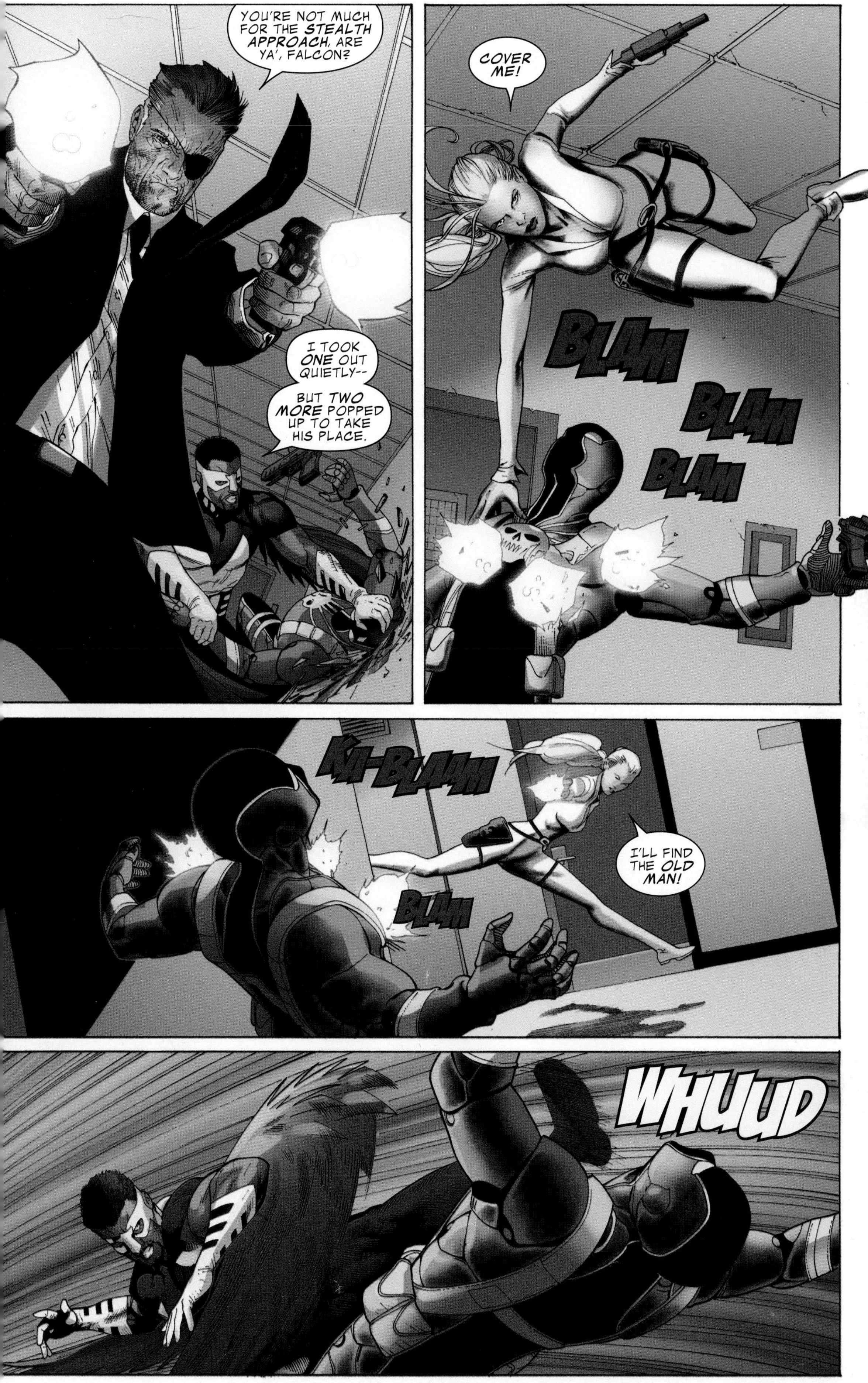
YOU'RE NOT MUCH FOR THE STEALTH APPROACH, ARE YA', FALCON?
I TOOK ONE OUT QUIETLY--
BUT TWO MORE POPPED UP TO TAKE HIS PLACE.
COVER ME!
BLAM
BLAM
BLAM
KA-BLAAM
I'LL FIND THE OLD MAN!
BLAM
WHUUD

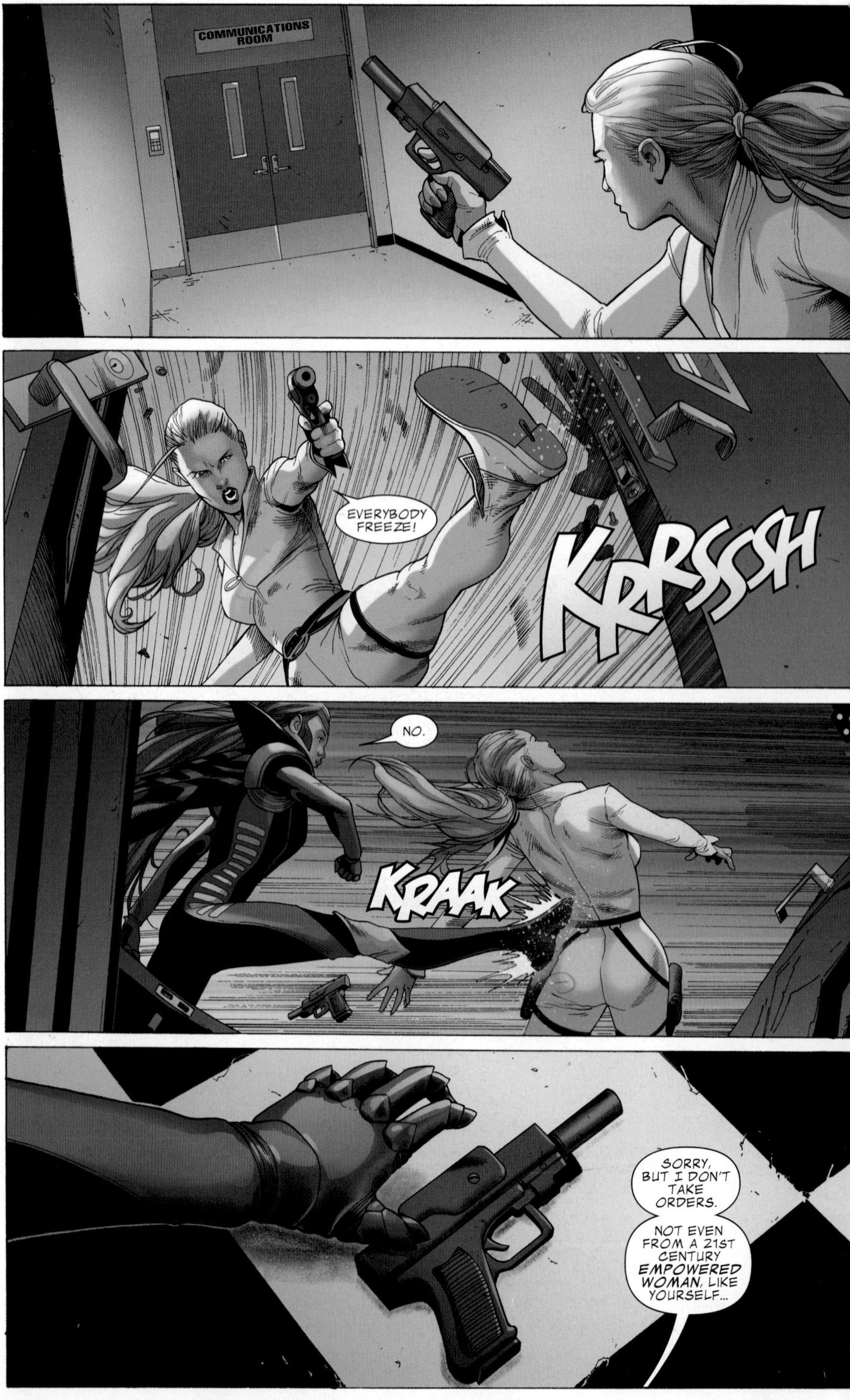
COMMUNICATIONS ROOM
EVERYBODY FREEZE!
KRRSSSH
NO.
KRAAK
SORRY, BUT I DON'T TAKE ORDERS.
NOT EVEN FROM A 21ST CENTURY EMPOWERED WOMAN, LIKE YOURSELF...

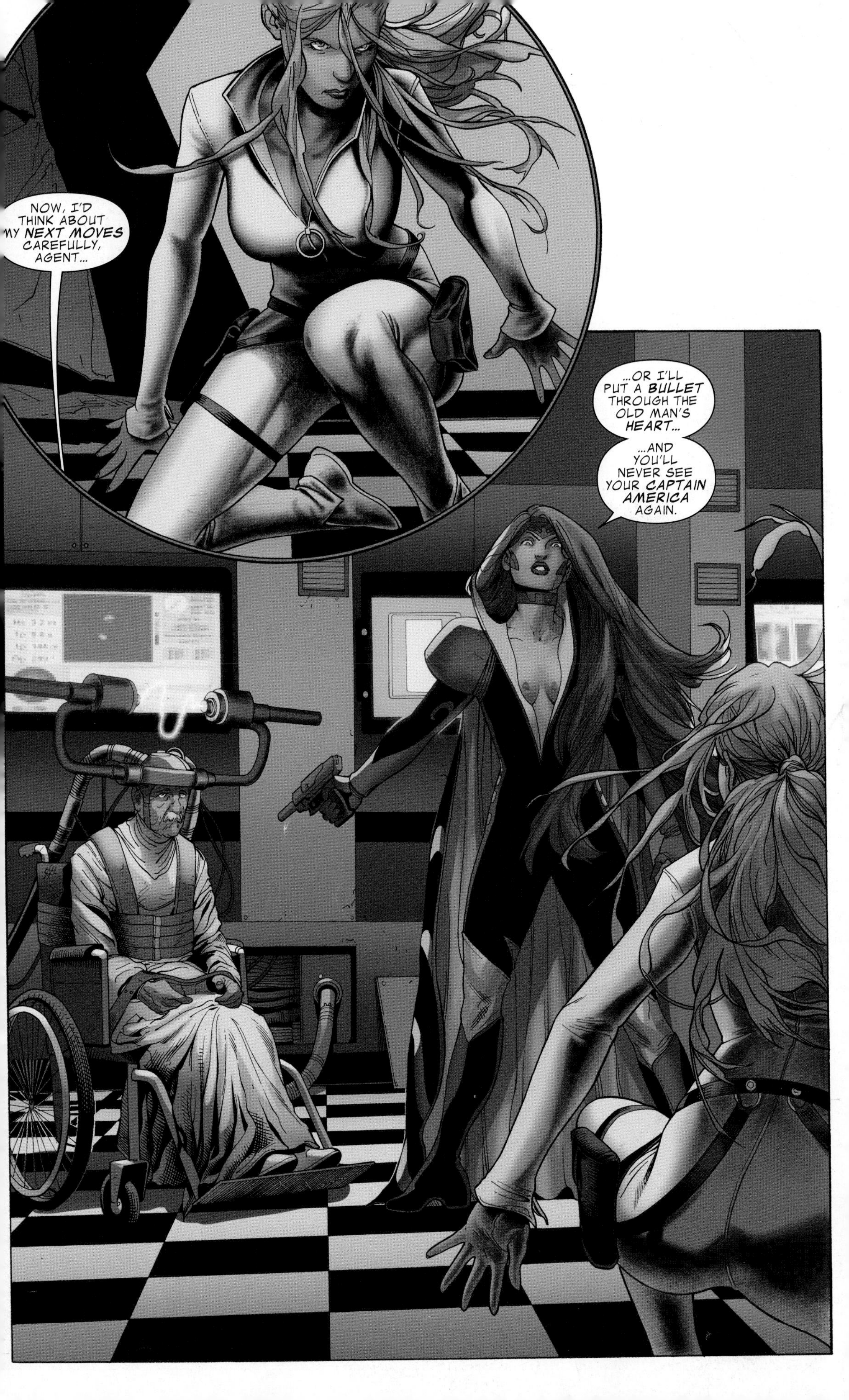
NOW, I'D THINK ABOUT MY **NEXT MOVES** CAREFULLY, AGENT...
...OR I'LL PUT A **BULLET** THROUGH THE OLD MAN'S **HEART**...
...AND YOU'LL NEVER SEE YOUR **CAPTAIN AMERICA** AGAIN.

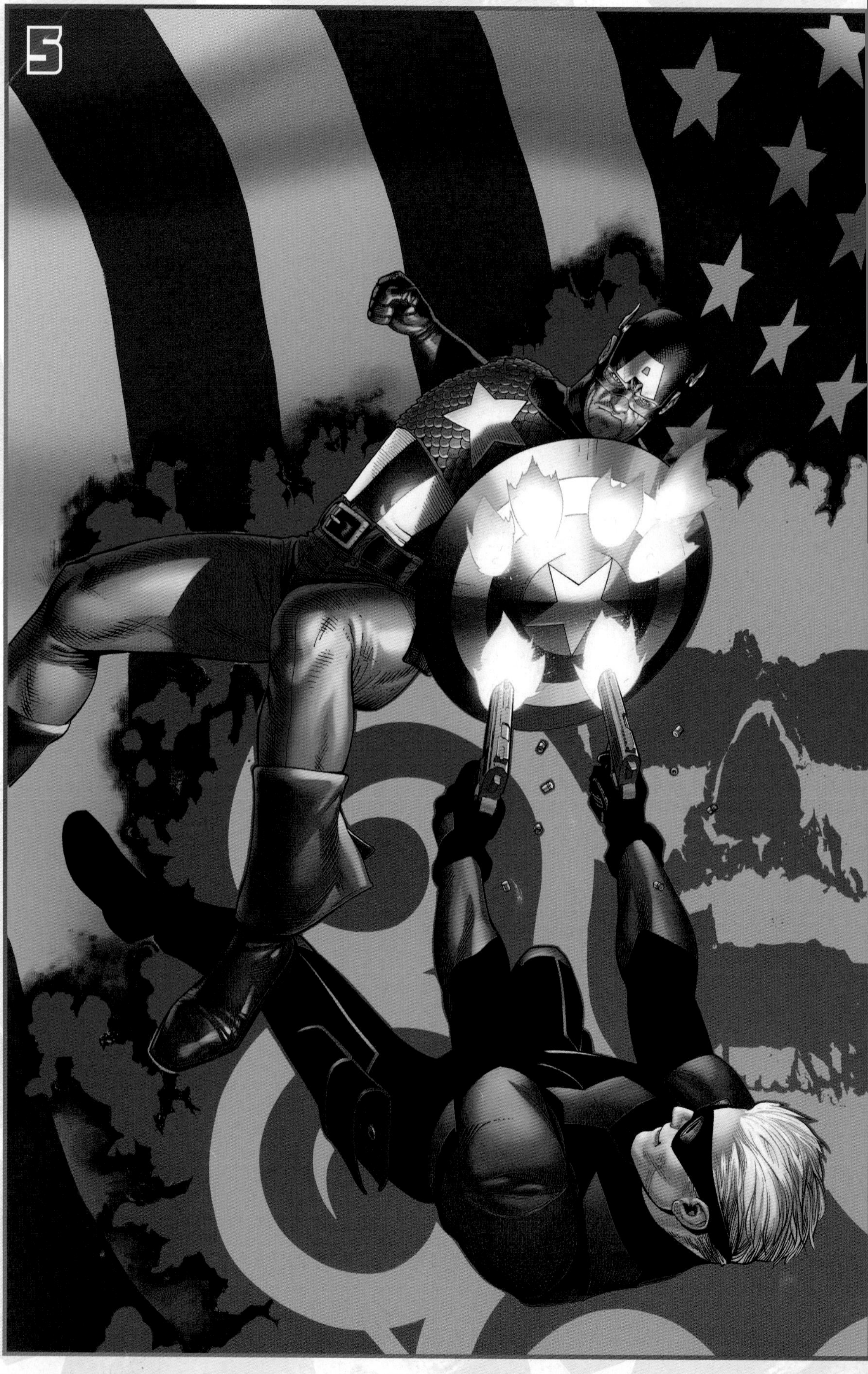
5

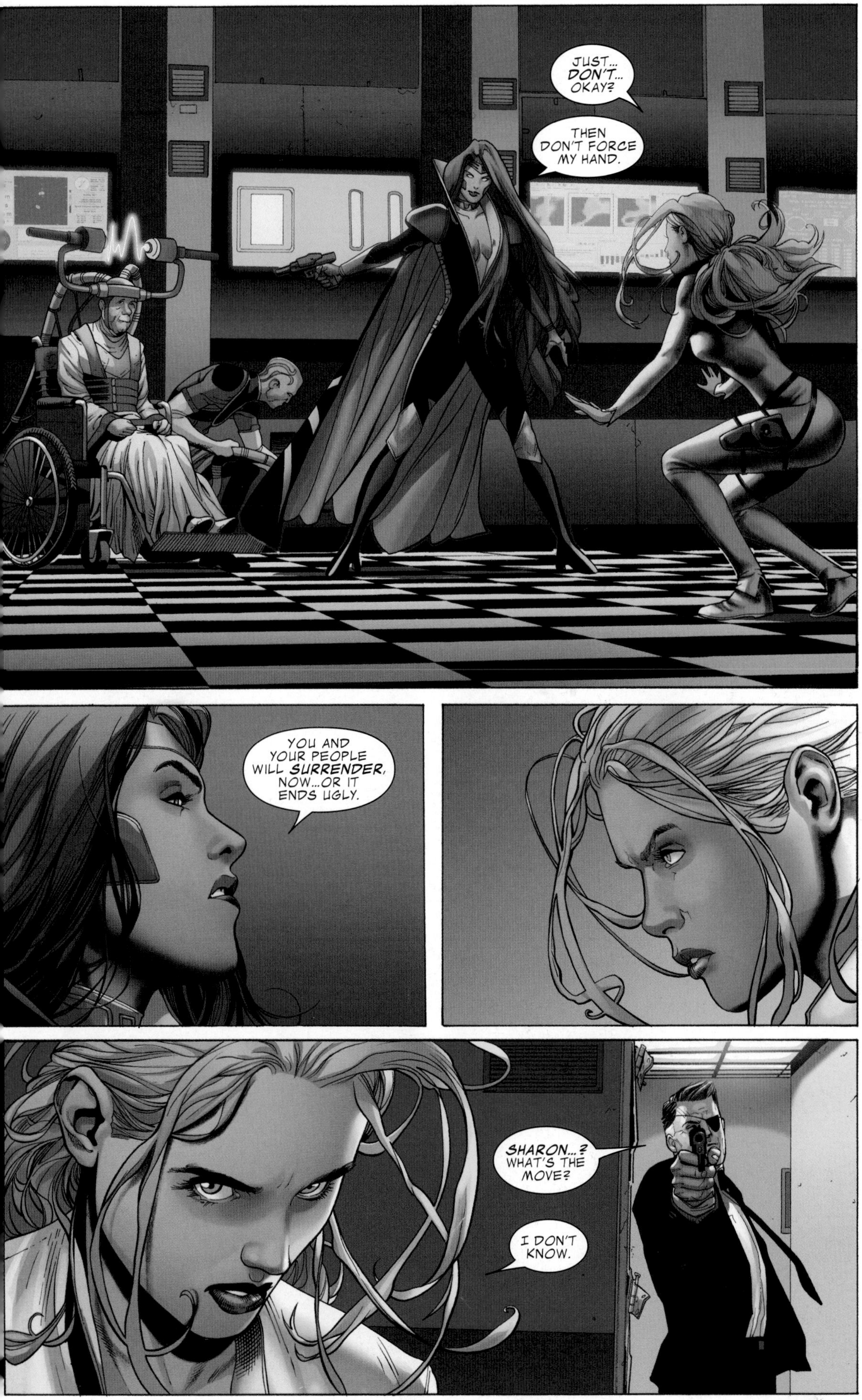
JUST... DON'T... OKAY?
THEN DON'T FORCE MY HAND.
YOU AND YOUR PEOPLE WILL SURRENDER, NOW...OR IT ENDS UGLY.
SHARON...? WHAT'S THE MOVE?
I DON'T KNOW.

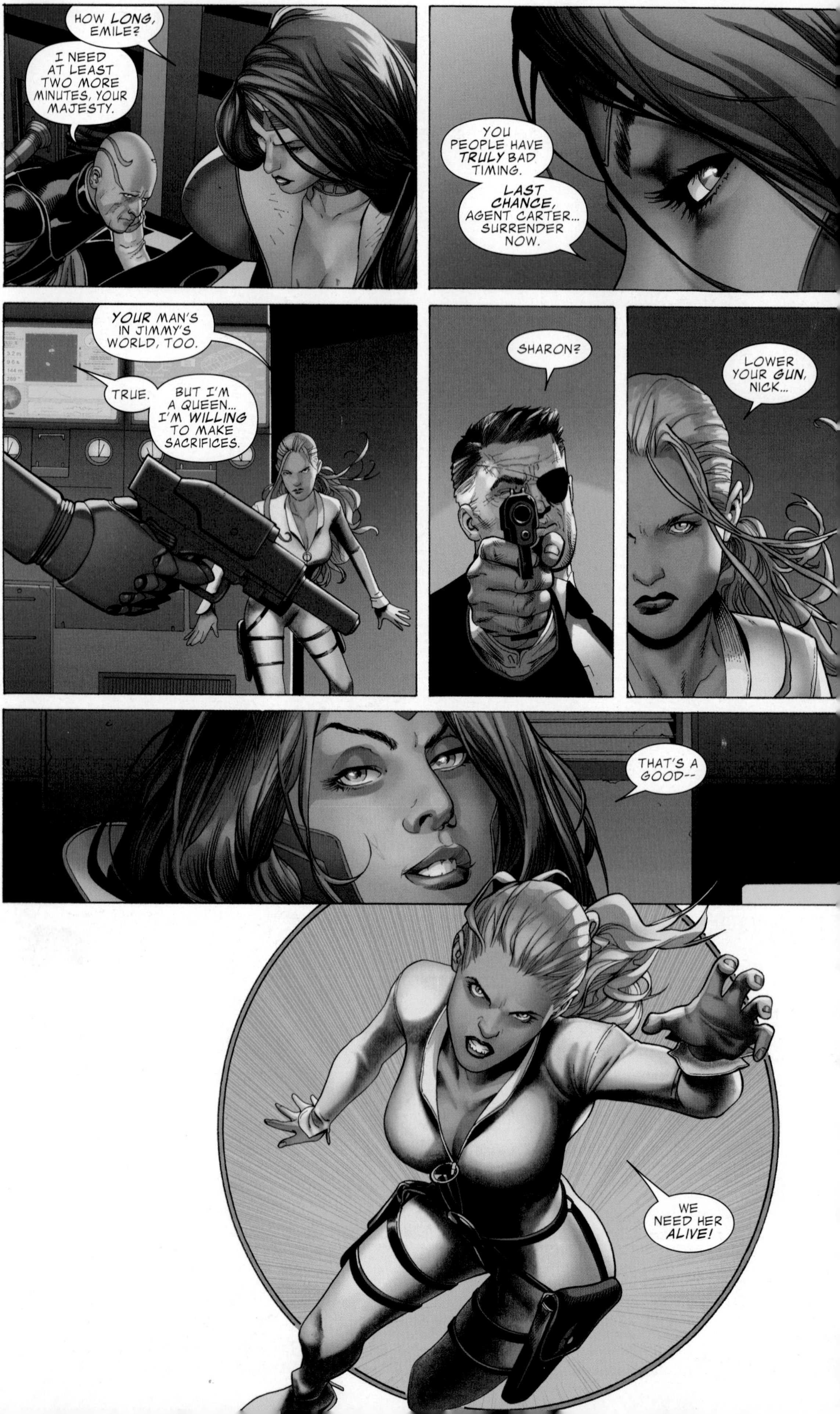
HOW LONG, EMILE?
I NEED AT LEAST TWO MORE MINUTES, YOUR MAJESTY.
YOU PEOPLE HAVE TRULY BAD TIMING.
LAST CHANCE, AGENT CARTER... SURRENDER NOW.
YOUR MAN'S IN JIMMY'S WORLD, TOO.
TRUE.
BUT I'M A QUEEN... I'M WILLING TO MAKE SACRIFICES.
SHARON?
LOWER YOUR GUN, NICK...
THAT'S A GOOD--
WE NEED HER ALIVE!

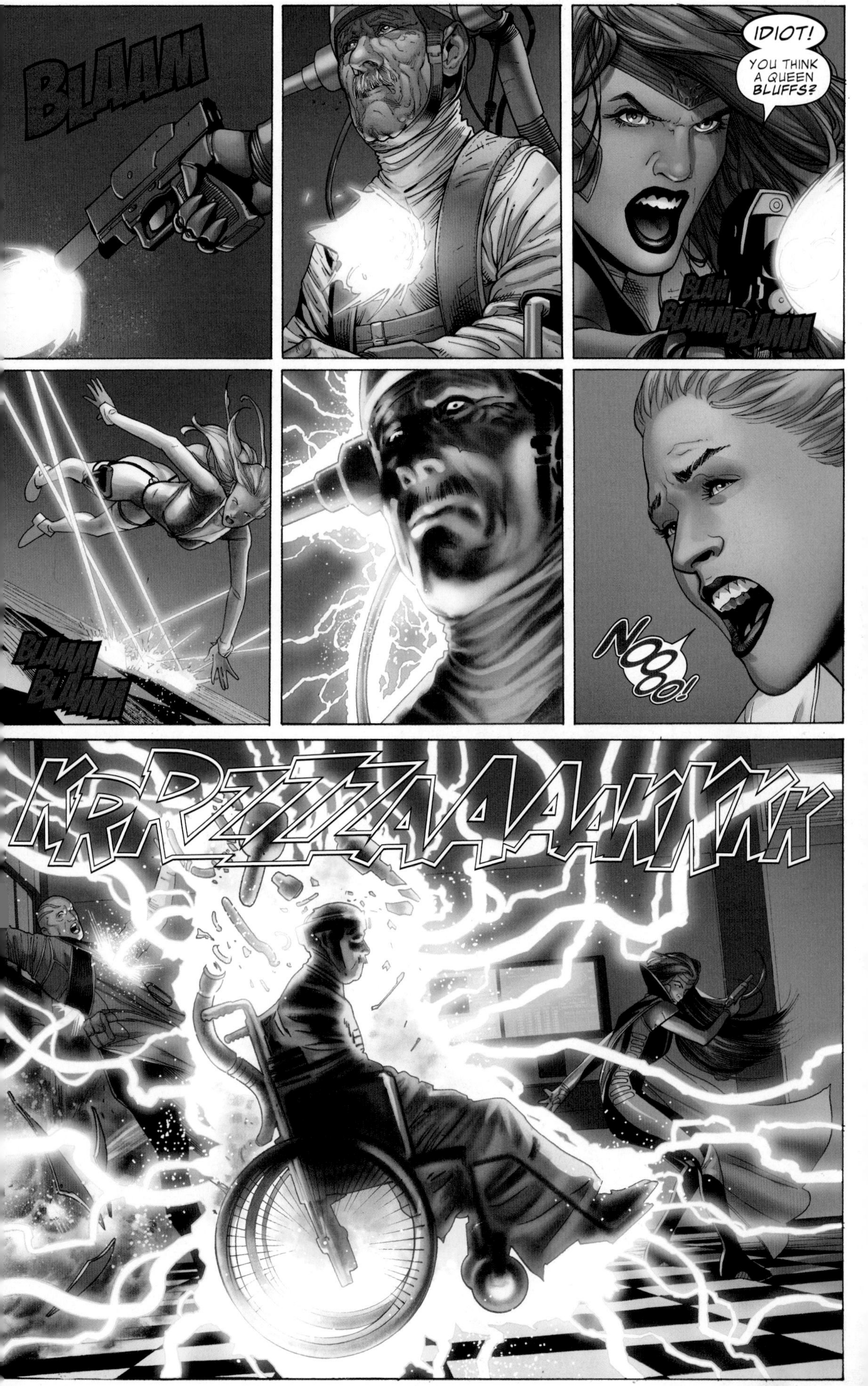
BLAAM
IDIOT!
YOU THINK A QUEEN BLUFFS?
BLAM BLAMM BLAMM
BLAMM BLAMM
NOOOO!
KRRZZZAAAKKKK

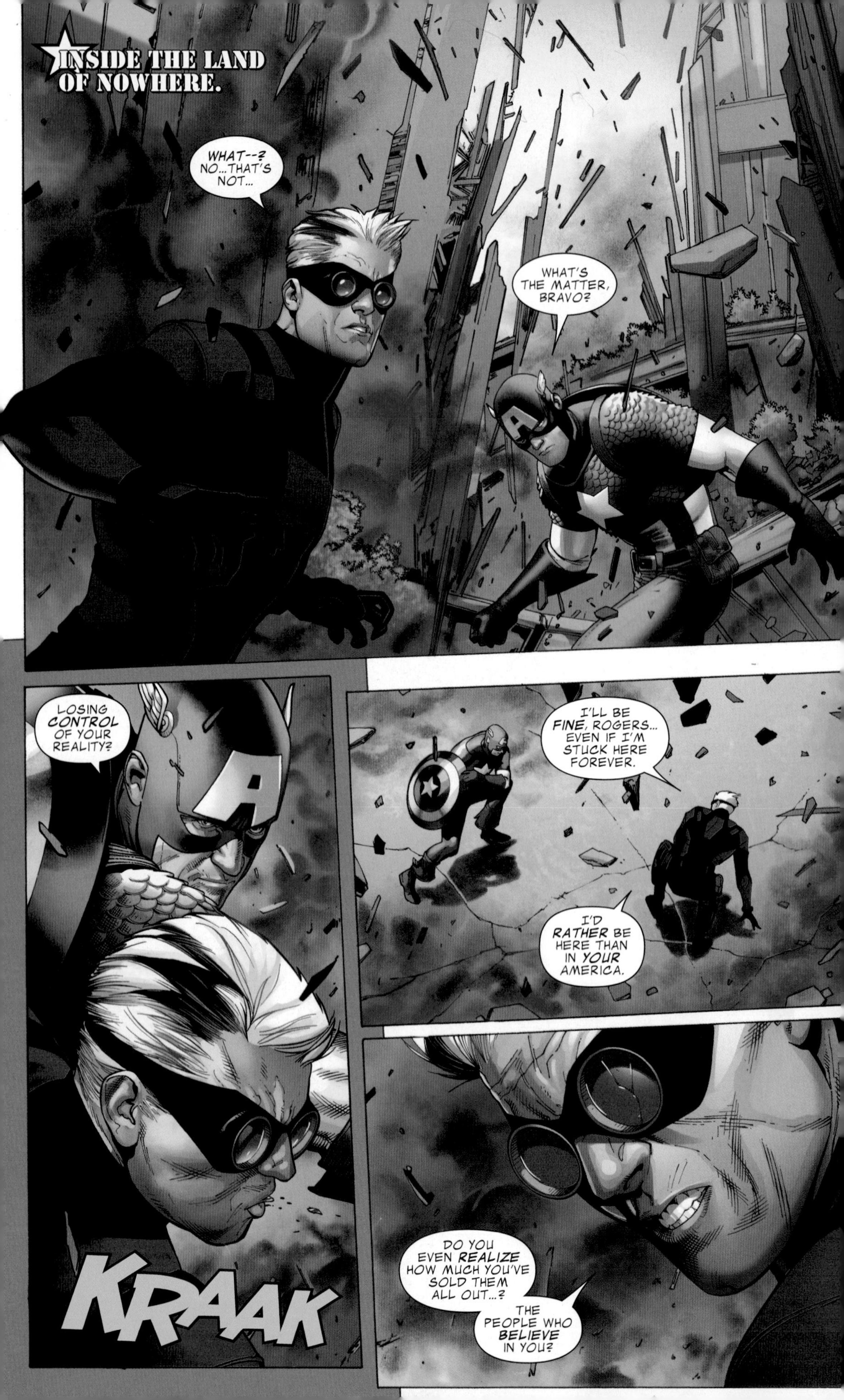
INSIDE THE LAND OF NOWHERE.
WHAT--? NO...THAT'S NOT...
WHAT'S THE MATTER, BRAVO?
LOSING CONTROL OF YOUR REALITY?
I'LL BE FINE, ROGERS... EVEN IF I'M STUCK HERE FOREVER.
I'D RATHER BE HERE THAN IN YOUR AMERICA.
KRAAK
DO YOU EVEN REALIZE HOW MUCH YOU'VE SOLD THEM ALL OUT...?
THE PEOPLE WHO BELIEVE IN YOU?

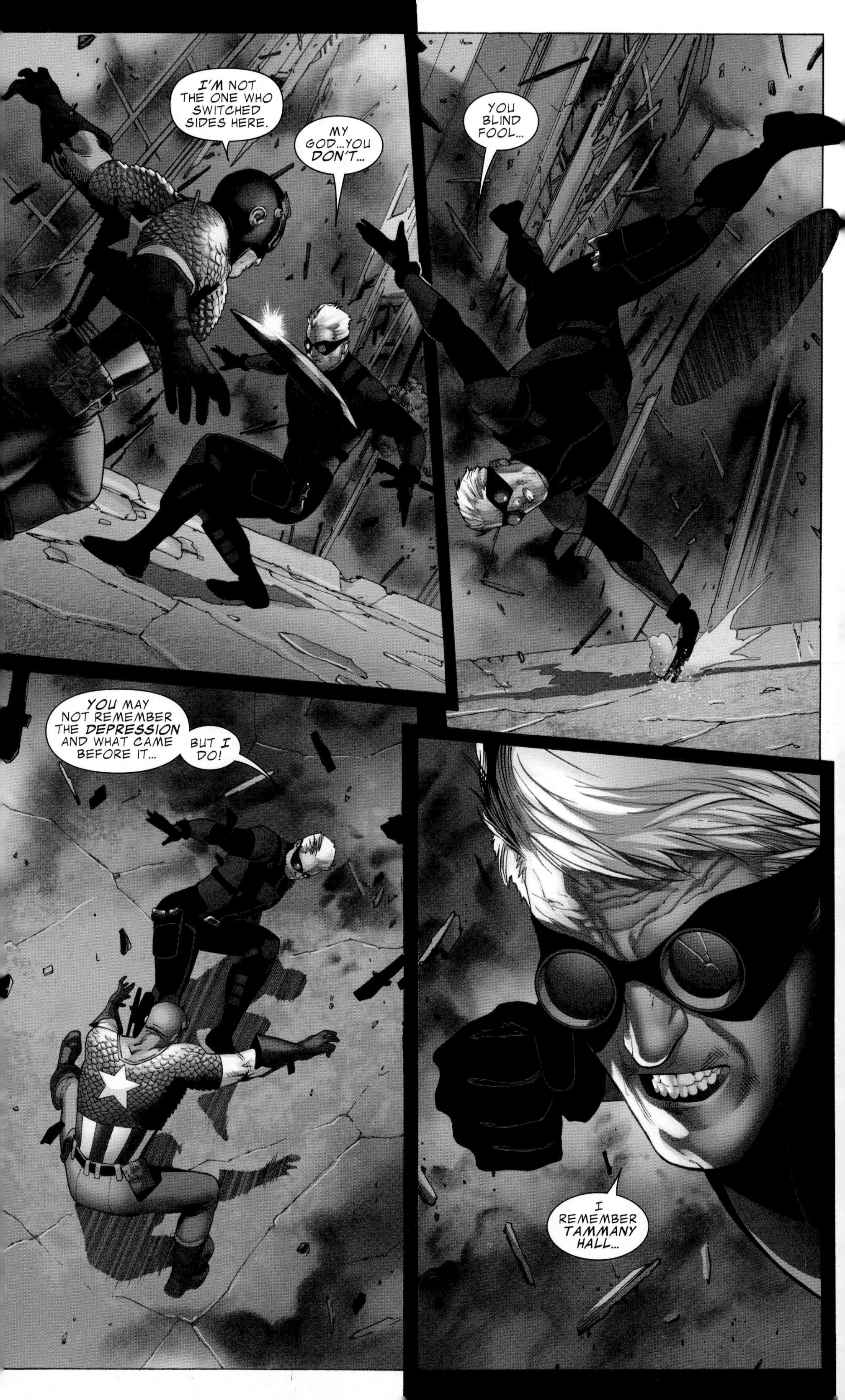
I'M NOT THE ONE WHO SWITCHED SIDES HERE.
MY GOD...YOU DON'T...
YOU BLIND FOOL...
YOU MAY NOT REMEMBER THE DEPRESSION AND WHAT CAME BEFORE IT...
BUT I DO!
I REMEMBER TAMMANY HALL...

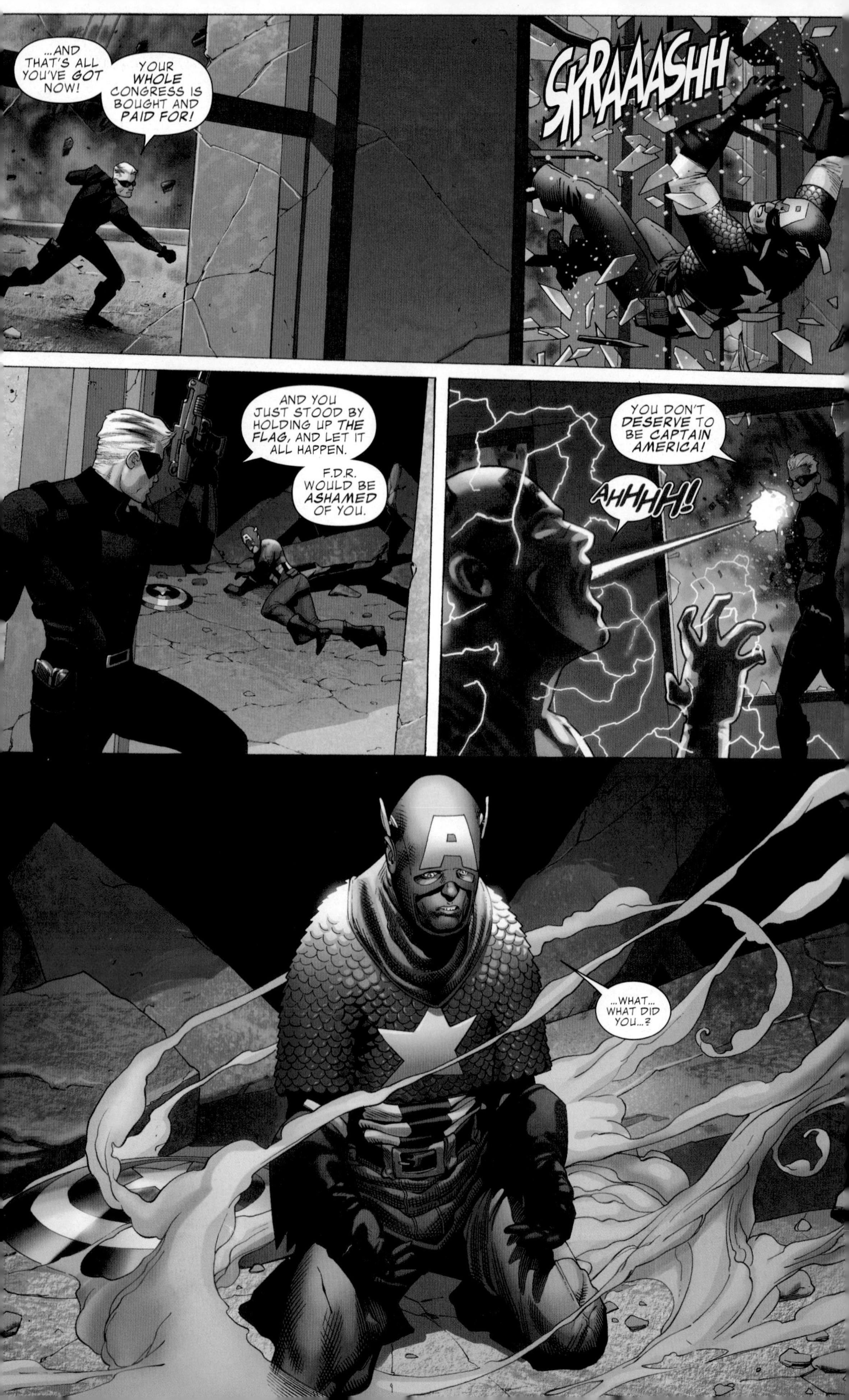
...AND THAT'S ALL YOU'VE GOT NOW!
YOUR WHOLE CONGRESS IS BOUGHT AND PAID FOR!
SKRAAASHH
AND YOU JUST STOOD BY HOLDING UP THE FLAG, AND LET IT ALL HAPPEN.
F.D.R. WOULD BE ASHAMED OF YOU.
YOU DON'T DESERVE TO BE CAPTAIN AMERICA!
AHHHH!
...WHAT... WHAT DID YOU...?

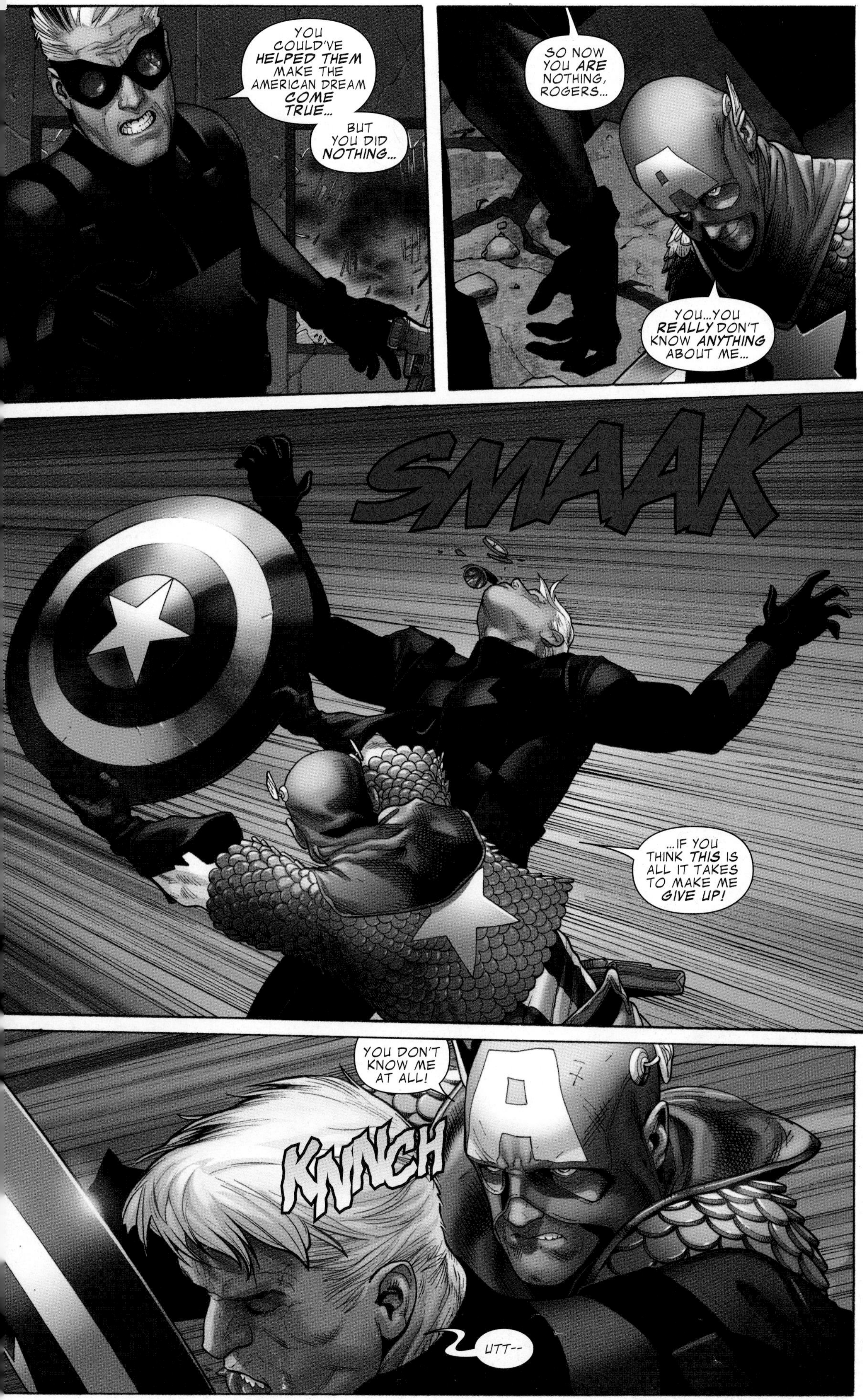
YOU COULD'VE HELPED THEM MAKE THE AMERICAN DREAM COME TRUE...
BUT YOU DID NOTHING...
SO NOW YOU ARE NOTHING, ROGERS...
YOU...YOU REALLY DON'T KNOW ANYTHING ABOUT ME...
SMAAK
...IF YOU THINK THIS IS ALL IT TAKES TO MAKE ME GIVE UP!
YOU DON'T KNOW ME AT ALL!
KNNCH
UTT--

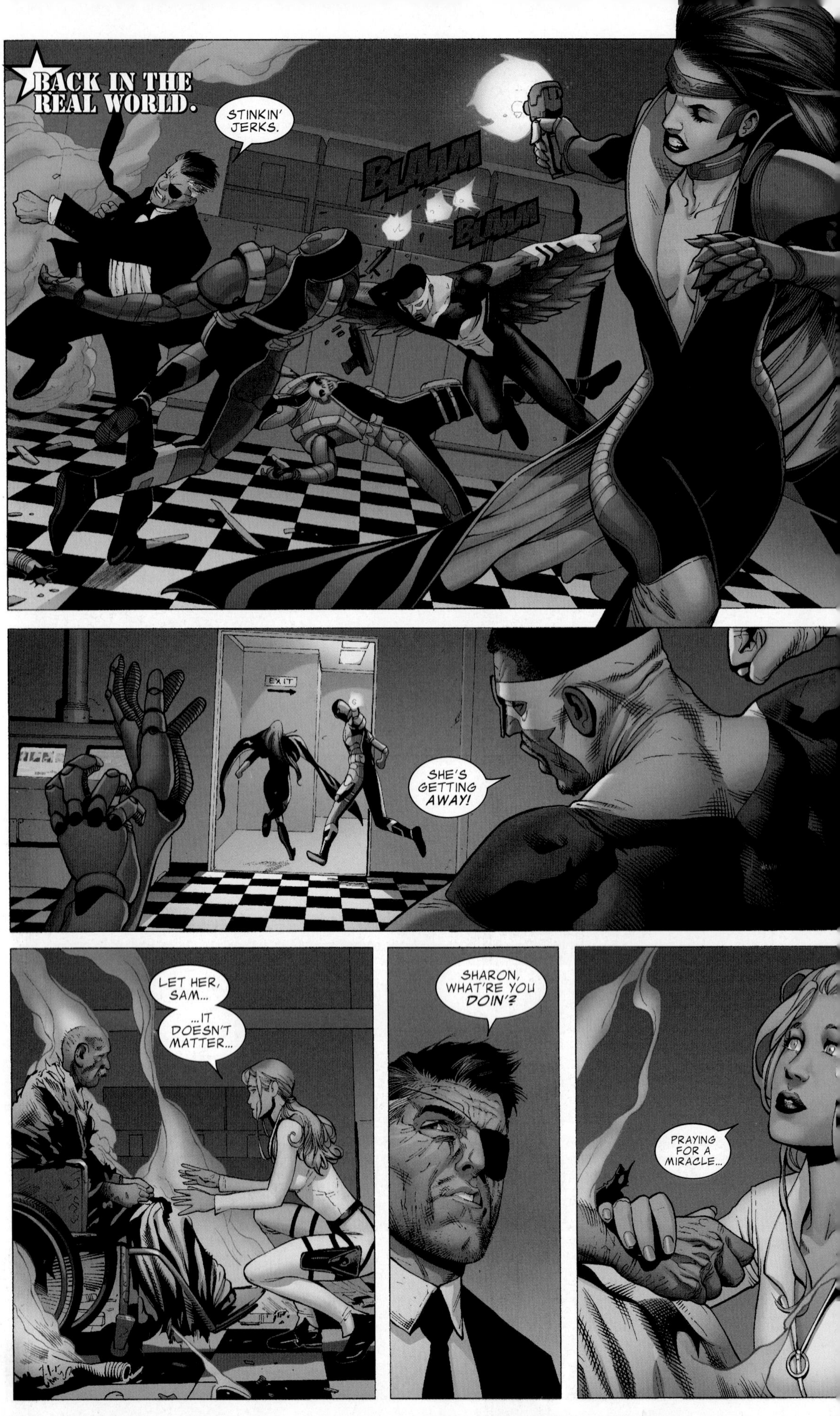
BACK IN THE REAL WORLD.
STINKIN' JERKS.
BLAMM
BLAMM
EXIT
SHE'S GETTING AWAY!
LET HER, SAM...
...IT DOESN'T MATTER...
SHARON, WHAT'RE YOU DOIN'?
PRAYING FOR A MIRACLE...

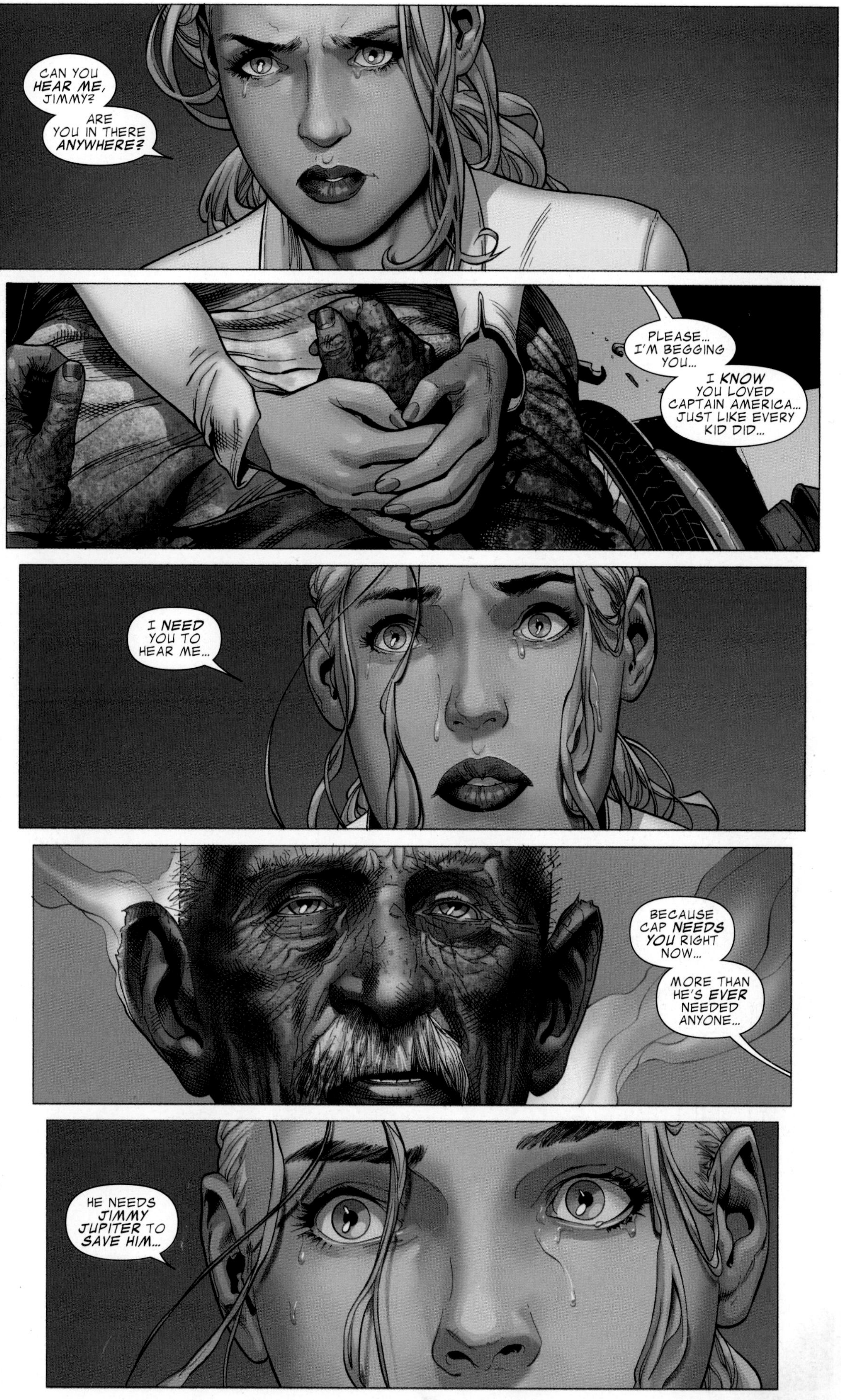
CAN YOU *HEAR ME,* JIMMY?
ARE YOU IN THERE *ANYWHERE?*
PLEASE... I'M BEGGING YOU...
I *KNOW* YOU LOVED CAPTAIN AMERICA... JUST LIKE EVERY KID DID...
I *NEED* YOU TO HEAR ME...
BECAUSE CAP *NEEDS YOU* RIGHT NOW...
MORE THAN HE'S *EVER* NEEDED ANYONE...
HE NEEDS *JIMMY JUPITER* TO *SAVE HIM...*

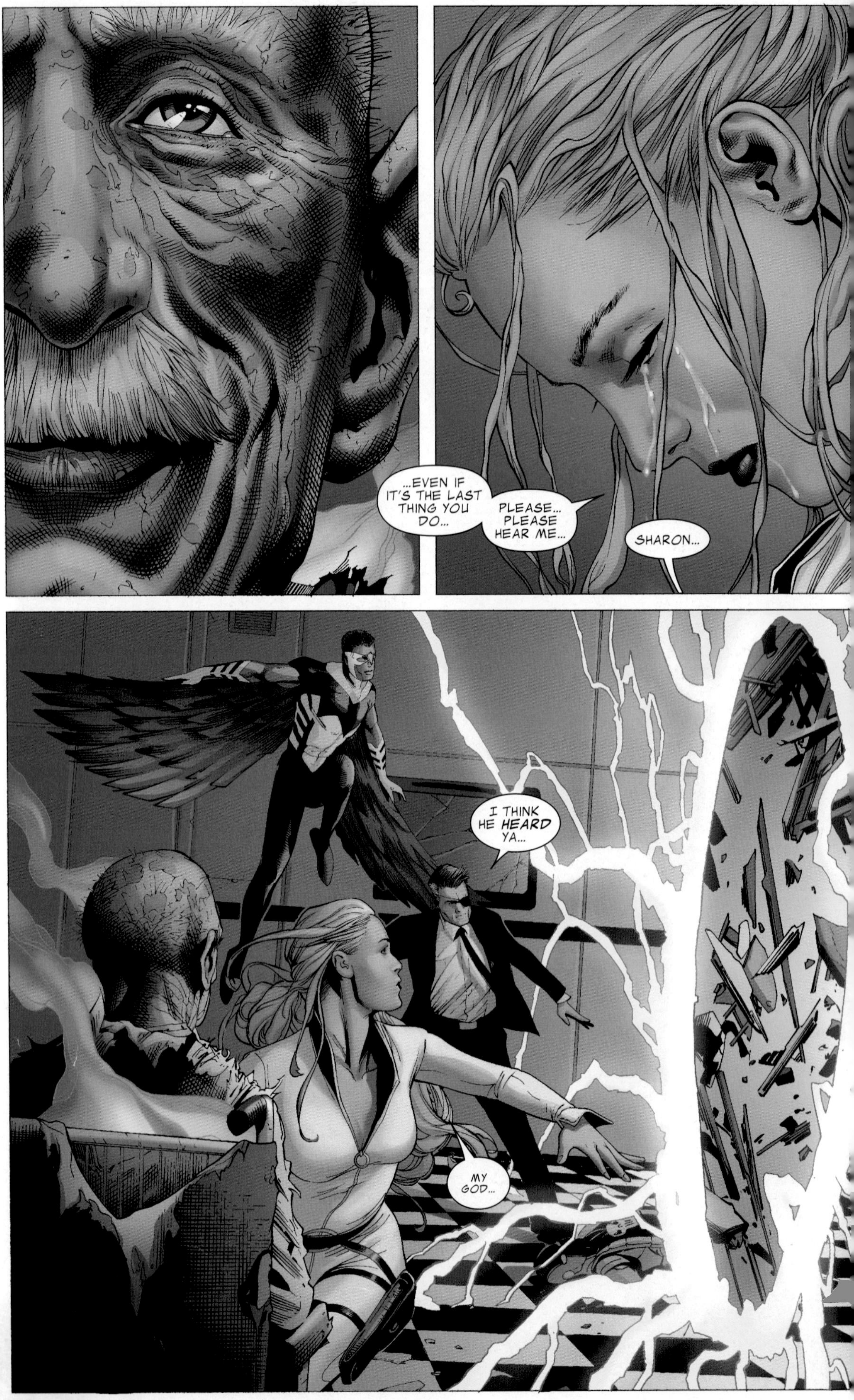
...EVEN IF IT'S THE LAST THING YOU DO...
PLEASE... PLEASE HEAR ME...
SHARON...
I THINK HE **HEARD** YA...
MY GOD...

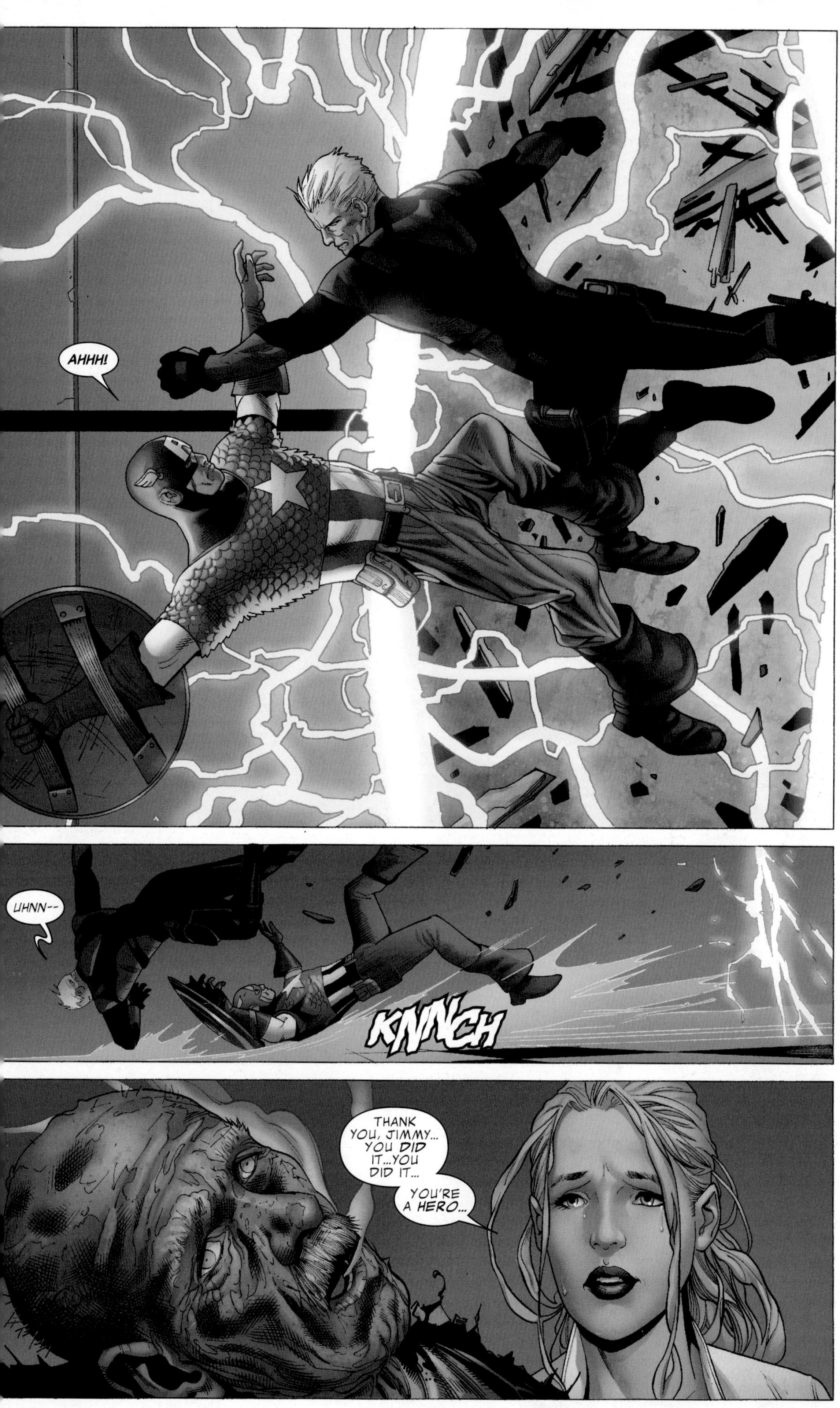
AHHH!
UHNN--
KNNCH
THANK YOU, JIMMY... YOU DID IT...YOU DID IT...
YOU'RE A HERO...

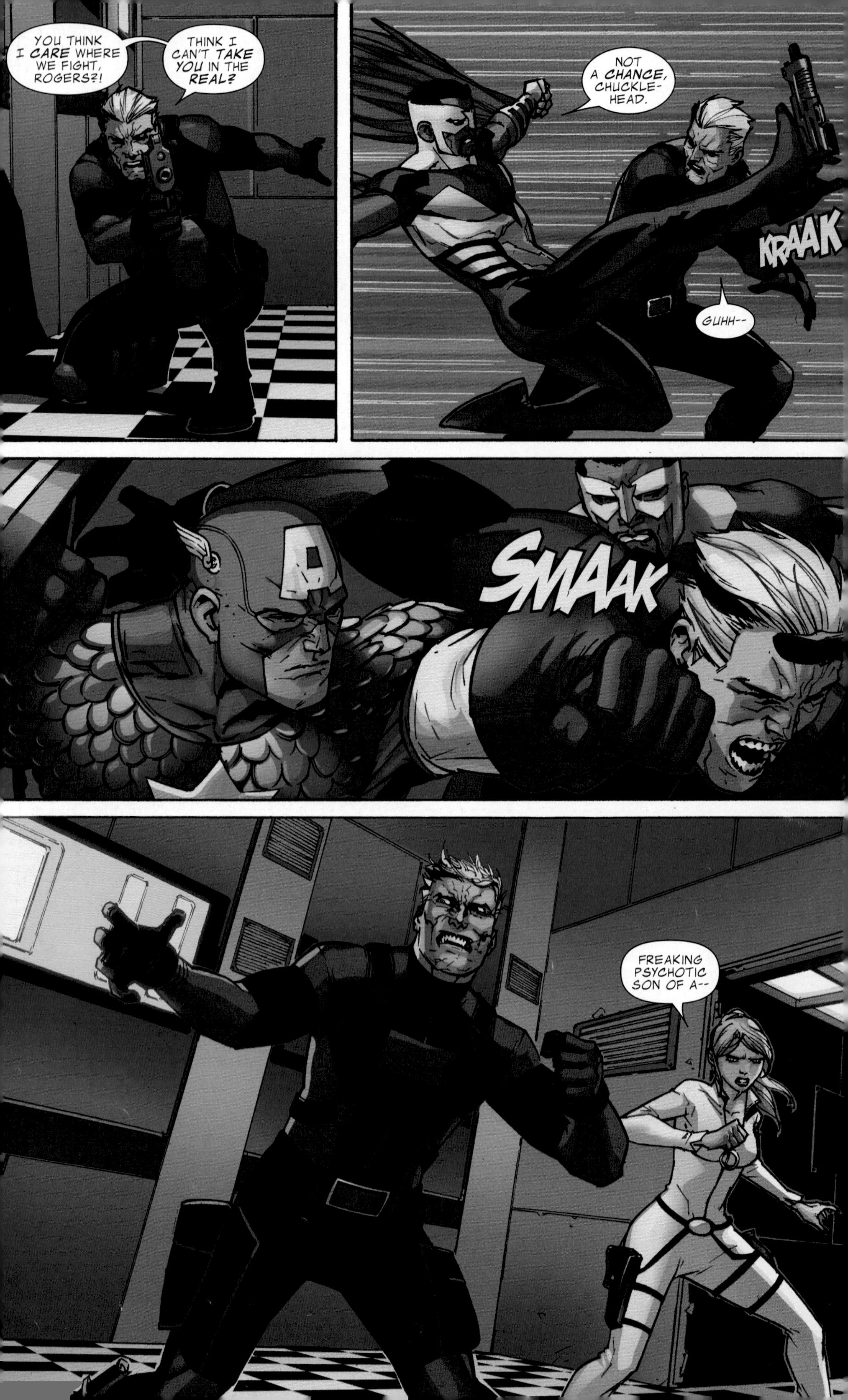
YOU THINK I CARE WHERE WE FIGHT, ROGERS?!
THINK I CAN'T TAKE YOU IN THE REAL?
NOT A CHANCE, CHUCKLE-HEAD.
KRAAK
GUHH--
SMAAK
FREAKING PSYCHOTIC SON OF A--

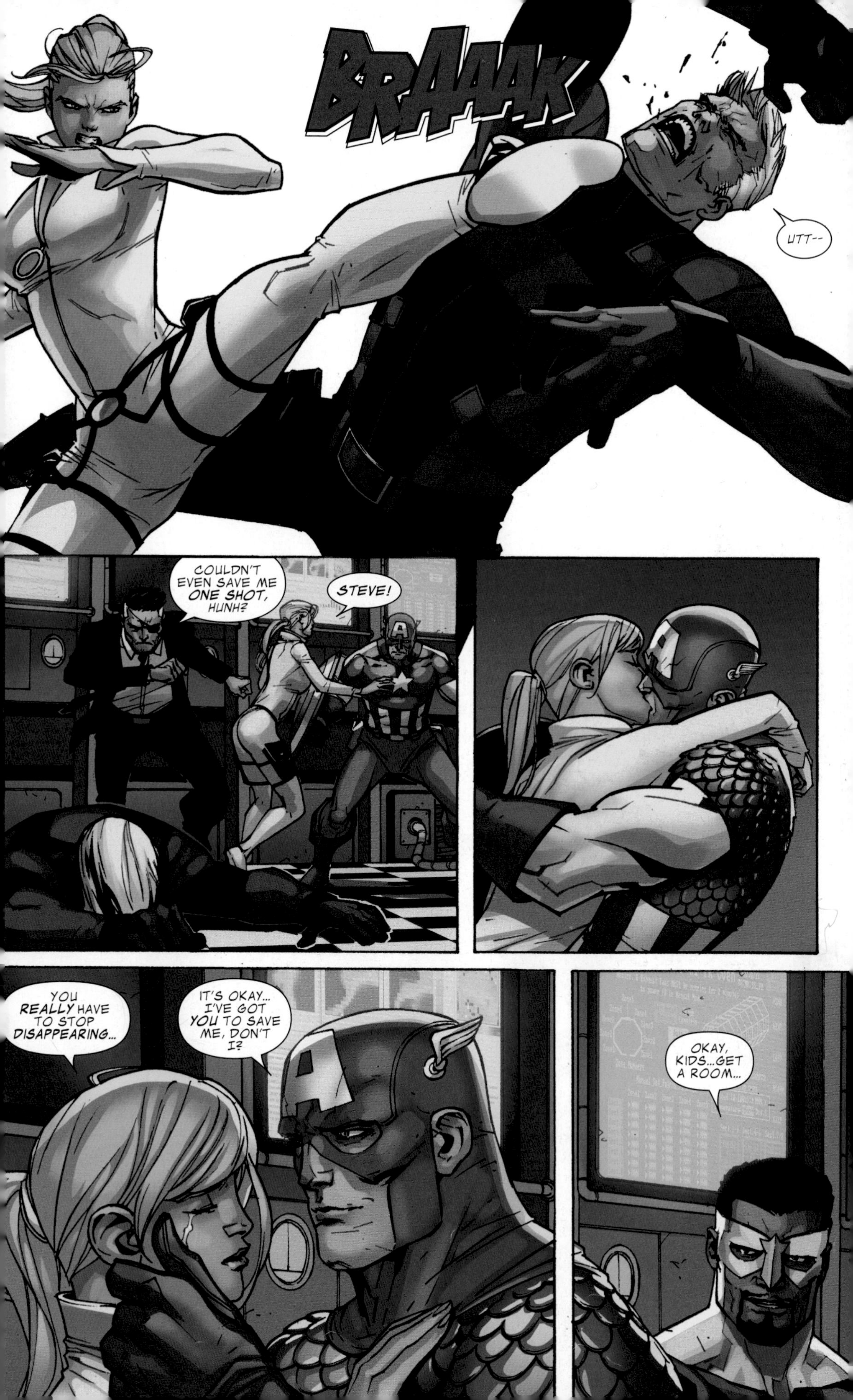

BRAAAK
UTT--
COULDN'T EVEN SAVE ME ONE SHOT, HUNH?
STEVE!
YOU REALLY HAVE TO STOP DISAPPEARING...
IT'S OKAY... I'VE GOT YOU TO SAVE ME, DON'T I?
OKAY, KIDS...GET A ROOM...

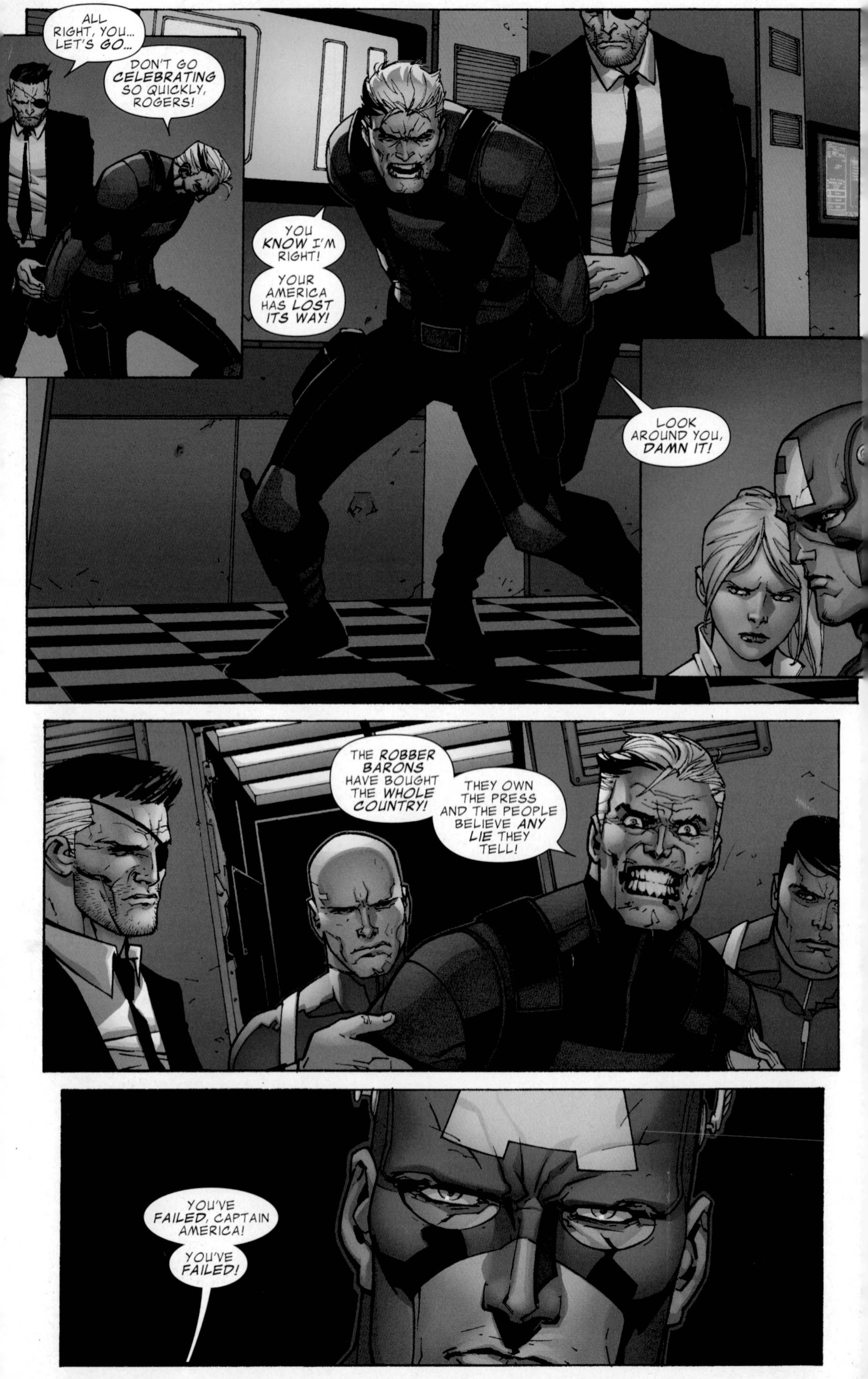
ALL RIGHT, YOU... LET'S GO...
DON'T GO CELEBRATING SO QUICKLY, ROGERS!
YOU KNOW I'M RIGHT!
YOUR AMERICA HAS LOST ITS WAY!
LOOK AROUND YOU, DAMN IT!
THE ROBBER BARONS HAVE BOUGHT THE WHOLE COUNTRY!
THEY OWN THE PRESS AND THE PEOPLE BELIEVE ANY LIE THEY TELL!
YOU'VE FAILED, CAPTAIN AMERICA!
YOU'VE FAILED!

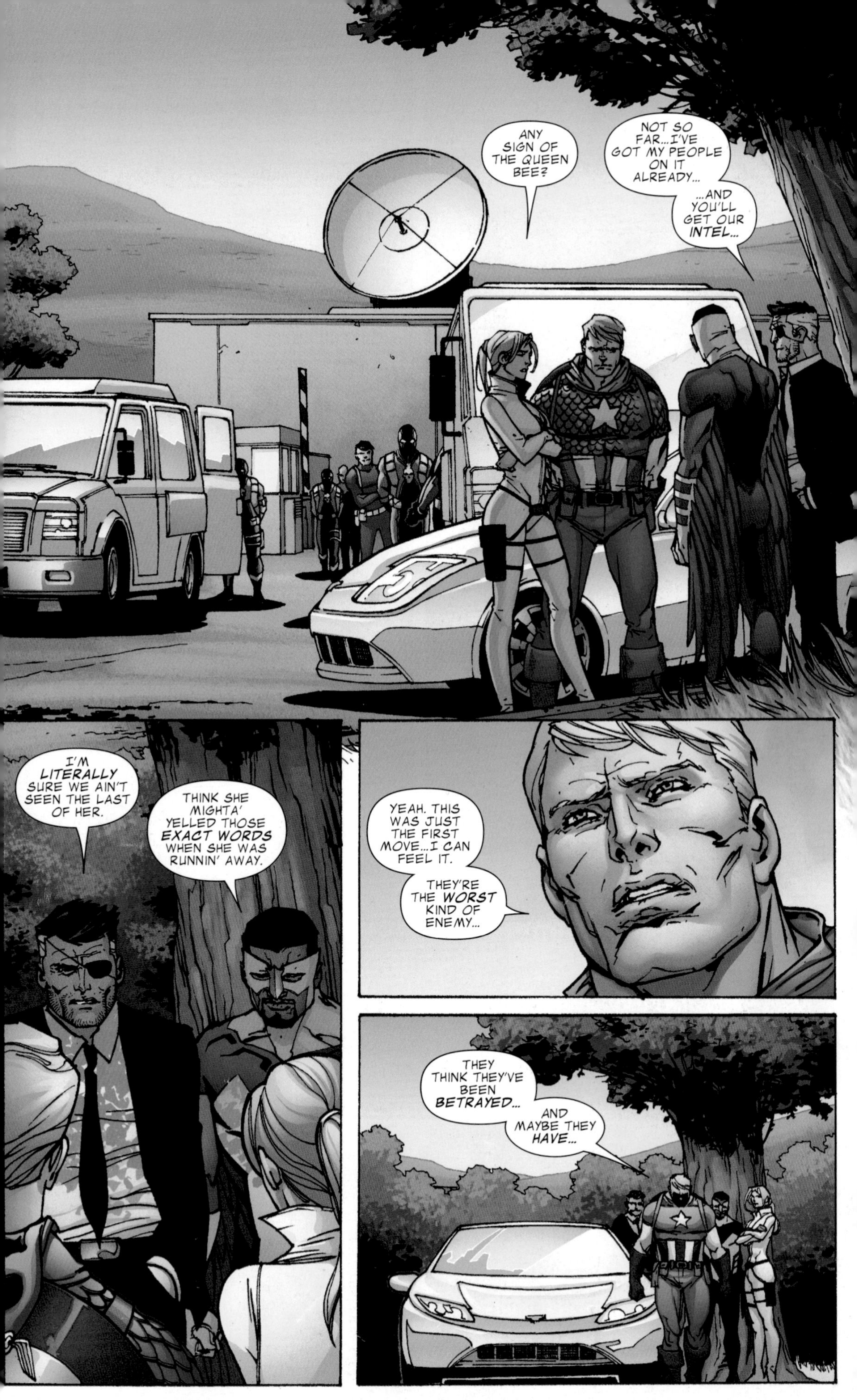
ANY SIGN OF THE QUEEN BEE?
NOT SO FAR...I'VE GOT MY PEOPLE ON IT ALREADY...
...AND YOU'LL GET OUR INTEL...
I'M LITERALLY SURE WE AIN'T SEEN THE LAST OF HER.
THINK SHE MIGHTA' YELLED THOSE EXACT WORDS WHEN SHE WAS RUNNIN' AWAY.
YEAH. THIS WAS JUST THE FIRST MOVE...I CAN FEEL IT.
THEY'RE THE WORST KIND OF ENEMY...
THEY THINK THEY'VE BEEN BETRAYED...
AND MAYBE THEY HAVE...

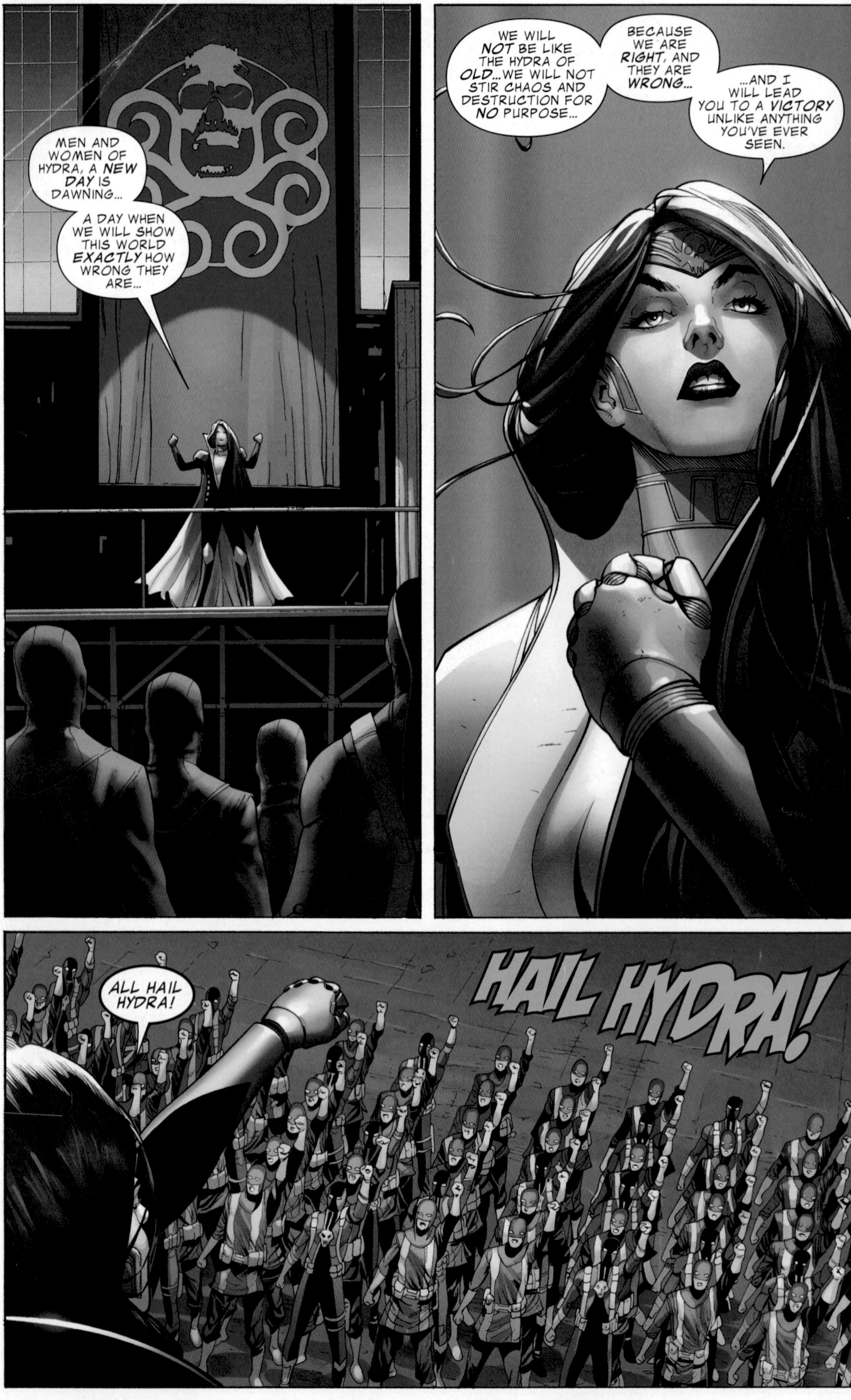
MEN AND WOMEN OF HYDRA, A NEW DAY IS DAWNING...
A DAY WHEN WE WILL SHOW THIS WORLD EXACTLY HOW WRONG THEY ARE...
WE WILL NOT BE LIKE THE HYDRA OF OLD...WE WILL NOT STIR CHAOS AND DESTRUCTION FOR NO PURPOSE...
BECAUSE WE ARE RIGHT, AND THEY ARE WRONG...
...AND I WILL LEAD YOU TO A VICTORY UNLIKE ANYTHING YOU'VE EVER SEEN.
ALL HAIL HYDRA!
HAIL HYDRA!

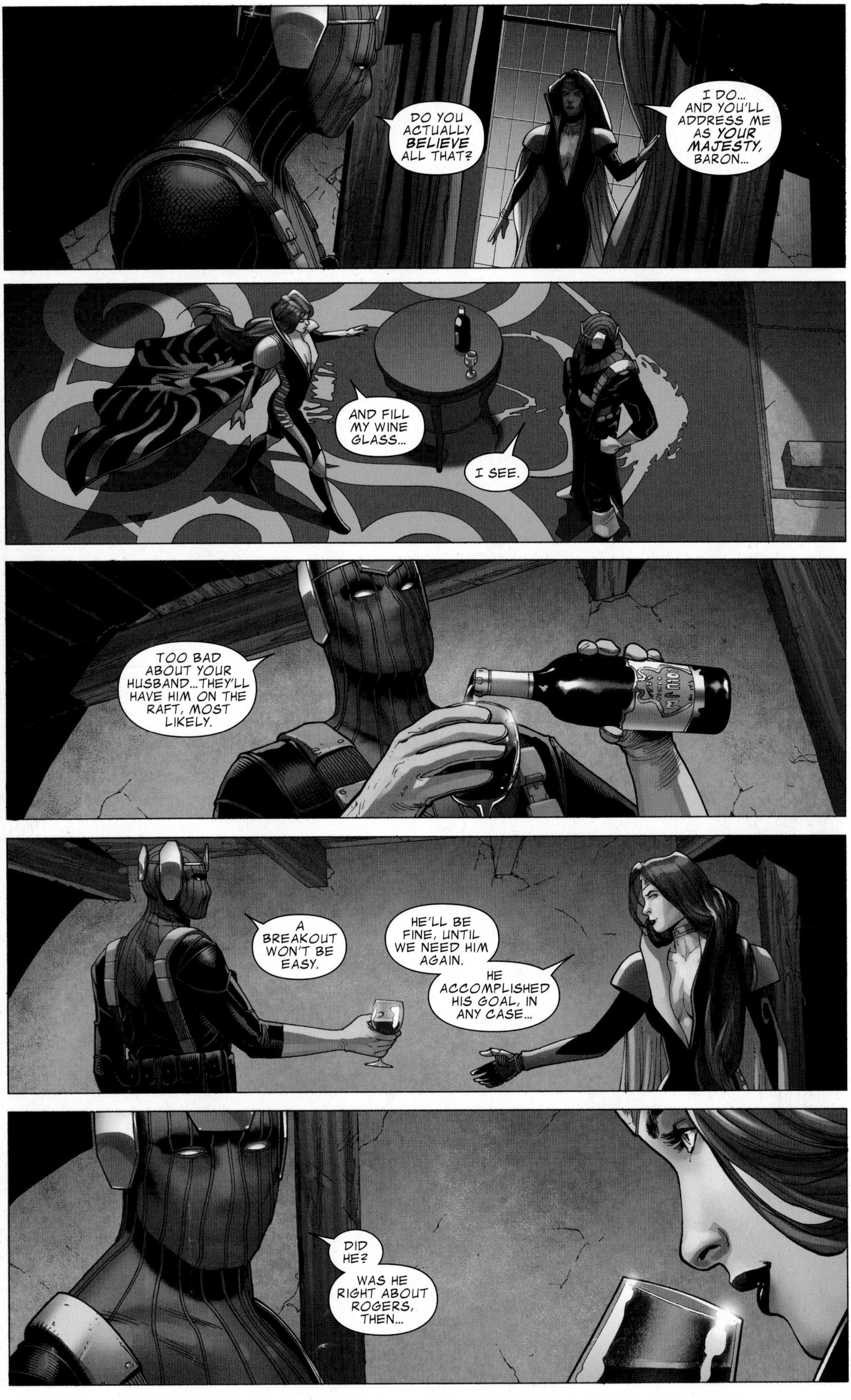
DO YOU ACTUALLY BELIEVE ALL THAT?
I DO... AND YOU'LL ADDRESS ME AS YOUR MAJESTY, BARON...
AND FILL MY WINE GLASS...
I SEE.
TOO BAD ABOUT YOUR HUSBAND...THEY'LL HAVE HIM ON THE RAFT, MOST LIKELY.
A BREAKOUT WON'T BE EASY.
HE'LL BE FINE, UNTIL WE NEED HIM AGAIN.
HE ACCOMPLISHED HIS GOAL, IN ANY CASE...
DID HE?
WAS HE RIGHT ABOUT ROGERS, THEN...

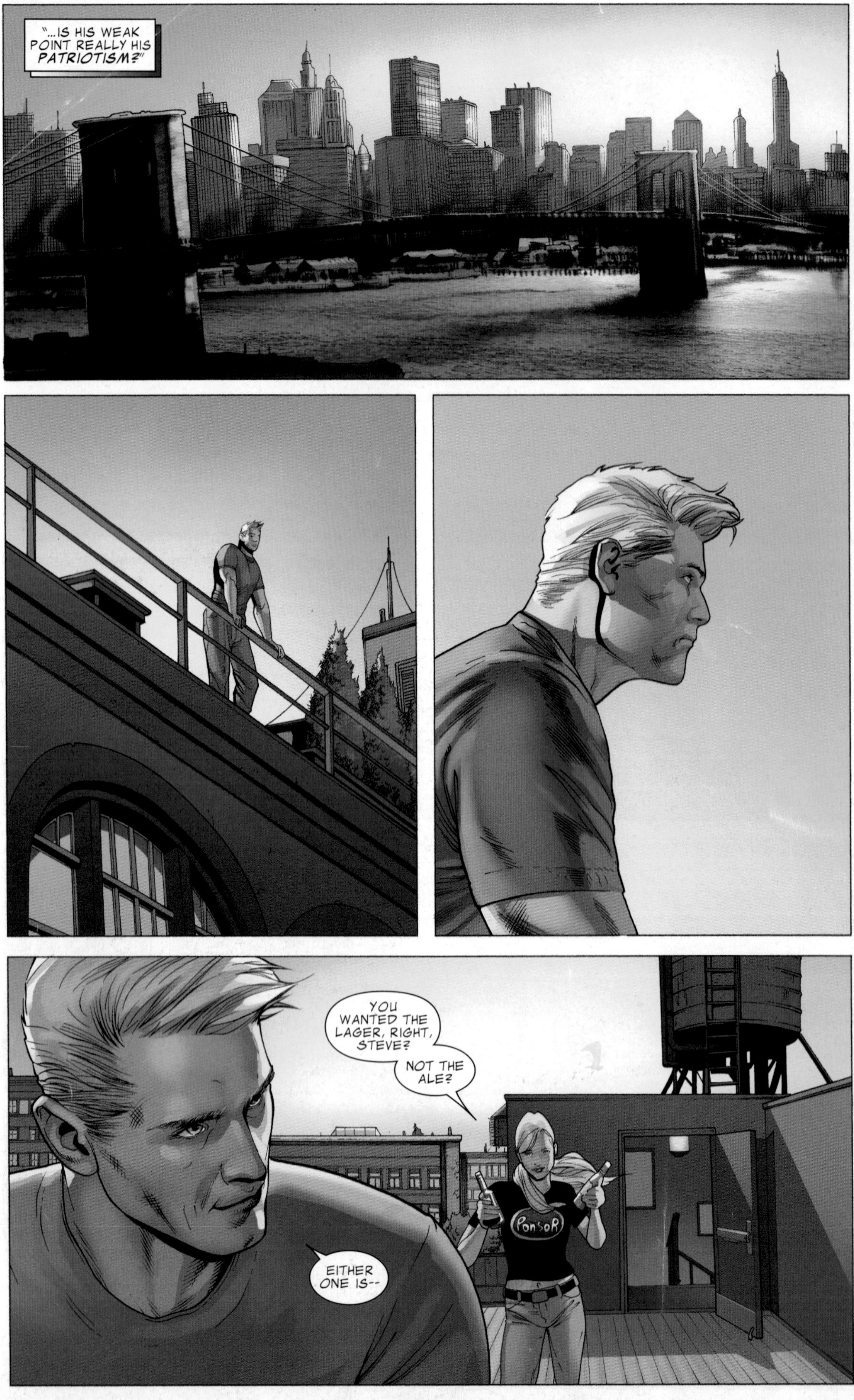
"...IS HIS WEAK POINT REALLY HIS *PATRIOTISM?*"
YOU WANTED THE LAGER, RIGHT, STEVE?
NOT THE ALE?
EITHER ONE IS--

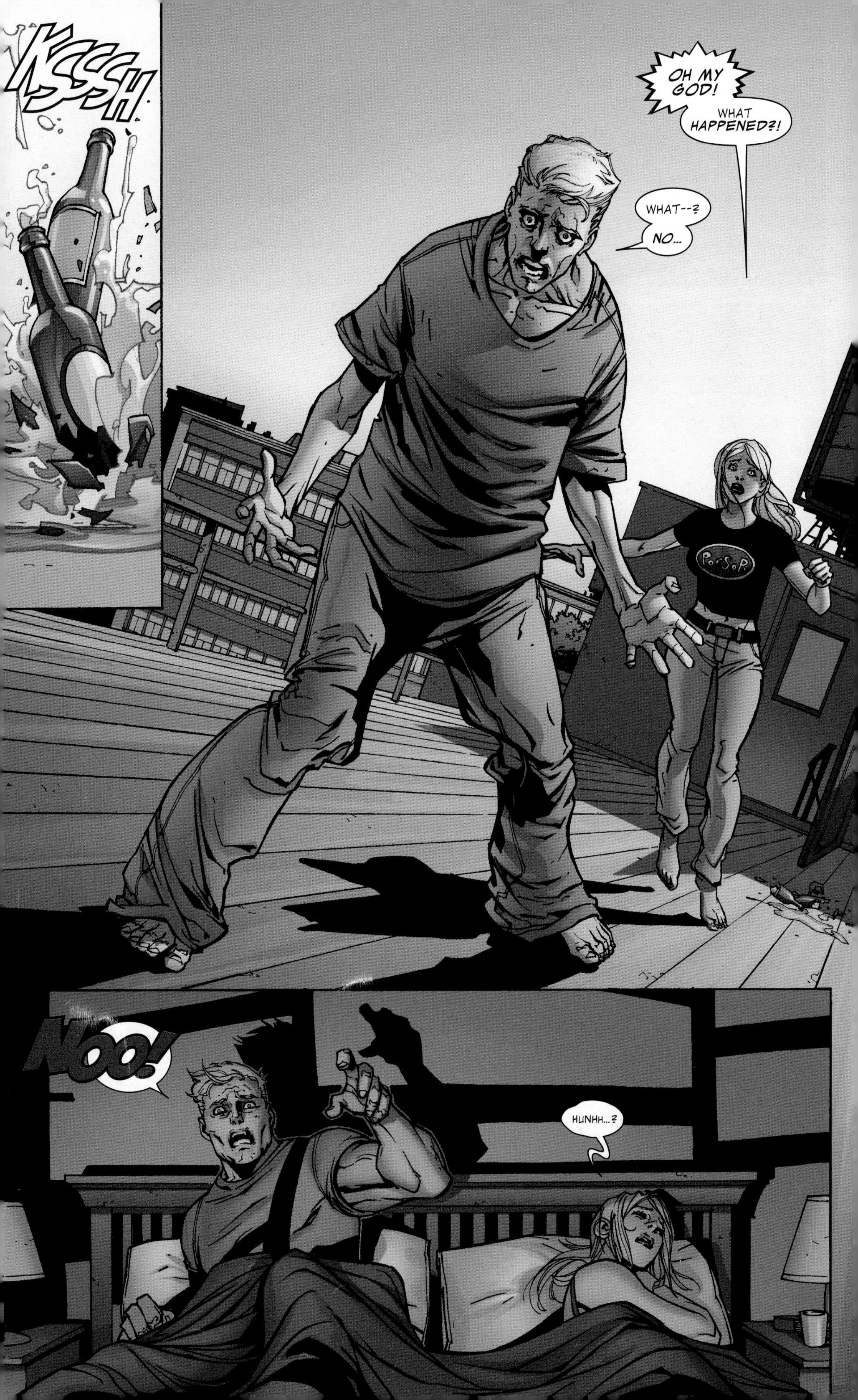
KSSSH
OH MY GOD!
WHAT HAPPENED?!
WHAT--?
NO...
NOO!
HUNHH...?

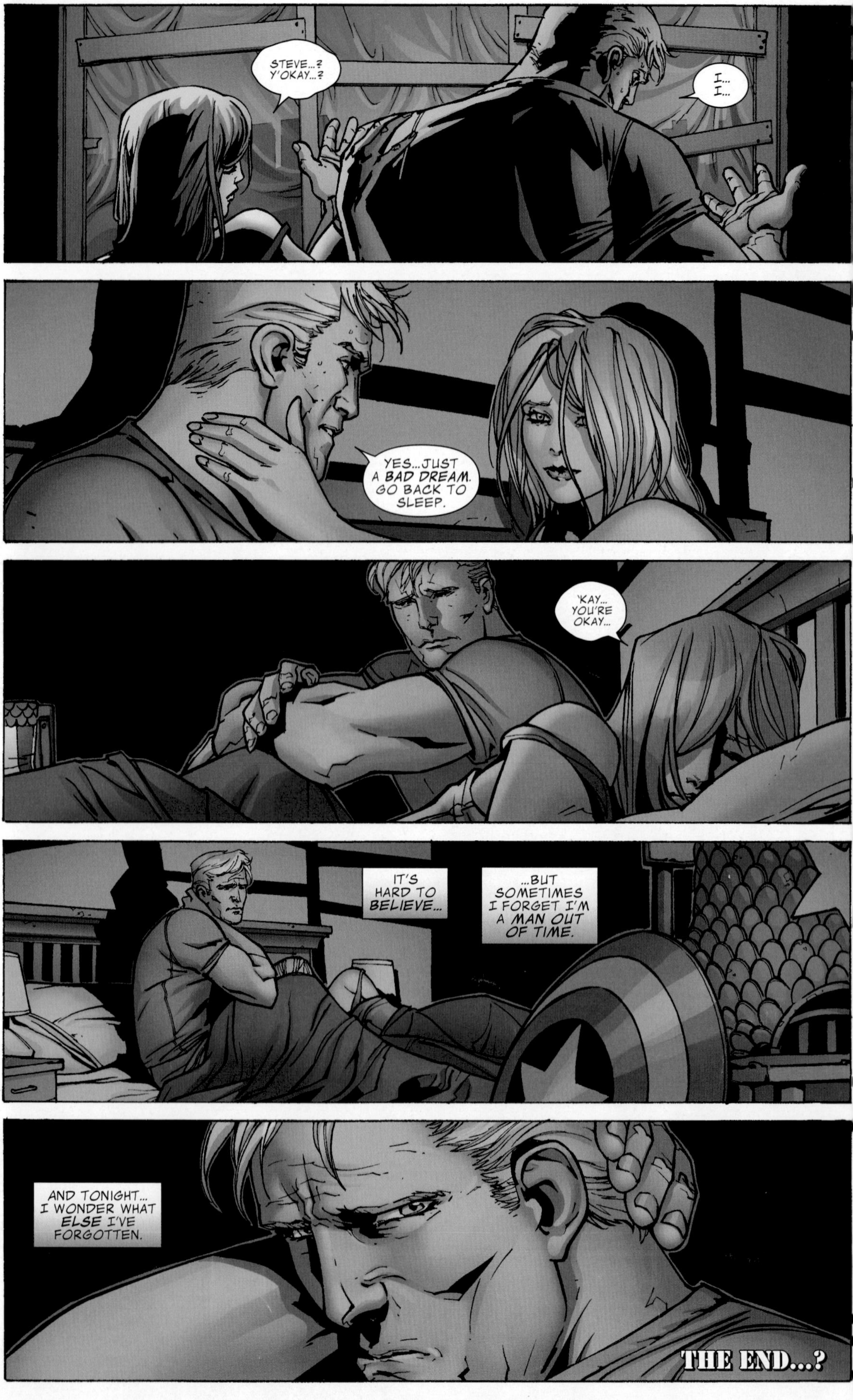
STEVE...? Y'OKAY...?
I... I...
YES...JUST A BAD DREAM. GO BACK TO SLEEP.
'KAY... YOU'RE OKAY...
IT'S HARD TO BELIEVE...
...BUT SOMETIMES I FORGET I'M A MAN OUT OF TIME.
AND TONIGHT... I WONDER WHAT ELSE I'VE FORGOTTEN.
THE END...?

#1 VARIANT BY **OLIVIER COIPEL**

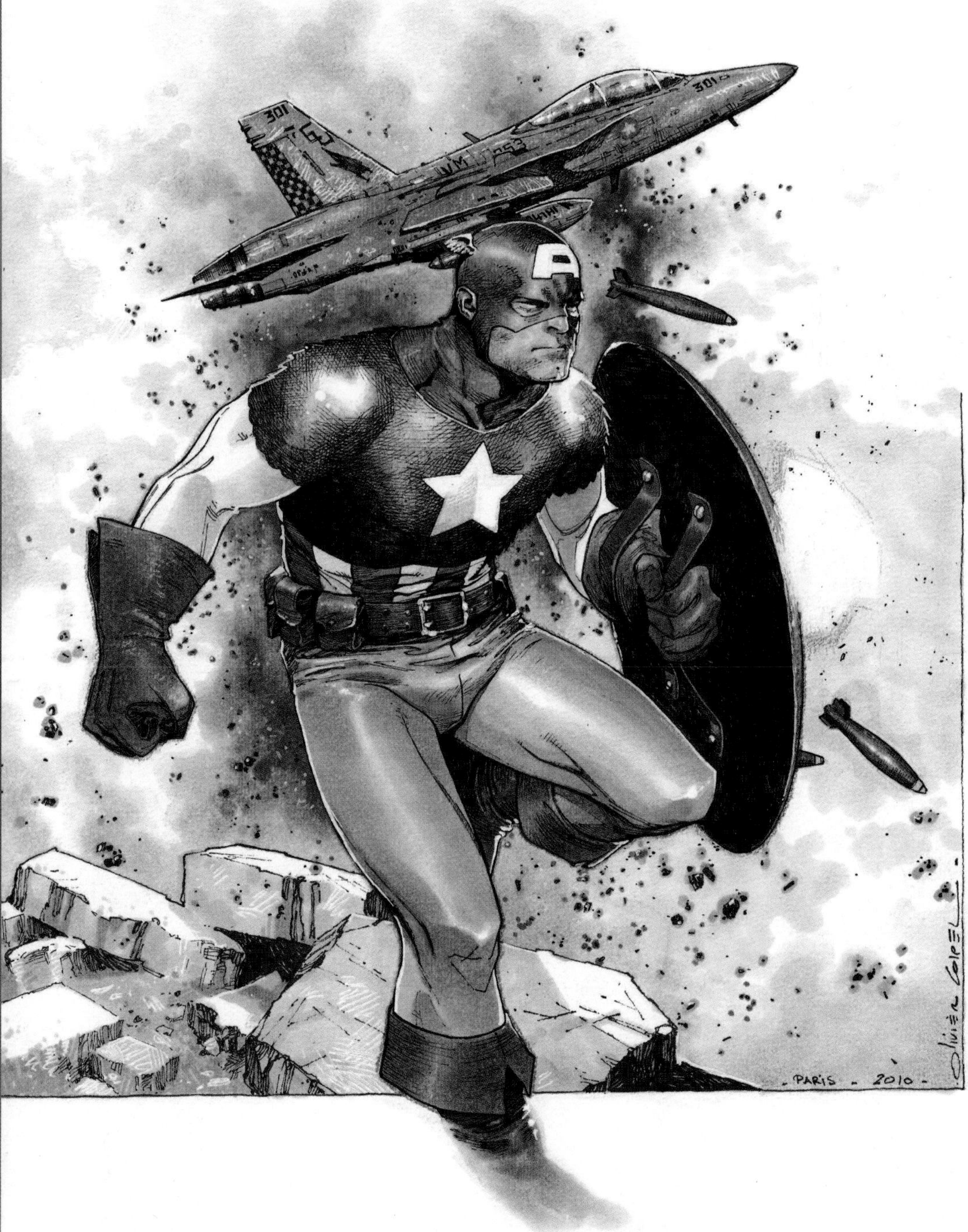

301
PARIS - 2010 -

#1 VARIANT BY NEAL ADAMS & JUSTIN PONSOR

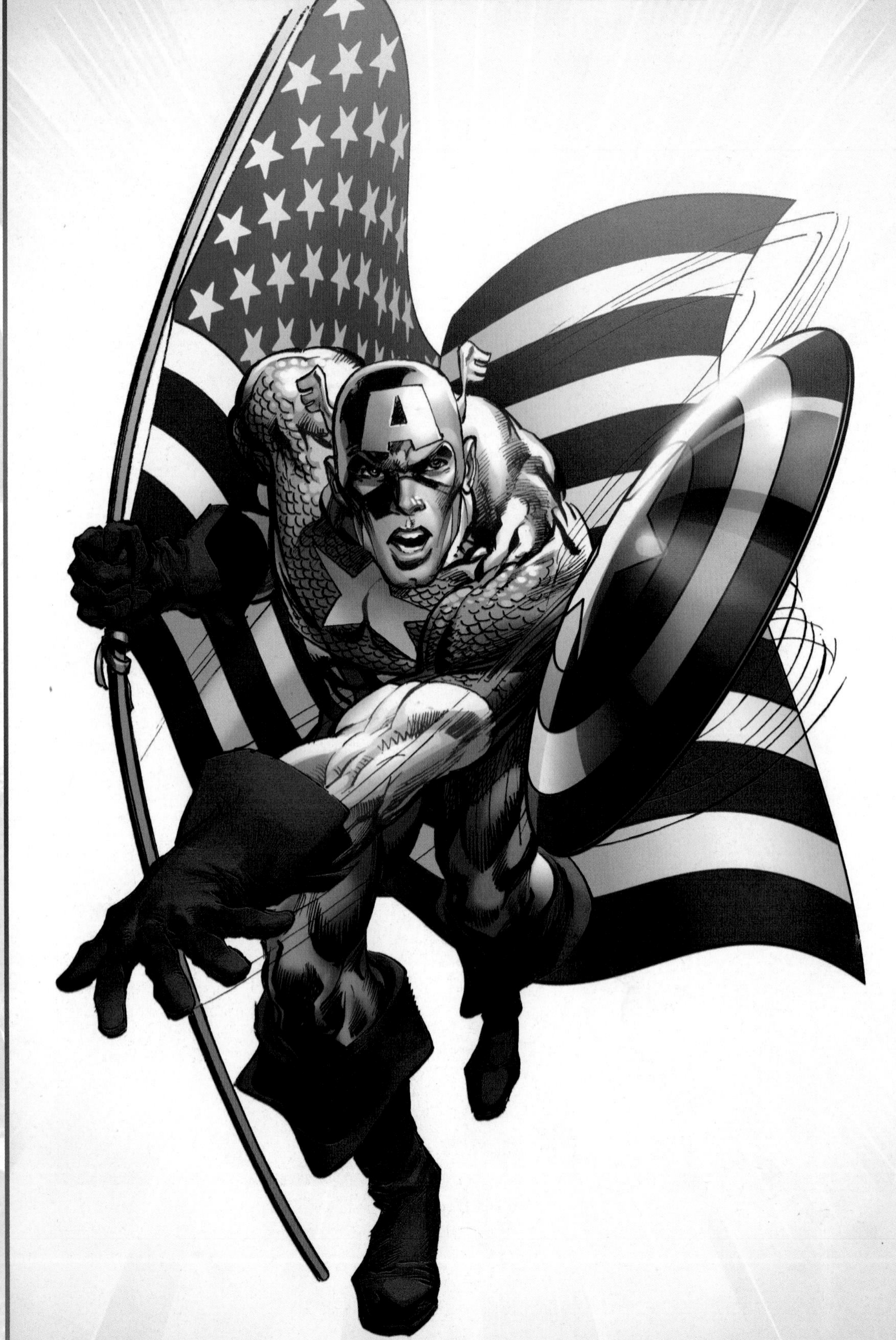

#1 SINGAPORE VARIANT BY HARVEY TOLIBAO & CHRIS SOTOMAYOR

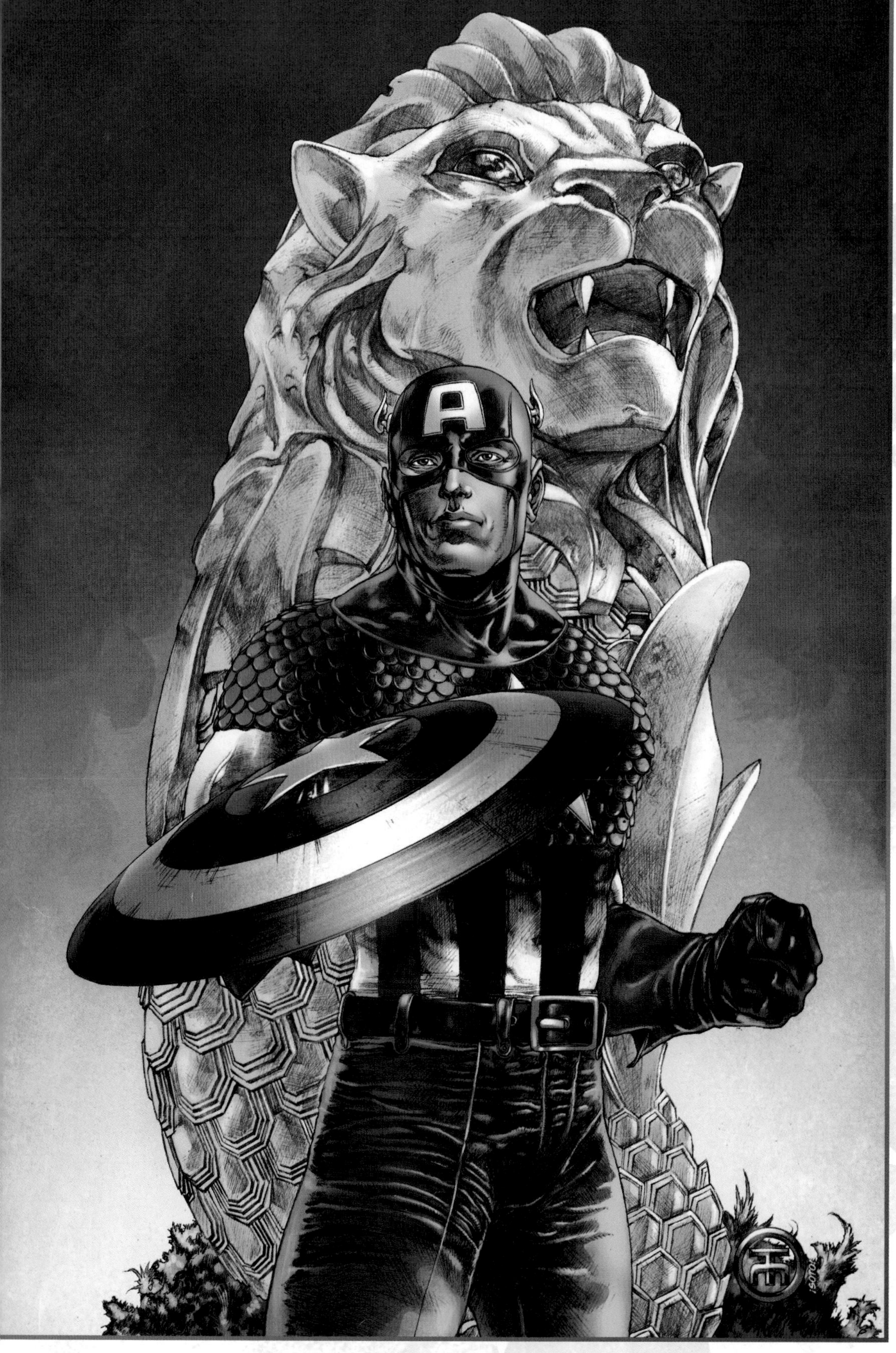

#1 MOVIE VARIANT

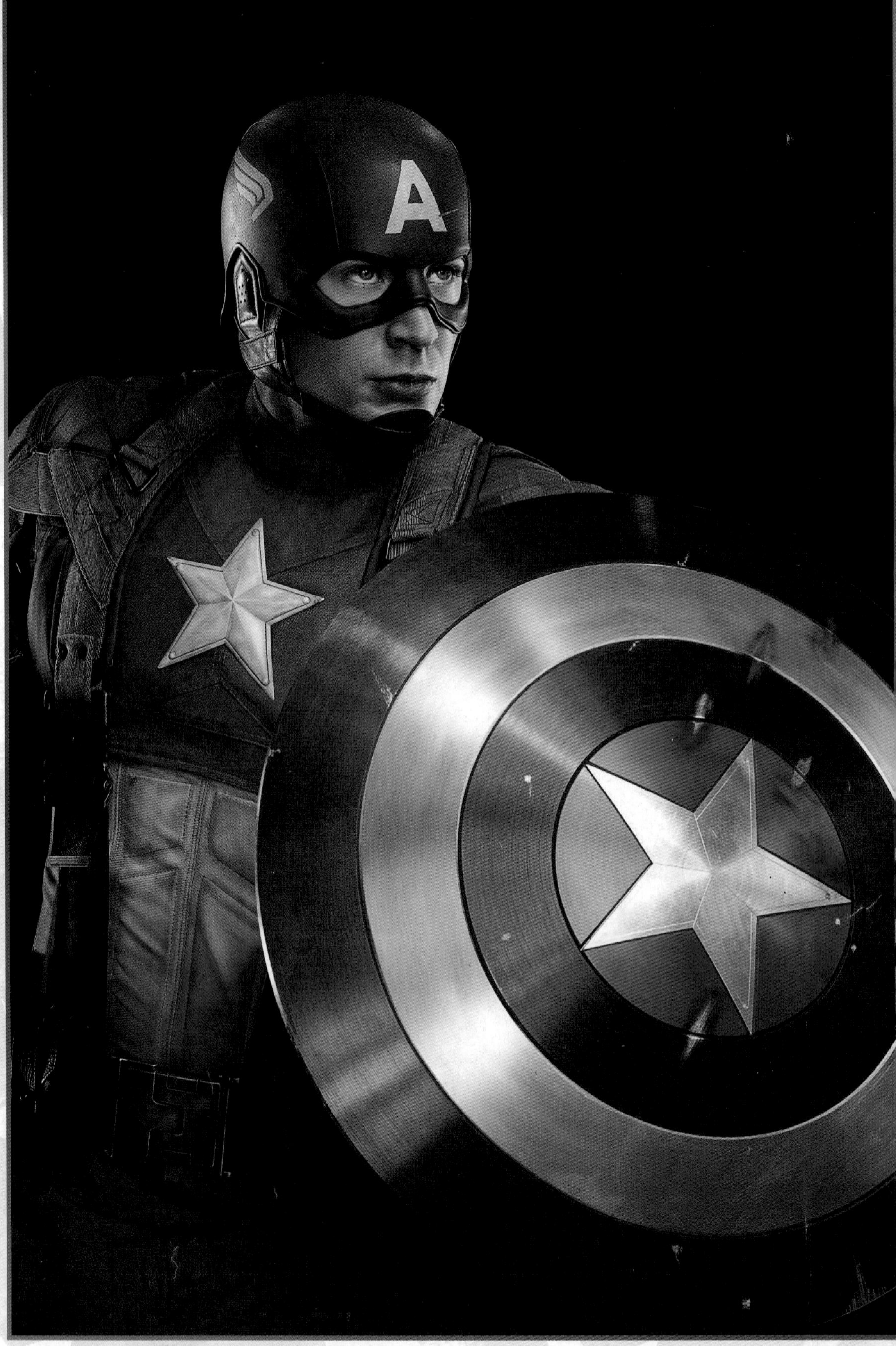

#1 FAN EXPO VARIANT BY DALE EAGLESHAM & SONIA OBACK

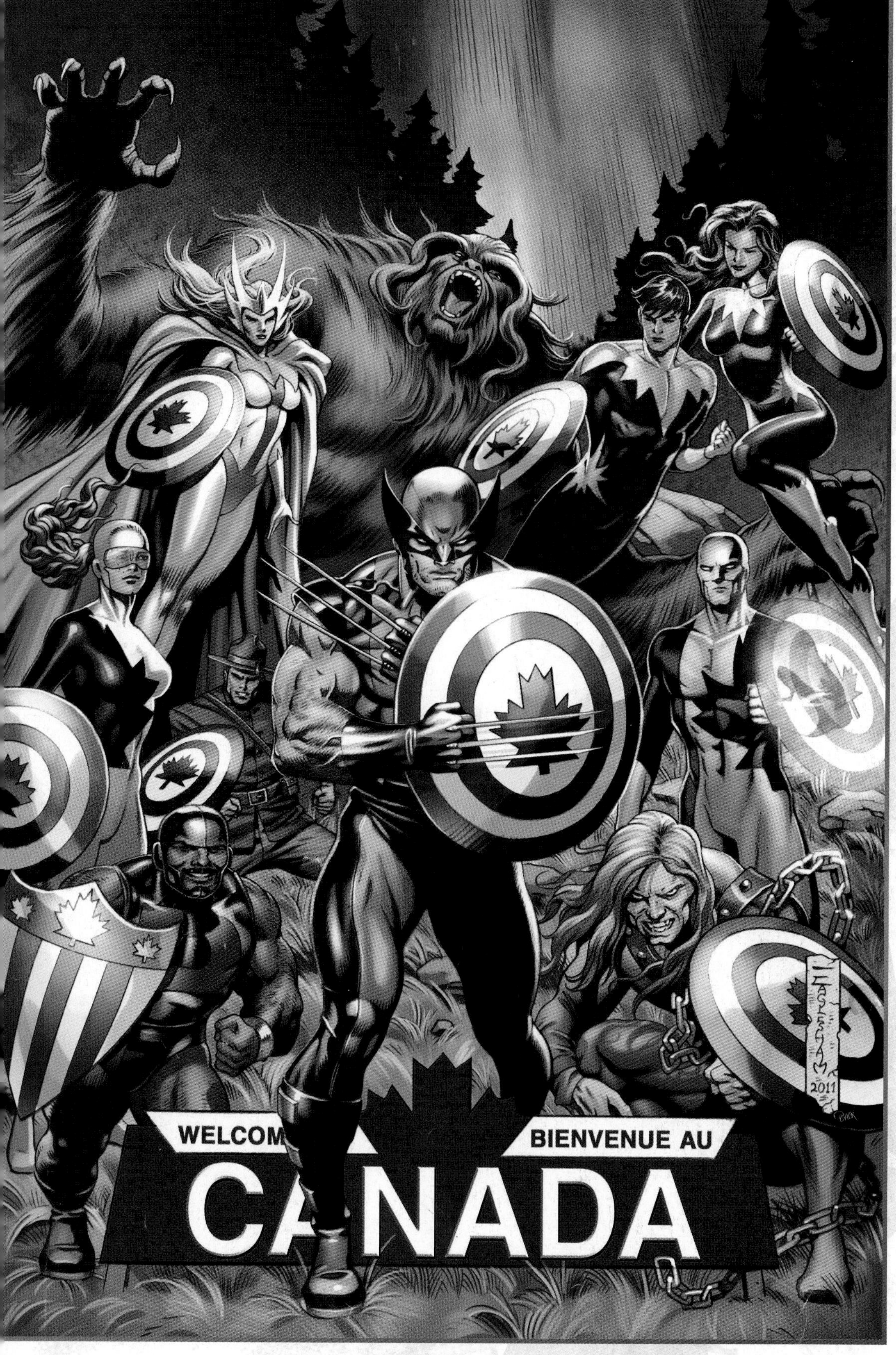
WELCOM
BIENVENUE AU
CANADA
EAGLESHAM 2011

#3 ARCHITECTS VARIANT BY SALVADOR LARROCA & FRANK D'ARMATA

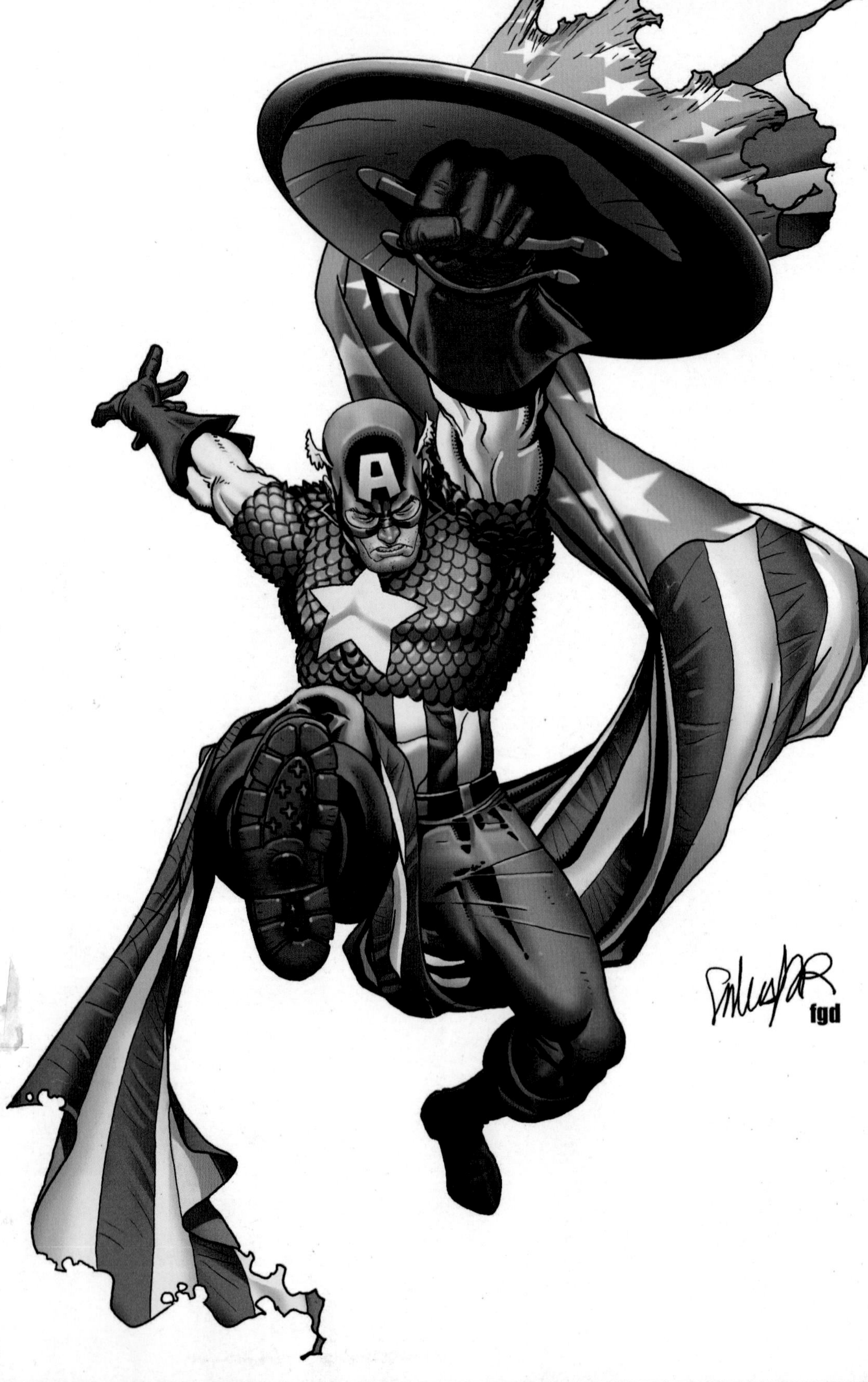